Praise for ~~~~~

The Men in My Life

"In this moving follow-up to her 1997 memoir, *Anything Your Little Heart Desires*, Bosworth comes into her own as a memoirist."

—*Publishers Weekly* (starred review)

"Looking back to her rampaging twenties, Bosworth chronicles how she repressed her grief and guilt, recklessly threw herself into harrowing situations, and embraced exhilarating opportunities, all of which she describes with stunning immediacy and valiant candor. . . . Lush with tales of Lee Strasberg, Marilyn Monroe, Gore Vidal, Elaine Stritch, Audrey Hepburn, and many more, and spiked with arresting observations about glamour and about toxic sexism and homophobia, Bosworth's riveting memoir brings the covertly wild 1950s into startlingly close focus."

—*Booklist* (starred review)

"Although Patricia Bosworth's new memoir is set in the 1950s, it is urgent and essential reading, especially for young women."

—*Los Angeles Times*

"[Patricia Bosworth's] life was a dramatic saga of ambition, sex, love, affairs, heartbreak, and abortion. She courageously reveals it all in *The Men in My Life: A Memoir of Love and Art in 1950s Manhattan*."

—*Wall Street Journal*

"Deliciously vivid."

—*New York Times*

"Bosworth's command of detail . . . makes the book more than merely a dishy showbiz memoir."

—*The New Yorker*

"Scorchingly honest."

—*AARP The Magazine*

"Highbrow and brilliant."

—*New York* magazine

"This exceptional account not only provides an in-depth portrait of the author, it also clearly illuminates a complex yet pivotal period in twentieth-century America."

—*Library Journal* (starred review)

"[Bosworth] recounts the glamorous highs and frustrating lows of trying to succeed as an actress, offering juicy anecdotes featuring a large cast of the actors, directors, and playwrights who comprised the important men in her young life. . . . A forthright memoir of pain and aspirations enlivened by sharp portraits of a host of colorful celebrities."

—*Kirkus Reviews*

" 'You won't be able to do it for a while, maybe not for a long time,' Gore Vidal warned the young Patricia Bosworth, suggesting she write a memoir of her charmed, tragic early years. He was right. She now has and it's a stunner, a searing, suspenseful meditation on acting, being, and the distance in between. Not every inner life can hold its own against the behind-the-scenes drama at the Actors Studio; Bosworth's steals the show."

—Stacy Schiff, author of *The Witches*

"What an emotional and remarkable journey! Bosworth is a dazzling writer—I came under her spell years ago when I read her biographies. Now, in her new book, Patricia has reached into the depths of her adventurous, sometimes terrifying life, to tell us a story that could not be fiction—too sad, too wildly happy at times, and in every way challenging. Bosworth tells us how it is to live a life of creativity and beauty when the hard times come, and when the good times roll. She has lived through both and come up shining and brilliant. Read this book! I loved it!"

—Judy Collins, author of *Sweet Judy Blue Eyes*

"I couldn't stop reading this book. It's terrific. There are fascinating characters throughout, and so much glamour and excitement, but also loss and tragedy. That unsettling combination fuels Patricia Bosworth's amazing story."

—Gay Talese, author of *High Notes*

"Honesty in writing is rare and precious. In telling us the previously untold story of her extraordinary life, Patricia Bosworth has added an important testament to the history of women. I read this book with tears in my eyes and a smile on my face."

—Erica Jong, author of *Fear of Dying*

"This memoir is so passionate, so discerning, so emotionally textured. Set in the fifties and early sixties, when constricting beliefs and traditions battled an urgent need for authenticity and experiment, the young women of Bosworth's generation were searching for their own destinies, fighting to do more than play supporting roles in the lives of powerful men. And yet, as she shows so poignantly, men like her brilliant father, and her gifted, tragic brother were also trapped. This is the kind of memoir we need now: the story of a life that's also the story of a culture."

—Margo Jefferson, author of *Negroland*

"Graced with a talent for delving into the truths of creative lives, Patricia Bosworth has now taken the truth serum herself. The result is a powerful, gutsy, tender, and mesmerizing memoir, wherein Bosworth bravely restores her romantic past to the jagged intensity of the present tense."

—Brad Gooch, author of *Smash Cut*

"Patricia Bosworth, one of our most accomplished biographers, has led a life that few could survive, including the suicides of her brother and father; an acting career marked by exhilarating highs and crushing lows; an abusive first husband; and many other heart-pounding and heart-destroying events recounted in this utterly absorbing memoir. Through it all, Bosworth remains ebullient, self-aware, even funny, and without dissembling. This is who she is, a bright spirit in love with life, whatever it throws at her."

—James Atlas, author of *My Life in the Middle Ages*

"In *The Men in My Life* Patricia Bosworth, who has given us such fine biographies of Montgomery Clift, Diane Arbus, and Jane Fonda, turns her lens on her own twenty-something self, and on the men—and women—she encountered during those extraordinary years. The result is a moving, revealing, unsparing, and enthralling book."

—Amanda Vaill, author of *Hotel Florida* and *Everybody Was So Young*

"A fascinating, vivid story. *The Men in My Life* is not only a page-turning self-portait, but also a nuanced cultural history of America in the 1950s."

—Philip Lopate, author of *To Show and to Tell: The Craft of Literary Nonfiction*

"As memoirs go, this one is TOPS. Vivid, beautifully written, evocative, and SO refreshingly frank about sex."

—André Bishop, artistic director of Lincoln Center Theater

The Men in My Life

Patricia Bosworth

The Men in

HARPER

NEW YORK · LONDON · TORONTO · SYDNEY

My Life

A Memoir

of Love and Art

in 1950s

Manhattan

HARPER

A hardcover edition of this book was published in 2017 by HarperCollins Publishers.

THE MEN IN MY LIFE. Copyright © 2018 by Patricia Bosworth. All rights reserved. Printed in the United States of America. No part of this book may be used or reproduced in any manner whatsoever without written permission except in the case of brief quotations embodied in critical articles and reviews. For information, address HarperCollins Publishers, 195 Broadway, New York, NY 10007.

HarperCollins books may be purchased for educational, business, or sales promotional use. For information, please email the Special Markets Department at SPsales@harpercollins.com.

FIRST HARPER PAPERBACKS EDITION PUBLISHED 2018.

Photographs are courtesy of the author unless otherwise credited.

Title page photograph © Paul Slade/Getty Images

Designed by Fritz Metsch

Library of Congress Cataloging-in-Publication Data has been applied for.

ISBN 978-0-06-228791-5 (pbk.)

18 19 20 21 22   LSC   10 9 8 7 6 5 4 3 2 1

For my beloved brother, Bart

Disclaimer

This is a work of nonfiction. The events and experiences detailed herein are all true and have been faithfully rendered as I have remembered them, to the best of my ability. Some names, identities, and circumstances have been changed in order to protect the privacy of those involved.

Though conversations come from my keen recollection of them, they are not written to represent word-for-word documentation; rather, I've retold them in a way that evokes the real feeling and meaning of what was said, in keeping with the true essence of the mood and spirit of the event.

Contents

Author's Note

FOR MOST OF my life I've been able to hide my feelings; indeed, I'd have to say I've been virtually defined by my ability to hold back. Until now.

I call this memoir *The Men in My Life* because two of the principal characters are my father, the lawyer Bartley Crum, and my brother Bart Jr.; they were the first men I cared for passionately and who passionately cared for me. When I was very young and struggling to be both an actress and a writer, my brother shot himself in the head, and six years later, my father took an overdose of sleeping pills. How did I survive their deaths? By shutting down completely.

Over the years I filtered my emotions through the biographies I wrote of Diane Arbus, Jane Fonda, Montgomery Clift, and Marlon Brando. I gravitated toward these subjects for good reason. One died by her own hand; another was a suicide survivor. All of them engaged in extremely self-destructive acts. Writing about them was one of the ways I coped with and tried to understand why the two men I loved most in the world had decided to kill themselves.

During the most traumatic years of my early life, I connected in person with three of the artists whose biographies I would eventually write. I was introduced to Montgomery Clift because he happened to be my father's client. I never forgot his enormous dark eyes or his strange hooting laugh. I suspected he had secrets and I wanted to find out what they were. The same was true with Jane Fonda; we were in classes together at the Actors Studio. I'd heard she had issues with her father, but then so did I.

Diane Arbus would be the most mysterious of my future subjects. I modeled for her when I was eighteen. She'd be barefoot, and with her husband, Allan, would duck under the focusing cloth of their heavy eight-by-ten view camera and start whispering conspiratorially before they photographed me. They were a shy young couple, symbiotically close. Their relationship reminded me of mine with my brother. I longed to find out if this was true, and these remarkable people stayed with me in my subconscious as I proceeded on my journey.

I often don't recognize the self I was back then, a skinny girl in leotards and an old duffel coat wandering around New York City. This book is set during a ten-year period in the fifties and sixties (1953–1963), which on the surface was dark and puritanical, but underneath was a seething ferment of creativity, with painters, poets, photographers, writers, and actors all clamoring to be heard. I longed to be part of that ferment, but I was so spoiled and privileged and in such a daze, it's a miracle that I accomplished as much as I did.

Suicide survivors are usually workaholics. I certainly was; I worked nonstop. Many different kinds of men helped me evolve, in many different ways. They were friends and colleagues—in some cases, lovers and husbands—and they were mentors too, like Gore Vidal, Elia Kazan, and Lee Strasberg.

Looking back on it, I can't figure out how I did everything I did because I seemed to be doing everything at once in those days. Before I turned twenty I'd earned my first paycheck, opened my first bank account, was in college and auditioning. I loved my independence and reveled in my vagabond existence. The problem was that part of me felt pressured to conform so as to be accepted as a woman; it was the fifties, after all. The push-pull of so many forces, especially from my parents—their demands and their needs versus my demands and my needs—is also very much a part of this story. Slowly but surely I learned how to stand up for myself personally and professionally, and my ambivalence and confusion lessened.

One of the high points of my life—maybe the highest—was being accepted as a member of the Actors Studio (not to be confused with the TV series *Inside the Actors Studio,* hosted by James Lipton). At the time the Studio, the birthplace of "The Method," was the most influential and talked-about workshop for actors in America. Passing my final audition was a singular honor. I was one of five to be accepted that year—five out of five hundred.

However, I couldn't participate in classes at first. Since my brother's suicide I'd hidden behind a silent, detached facade. Instead I'd sit in the back row of the brick-walled theatre, writing down everything I was observing, listening to the Studio's master teacher Lee Strasberg as he challenged actors to dig for "internal truths." Back then I was a watcher more than a doer. Lee was the first person to encourage me to write. Once he came by as I was scribbling into a notebook and murmured, "Darling, maybe you should do what you are doing instead of acting. You seem to be enjoying it more."

Did I hear what he said—really *hear* him? No, not yet, because I wanted to prove to him that I could act.

By then I had worked for Lee and he'd been surprisingly gentle with me, although we both knew I'd been awful. He got tougher with me as time went on. He wouldn't let me get away with faking. He was always talking about behavior, behavior, behavior. Truthful, genuine behavior. *Real* behavior. I was already acting professionally when I got into the Studio, so I knew how to project externally, but working at the Studio forced me to open up and tap into my inner self. For the next ten years I appeared on Broadway and off, directed by Garson Kanin and Harold Clurman; on TV with George Roy Hill; and then I was featured opposite Audrey Hepburn in *The Nun's Story*. The memories of these experiences in theatre and film remain vivid to me decades after the fact. I've always wanted to share them.

But in the end, what I've needed most is to share the bittersweet recollections I have of my beloved little brother, Bart. He is at the heart of this journey. We were as close as twins. I confided in him, depended on him, adored him. But I can't explain what he did. I refuse to be an armchair shrink.

I don't think I've been self-indulgent in these pages. I dislike sentimentality. Instead I truly believe I've shown how the glories in my life outweigh the bleak and terrible. Writing this book has been cathartic. It's finally caused me to *feel*. I've cried and cried as I've written it, but that's good. My emotions were rock-solid for so many years. Now, as I finish *The Men in My Life*, my body feels lighter. I walk with more of a spring in my step. I've been carrying around a huge burden of grief and guilt for much too long.

Now it's almost gone.

The Men in My Life

Prologue

I HAD LEARNED the news in the middle of a dance rehearsal at Sarah Lawrence College; I was choreographing a piece to the tune of Frank Sinatra's exuberant "I've Got the World on a String." The studio I was working in was walled with mirrors so I could see the dancers from every angle, twirling and bending, and I could see myself too, skinny then, freckle-faced, serious. Suddenly my teacher Bessie Schönberg was pulled almost bodily out of the studio by the dean of students, Esther Raushenbush, who ordinarily didn't attend dance rehearsals.

Bessie returned moments later with a strange look on her face. She told me I had a phone call I must answer immediately. I ran out into the foyer and the next thing I heard was my father on the line saying, "Your brother, Bart, has killed himself with the .22 rifle Granddad gave him for his birthday." He had died in his room at Reed College. He was eighteen.

I didn't react. I couldn't cry. I found myself shivering uncontrollably because it was cold in the hall and I was barefoot and wearing only a leotard. "Go home to Mama right away." "Yes, Daddy, of course I will." Someone put a coat on my shoulders, and then, as if I were in a dream, someone else led me across the snowy campus to my dorm, where I dressed. My best friend, Marcia Haynes, had appeared out of nowhere, saying she would drive me to New York so I could be with my mother.

We didn't speak in the car. Marcia turned on the radio so we could listen to the news. Something about Sir Winston Churchill winning the Nobel Prize for Literature and Sir Edmund Hillary searching for the Abominable Snowman in the Himalayas. I couldn't absorb anything. Instead I stared out the window at the banks of trees glittering with ice that lined the Saw Mill River Parkway. It was December 13, 1953.

I kept thinking of Bart at target practice. That previous summer at our weekend home in Garrison, high on a hill overlooking the Hudson, Bart had practiced shooting tin cans set on a crate. The incessant crack of gunfire was so unnerving I'd run into the woods a quarter of a mile from the house and beg him to stop. He would be standing there in jeans and a T-shirt, emaciated, his head shaved. He would glare at me, take aim at his target, and fire. On those afternoons he'd go on firing that .22 rifle for hours. He never missed. He was a crack shot.

MY HEAD STARTED to ache; it was as if somebody was squeezing my brain very, very hard. There was a tightness around my eyes. I panicked. I had always been disgustingly healthy. Could I be having a stroke? A heart attack? I was twenty years old.

My head throbbed more the minute Marcia and I entered the so-called family brownstone on East Sixty-Eighth Street and I faced my reflection in the smoky mirrors that covered the halls of the foyer. ("So-called" because we had lived in so many places and never remained in any of them long enough to call them home.) My mother blamed her "restlessness." "I need to change my settings constantly!" she'd exclaim. But the moves invariably occurred after some crisis in my father's fast-paced, ever-changing career.

His name was Bartley Crum and he was a high-priced left-wing lawyer who dabbled in politics. His wealthy corporate clientele virtually disappeared with the advent of McCarthyism. Since we'd moved from San Francisco to New York in 1948 he'd been hired and fired by two Manhattan firms because he kept on defending communists. His luck changed briefly when he secured a partnership in a Wall Street office. The main reason: He had been able to bring them movie star Rita Hayworth as a client. He had been asked to negotiate her divorce from Prince Aly Khan.

At this very moment he was in Los Angeles meeting with Rita. I wondered when he'd be home. I imagined the three of us flying out to my brother's funeral in Portland—my mother, my father, and me, how we'd rush to the plane and might even be holding hands. Maybe for once we'd be a family. Together we'd grieve over the inexplicable death of someone I loved more than anyone in the world.

As Marcia and I climbed the stairs to the second floor, my heart beat rapidly, as it always did when I had to confront my mother. We found her pacing the floor of the living room. I was always surprised by how tiny she was because she had such a huge presence. Big protruding eyes, thin scornful mouth, trim little body— she had been a champion golfer long ago. My father often told her she reminded him of Bette Davis because of the brisk way Mama clipped her words, then paused between syllables. That evening she sounded exactly like Davis as she intoned, "Lamb-pie, what are you wearing?" (Skirt and sweater over my leotard) "When did you last take a bath?" The tone was affectionate yet mocking, and her shoulders twitched impatiently. Those Davis mannerisms drove me and my brother crazy.

I didn't answer, so she stopped pacing and offered me some hors d'oeuvres. "Delicious cheese ramekins." Another long pause. Marcia moved to the bar. "I'll fix us some drinks. Okay, Mrs. C.?" I think we all had vodka on the rocks.

So far there had been no mention of my brother. The Christmas tree was up. As always, Mama had done an amazing job of decorating; the branches were heavy with ornaments and twinkling lights, presents piled about. I tried to think of something to say. "Everything seems ready for the holidays," I murmured.

The phone rang, but Mama let it ring. Marcia picked it up. "Long distance from L.A." It was my father calling. "He wants to talk to you," Marcia said, handing the receiver to my mother, who grabbed at it. Silence for a moment and she began crying out, "No! No! No, I won't go . . . I can't go . . . I don't believe any of this. Bart was murdered, you fool! He was murdered."

I ran into the adjacent room so I could pick up the extension and hear what my father had to say. He was telling her sorrowfully, "No, Cutsie [her nickname—pronounced 'cutes'], it was not murder. Bart . . . killed himself."

"No!!" Mama repeated angrily. "No, I do not—will not believe it. He would never do that to us. He would never hurt us like this. He loved us too much to do this." Only then did her voice break.

"The funeral will be in Sacramento tomorrow," my father said. "You and Patti will fly out. I have made all the arrangements. We are booked into the best hotel. Bart will be buried in the family plot."

Another silence, and then Mama announced very coldly, "Well, I am not going. I am not going. Funerals are . . ."

"My darling," I heard my father say very softly, "this is our son." No answer.

"Gertie. Gertrude." For once my father addressed her by her real name. He was trying to be stern and commanding. It didn't work.

"I will not change my mind." And then she hung up and began her pacing again. I came back to the living room and faced her. "Mama, I want to go to the funeral. I think we should all go to the funeral."

"You are *not* going to the funeral. You are going to stay right here and be with me. I cannot be alone now." She was glaring at me.

Marcia stood by the fireplace, observing, implacable.

I DIDN'T ARGUE or fight back. At the time my mother was angry at me for not "living up to my potential" or appreciating my "privileged life" (a life I had been born into but was choosing not to live in). Even so, I couldn't bear her being angry with me. I agreed to stay with her and not go to the funeral. I knew even then that I would regret this decision for the rest of my life.

I gulped down my vodka and then poured myself another. Suddenly I imagined I could hear my brother's soft mocking voice in my ear. *You could be a drunk like our father if you don't watch out.* I heard myself answering back, "Daddy is not a drunk. He knows how to hold his liquor—he's under a lot of pressure."

Sure, sure, my brother singsonged. *How many times do we have to hear about him being blacklisted and losing all his money when he bought the newspaper?*

"Our father is a brave, gallant man."

Spare me your sentimentality, Attepe, Bart said in our private language. We'd invented it when we were kids and thought we were the only ones who could speak it. It was Pig Latin, and we spoke it so fast it used to drive our parents wild.

MARCIA AND I spent the night on the fourth floor, where my brother and I had a suite of rooms. I couldn't sleep, so I got up and wandered into his room. A single bed covered with a blue spread. One book on the desk, a copy of Einstein's biography, and next to it Frisky Jr.'s leash. He was our cocker spaniel who'd been run over by a car.

I felt numb, inconsolable. I wondered how I could go on without my brother. We'd been as close as twins, although we were as different as night is to day. I was agreeable, talkative, curious about everything. Bart was silent, moody, detached. He had a genius IQ. I was a lousy student, failing my classes, especially when we were in grammar school.

"Why? Why? Why?" I found myself choking out the words in the empty room.

What a stupid question, Attepe. Again I heard my brother's voice mocking softly in my ear.

I sank down on his bed. "I want to know. Why did you do it?" I heard myself talking to Bart as if he were still alive.

Mama says I was murdered. That's one way of putting it.

"I want to be with you." I'd begun to sob.

"Patti! What are you doing?" It was my mother, pulling open the door to my brother's room and marching in. "Who are you talking to?"

I turned to her, tears streaming down my cheeks. "I had to be in his room. Had to."

With that, Mama let out a groan and folded me into her arms.

OVER THE NEXT decade my brother and I would go on talking to each other, and each time I heard him, it would be a comfort. Oh yes, it was eerie too. He'd show up when I least expected it and then I'd whisper, "Are you here or everywhere now that you're dead?"

He didn't always answer, but I didn't care. The point was that we were together, if only briefly, and his visitations were as real to me as the traffic outside my window, the rain pelting against my cheeks.

Part One

Waking Up

Chapter One

DADDY USED TO say, "Our Bart was born with an angel on his shoulder." That seemed to be true (if you believed in angels). When he was three weeks old, Bart was fast asleep in his bassinet when a fire broke out in our nursery. We were living high in the Berkeley Hills then. Within minutes the room was an inferno of flames, and Daddy rushed in, scooped Bart up in his arms, and ran through the blaze to safety.

The next time Bart almost died, he was two. We were visiting friends in Napa Valley and he had toddled off by himself. Daddy noticed Bart was gone, ran to the swimming pool, dove in, and with a great splash and a cry, pulled his tiny son up out of the water.

These stories were part of family lore, like the time I ate rat poison when we were vacationing at Lake Tahoe and Mama noticed I had blue around my mouth and stuck her finger down my throat until I vomited. I was sent to the hospital and Mama was told that I'd ingested enough poison to kill nine men. When we were in our teens, Bart and I loved to tell each other these stories of our near-death experiences. "Mine were worse than yours," he would say. "I believe I am destined to die many deaths."

* * *

AS A LITTLE boy, Bart was small and delicate, with tawny skin and huge questioning gray eyes. Shy in the complicated way exceedingly intelligent people are shy, he was also as quiet as a shadow. He didn't want to speak to anyone but me until he was four, so we created our secret language together. But Bart preferred being alone, curled up with a book (he began reading very early) or looking through his telescope. He was fascinated by the heavens, the stars. Later music and science became his main interests. Eventually he would barricade himself within his eccentric mind while I lived out every reckless desire.

We spent much of our early childhood in our nursery in Berkeley, a wondrous place of books and toys and a hobbyhorse I rocked back and forth on continuously. I chattered happily to my parents whenever they came to visit. Bart, however, existed in utter silence. His main occupation was bouncing a big blue rubber ball up and down or staring out the window at San Francisco Bay.

By the age of four he still hadn't spoken a word. Mama was worried. She enrolled him in Erik Erikson's special nursery school on the university campus near our home. Erikson (who would become one of the most influential developmental psychologists and psychoanalysts in the country) was studying so-called normal children in long-term play situations. He became interested in Bart because he enjoyed playing by himself (and occasionally mouthing words as he did), but he never played with other children. Erikson had many sessions with my brother and finally he began to talk. But it was only when Daddy began reading to us from some of our favorite books—the Greek myths, *Peter Pan,* and *Mary Poppins*—that Bart opened up.

We were fascinated by the acerbic English nanny who took her charges on flights around London soaring above shingled rooftops, bobbing and dancing through the sky astride her parrot-handled umbrella. And the enchanter Peter Pan, who taught

Wendy and John and Michael how to jump into the wind—up, up into the air—though he never taught the children how to stop. And then he'd just disappear to Neverland, a place for adventures and memories.

One story captured my brother's fancy. It was the tale of the mythical Icarus, who didn't know his own limits; who flew so close to the sun that the heat melted the wax that bound his wings and he plunged to his death into the sea. Bart loved that scary image. When we were alone in the nursery, he'd stretch out his little arms and flap them and then run around and around the nursery until he got dizzy and sometimes fell down.

One day he began building an enormous pair of paper wings. "To fly away on," he told me excitedly. In the following weeks he would spend hours sitting on the floor of the nursery surrounded by rolls of white shelving paper, nails, bits of wood, string, pots of glue. He had no blueprint, no plan (he seemed to be working from some illustration in his head), but soon, miraculously, the wings began to take shape and spread like some monstrous prehistoric bird half-covering the nursery floor.

After they were built, he attempted to attach one wing to his little arm; he couldn't do it himself, so I tried to help, but the wing was so cumbersome we both toppled to the floor. We tried again, but the wings were obviously much too big. As soon as he realized this, Bart methodically began to destroy them, and then he started all over again.

It took him close to five months to rebuild those wings. When he did, he smiled triumphantly. "Now I can fly out the window," he told me.

It was early evening. I ran downstairs to tell my parents (they knew about the building of the wings and they were concerned, because my brother had already told them he wanted more than anything to fly out the window like Mary Poppins, like Icarus).

Daddy happened to be home; I remember he kissed me and said, "Oh thank you, baby," and he raced up to the nursery and knelt beside his little son, who was struggling unsuccessfully to attach one gigantic wing to his arm.

Daddy raved about the wings. "Goddamn feat of genius—so beautiful," he told him, but then he added that although Bart's plan to fly into the clouds was very brave, it would be unwise to try it now. Night had fallen. It was pitch-black out, "not even a moon to light your way," my father told him intensely. He gently advised him to wait until the sun came up. When it was light they would talk again.

The next morning came and we all assembled in the nursery: Bart and me, Mama and Daddy, and an engineer from the University of California whose help my father had enlisted. A middle-aged balding man with horn-rimmed glasses, he proceeded to explain to Bart that it was impossible for him to fly properly in those wings. That frankly it just wasn't safe. Bart listened, a frown on his face. After a while he nodded. He threw the wings away that very morning.

But he never stopped dreaming about the mysteries of the sky, the firmament. Years later, when we were at our country home in Aptos, California, we would often sleep outside in sleeping bags on the sun deck. Oh, it was beautiful, so clear and dark, millions of stars twinkling above us in the heavens. Every so often we would see a shooting star, and Bart would say, "I wish I knew where it was going."

WHILE BART WAS building those wings, our father was becoming one of the most successful and publicized young lawyers in San Francisco. He represented corporations like Hearst and Crown Zellerbach, but he also took on pro bono cases: Chinese immigrants with passport problems, teachers who didn't want to sign loyalty oaths. By 1940 Daddy started his own firm and he was part of the newly formed National Lawyers Guild, an association of progressive lawyers who supported Roosevelt's New Deal. There were rumors Daddy might be offered a federal judgeship or might run for Congress or even governor. The FBI began surveilling him after he became president of the guild's San Francisco chapter.

At this point Mama was achieving her own bit of celebrity. She'd just had her first novel published, a book called *Strumpet Wind*, and it was a bestseller. It was based on her experiences as a crime reporter for the *San Francisco Call-Bulletin*; she'd covered the trial of a sexy mail-order bride who took a lover and then shot her weak rancher husband.

After *Strumpet Wind* was published, Mama was on the radio and her picture was in the paper. Then Bette Davis phoned, saying the novel would make a perfect film vehicle for her. They met for drinks. Davis said she'd asked Jack Warner to option the book. Mama was ecstatic.

But then a month went by, and another, and another. Mama never heard from Davis again. She began suffering from migraines; she took to her bed moaning, but then she pulled herself together and doggedly started writing another novel.

That's when I decided to copy her. I'd tiptoe into her bedroom where she'd be typing furiously away and I'd sit on the floor with pad and pencil scribbling words on a page. Mama would eventually look down at me and order, "Write something down. An observation, a detail." And then she'd go back to her typing.

I'd try to describe the white rose drooping in a vase on Mama's bedside table. I loved having the pencil in my hand, loved pressing it down on the paper and seeing a word appear. "The rose has brownish petals." The act of writing made me feel good.

For my eleventh birthday Mama gave me a white leather diary with a lock and key, and I began jotting down my thoughts; in time I would keep yearly journals. After I left college I switched to loose-leaf notebooks. Every so often I'd reread some passages. There was a lot of daydreaming in those pages, as well as meandering questions where ambition, luck, desire—not to mention incipient storytelling—played a part. Mama called her journals "a lonely woman's habit." My journals seemed to be a record of my painful attempts to *think*.

AFTER THE JAPANESE bombed Pearl Harbor, we moved from Berkeley to San Francisco, to an apartment at the top of a very steep hill overlooking Fisherman's Wharf; we had to climb sixty-five steps to get there. I was enrolled in the Convent of the Sacred Heart, my brother at the Town School.

I was at my most idealistic, my most malleable. Catholicism was important to me because Daddy was so devout. He took us to Mass and taught us special prayers. I got caught up in the pageantry and imagined I could be a nun like Mother M, my favorite teacher at Sacred Heart. The absolute certainty of her faith carried with it a wonderfully heady sense of freedom and courage.

MEANWHILE, MAMA'S THIRD novel didn't sell and she took out her disappointment on us, flying into rages and slamming doors. Daddy finally insisted they go away by themselves for a few days. When they returned, they announced excitedly that they'd bought a country place across the Santa Cruz Mountains in a tiny hamlet called Aptos. For the next four years we spent every weekend there, as well as holidays and summers. We became very attached to our funny shingled house guarded by redwoods and we loved hearing the waves boom and crash on the beach nearby—the Pacific Ocean was less than a mile from our home.

At first Mama and Daddy spent all their time together at Aptos, cultivating the wild untamed gardens that spread out over the property. They cleared and pruned and planted. Soon there were orchards on the hill and a line of poplars on the driveway, and Daddy built a lathhouse for Mama to grow fuchsias in.

But Daddy was at his peak as a lawyer then; he had clients all over the state and he was active politically too. He'd disappear to New York or Washington for weeks, and then we'd get word he was coming back to us and Mama would invite friends over for elaborate meals. There was so much expectation, tension, concern—the train would be late or the plane couldn't land—he'd appear, briefcase bulging, coughing from too many cigarettes. It would take a while for him to relax, calm down, and then he would start telling everybody what he'd been doing: organizing a Fight for Freedom committee with Orson Welles; joining Paul Robeson in his anti-lynching campaign; starting to discuss a possible project with President Roosevelt . . .

Bart and I decided our father must be very brave, speaking out and trying to make the world a better place. When he was home he was the most lenient of fathers, letting us play the radio loud and eat all the candy we wanted. But we were glad Mama stayed home and created such a beautiful nest, even though she was the disciplinarian—having us tutored in French, standing over us as we practiced piano.

ALTHOUGH I DIDN'T realize it then, the differences between my parents were very important to my development. I wasn't taught to think there was any one model I had to follow. This allowed me to make my own synthesis from two very different kinds of minds. I learned from listening to their conversations; it was all vague and dreamy in my head, hearing the two most important adults in my life talking intimately to each other and not to me. Daddy was often placating Mama after his long absences—making excuses, giving her a diamond bracelet, which she threw back in his face.

"I don't want this!" she cried angrily. "I want *you*!"

He often made grand statements to her like, "You can do anything you want—anything your little heart desires." Later, he'd repeat that thought to me and I remembered Mama's response. She would argue, "Life isn't like that."

I felt very close to Mama in those years at Aptos. Physically, emotionally close. We painted our toenails with Revlon's Fire-Engine Red polish; we wore identical mother-and-daughter Lantz patterned dresses and Bart took a snapshot of us with our Brownie camera. Mama was struggling to write another novel. She'd type for hours on the sun deck and then she'd have a hard time sleeping, so she was up half the night reading Willa Cather's *Song of the Lark* (about a woman who gives up everything to become an artist). She'd underline passages in the book; her mind teemed with ideas and opinions, which she didn't always voice, especially when Daddy was around. He often addressed her as his "child bride." She behaved accordingly—most of the time.

Cooking became another obsession for her. She'd graduated from the Cordon Bleu in Paris; she was already a celebrated hostess in San Francisco and now Aptos, where she gave a swirl of brunches, cocktail parties, and suppers. She taught me how to cook. I learned to roast chicken so it's always tender; I made soups, baked pies.

By early 1945 Daddy was gone again on special missions, first for President Roosevelt, and then for Truman after the former's death. Mama would remain outside even when it was foggy, overseeing our new gardener, Happy Kanta. A mysterious drifter with a "green thumb," he could make anything grow. Our gardens bloomed magnificently that year and Mama would stay outside with Happy until it got dark. Then another man appeared at Aptos, a sardonic bearded psychiatrist named Dr. Saul. I'd been introduced to him first in San Francisco, and then at Aptos I saw them kissing in broad daylight on the patio. This upset me very much. Didn't she love Daddy anymore?

When Daddy came home he and Mama quarreled about Saul. But months went by then something strange happened. Daddy stopped caring. He'd return from Washington or New York and appear at Aptos—and, though Saul might be there, he didn't bat an eye. The two men would shake hands. Mama seemed relaxed and loving to them both. She'd mix them drinks and they'd join her in the kitchen to help prepare supper. My brother and I would watch as Saul tossed the salad and Daddy fried the burgers (I'd throw in chopped onions and garlic and toast the buns). Meanwhile Mama and Bart would be setting the table.

Everybody *seemed* to be having such a good time, but I grew bewildered and afraid. Afraid that Mama and Daddy would break up, that our family would be no more. I couldn't bear that idea. I wonder if my confusion about power and powerlessness, authority, obedience, and evasion came from the way our parents operated with each other and us.

Looking back on it now, I seem to want to remember only the beauty of the gardens at Aptos and watching the fog roll in from the ocean. I'd like to forget Daddy passing out drunk after Saul left us and Mama beginning to scream and cry. Remembering the beauty that was part of my childhood and forgetting the dark stuff—that's how I survived.

BESIDES, WHEN YOU'RE a kid you deal with circumstances the way they are. So Bart and I didn't give our parents too much thought; we had our own lives to lead. Whenever we were at Aptos, we'd sometimes spend entire days with our beloved cousin Elena Bosworth, a rambunctious freckled blonde. We loved exploring the woods behind our property with her.

Otherwise my brother and I would escape to our hideout, a

one-room shack we shared next to the abandoned guesthouse about a quarter of a mile from the main house. We loved our hideout; it was a place where we acted out our fantasies of what we might be when we grew up. In one corner of the room Bart "invented" potions with his chemistry set or studied bugs and dead snakes under his microscope.

On the other side of the room, which I'd papered with photographs of my favorite movie stars, I'd propped up a big cracked mirror on a dressing table. Mama had given me an elaborate makeup box and a book filled with illustrations of exotic women. I'd spend hours transforming myself into a clown, painting red dots on my dead-white cheeks, or into a ballerina, with exaggerated eyebrows and fake eyelashes. I loved pretending to be different people.

When I was eleven, I performed in a musicale at the Convent of the Sacred Heart. It was set in a toy shop and I played a wooden soldier who breaks into song in the middle of the second act. I remember the experience of standing center stage, belting out the number in a loud, clear voice. I could sense the audience was delighted and I received applause before I had even finished singing. At the curtain call, a warm rush of love and approval rolled over me as I took my bow. I heard my father call out, "Brava!"

Afterward Daddy told me I'd "stopped the show. You have star quality. Think about becoming an actress!" I'd already been dreaming about it (what little girl doesn't?) and had decided my favorite actresses were Greer Garson and Ingrid Bergman.

I thought more about acting after Daddy took me to see my first play, *Harriet*, at the Curran Theatre in San Francisco, with Helen Hayes as Harriet Beecher Stowe, the author of *Uncle Tom's Cabin*. My heart pounded in expectation as the curtains parted, revealing a brilliantly lit stage. I'll never forget Helen Hayes's entrance. She was a tiny, determined woman who grew in stature as she walked around and around in a circle pontificating about the evils of the

Civil War and slavery. What a hold she had on her audience. Every-one sat in rapt attention until the curtain came down.

For days I pretended I was Harriet, walking around my room in a circle. Then Daddy hired a Shakespearean coach and I learned speeches from *The Merchant of Venice*. I'd perform them in front of guests and Daddy would beam; I was his "beautiful baby." My brother stood on the sidelines glowering. I was afraid he might be jealous. I didn't want him to be, although it was clear that Daddy did favor me. He couldn't seem to communicate with his son.

Once I heard my parents discussing me after I'd been kept back a grade and Bart had been pushed ahead. "Patti's the pretty one," Mama said. "Bart is smarter." Daddy argued, "I'm not so sure." Still, I got it into my head that I must be stupid, even though I didn't *feel* stupid. But sometimes I pretended to be.

AFTER OUR GRANDDAD Bosworth, a gruff imposing figure, heard me recite at parties, he complained to Mama that I was getting too much attention and that Bart, then age nine, was not getting enough. "I'm going to do something about it," he declared.

In the summer of 1945, Granddad bought my brother a .22 rifle and they drove to target practice in Marin every Saturday afternoon for months. Bart confided that the noise of bullets exploding upset him at first, but after a while he began to enjoy hitting the bull's-eye. He refused to shoot at birds, but he became a crack shot.

Granddad also took Bart to a gym; Bart exercised with weights and a teacher came over to teach him boxing. He would come home from these outings flushed, eyes sparkling, and then he'd beat away at a punching bag in his room. Learning to shoot and box gave him confidence, and he grew very strong.

So much so that when I tried to wrestle with him, he could pin me to the ground even though he was smaller than I was. I'd keep on struggling and he would laugh; our bodies would press together and this aroused me. Sometimes I'd wrap him onto my back and gallop around with him through the gardens at Aptos.

I was something of a tomboy then; so was my best friend, Terry Ashe. We exercised polo ponies together in Golden Gate Park and played frenetic volleyball games at the convent. For a while we were two against the world, even when we fought; we knew we'd be friends for life, and we still are. I had first spotted her at chapel and decided she was the most beautiful girl I'd ever seen—thick, dark curly hair and perfect features. I already knew she was the smartest student—A-plus in Latin and math—and was on scholarship; she was the best Catholic too. Oh, she was so capable, but she was also fun. She visited me at Aptos; she was the only person aside from Bart who I allowed into the hideout. Terry dreamed of becoming an actress too.

Then when we turned thirteen, we went through all sorts of mood swings. My breasts started swelling and I got my period. Mama didn't explain; she just handed me a Kotex—she was not about to talk to me about what it was like to live in a female body. Her way of teaching me about sex was giving me Colette to read. The great novelist believed that love and passion were the paramount experiences in a woman's life, more important than marriage or children. I wondered if Mama felt that way too.

I remember having incoherent discussions about sex with Terry. We'd read a pamphlet called *The Facts of Life* about sexual intercourse and where babies came from; the word *love* wasn't mentioned. We came away feeling confused. Sex in those days was such a big secret. We imagined that the act itself (although we didn't know exactly *what* the act was) could be sublime. Exhausting, crazy-making. This was implied in the movies we were seeing such as *Duel in the Sun*, a garish Western with Jennifer Jones as the panting half-breed Pearl Chavez, totally hung up on the taunting sexy cowboy Lewt McCanles (played by Gregory Peck).

Duel in the Sun didn't give us any answers, so we practiced kissing our pillows. Then in dancing school I flirted with various boys because I fantasized I could be a "sexpot," but I was also pretending to be a "good girl" because that was how I was expected to behave. Even so, when I'd practice the samba with Clark Smith, who had rosy cheeks and a shock of blond hair, I'd feel a tightness between my legs and I'd wonder if I should go to Confession. The taboos against sex were fierce, and to make matters more serious I was Catholic. The Church said it was a sin to have sex before marriage, and no man would ever marry a woman unless she was a virgin. Clark and I attended swimming parties together in Marin and he gave me a corsage, but we never kissed.

Then I met Pete when I was fourteen. He wore a leather jacket and had the beginnings of a scruffy beard. Mama disapproved of him ("He's from the other side of the tracks"), but that didn't matter to me. On our first date we rolled around in the grass in Golden Gate Park like a couple of puppies. Then we drove up to Twin Peaks in his jalopy and began kissing; Pete kissed me until my mouth grew swollen. He kept saying I was "hot" and he wanted to "go all the way." Once he tried to pull my panties down and we began tussling in the car. I got scared and tried to wriggle free, and he banged my head against the dashboard. I cried out in pain, stunned by the violence. He said he was sorry over and over again, but I told him quietly to take me home, and I refused to see him again.

I felt so lost after that experience. I missed the excitement and the tension as much as it overwhelmed me. I began spending more time with Terry again. We'd ride horseback with another friend, Pat Harrison, at her ranch in Marin, but Mama wanted me to stay home and study. By now we'd moved to a big house on Green Street near the Presidio. I'd be in my room, too restless to do schoolwork, so instead I'd wander through the silent, immaculate rooms in the late afternoons talking to myself. My fantasy life blossomed and I created an imaginary character, a "husband" I named Bill, to keep me company. Bill was sympathetic and kind and let me ramble on. Once Bart came upon me yakking to Bill. He told me I was nuts and should concentrate on my homework.

Except for composition, I wasn't doing well in school, but Bart was an A student and helped me raise my math grades. I stopped talking to Bill so much and spent more time with my brother.

Bart allowed me to do so, even though he now had a best friend, Arthur Mehija, a small handsome boy who appreciated his wry humor and taciturn ways. Sometimes I'd watch them play tennis in the park and then we'd go to Blum's for hot fudge sundaes. Bart talked about his new heroes, Mozart and Albert Einstein. In these men he saw what human beings were capable of.

"I don't want to be like you," he'd say to me, commenting on my ambitions. "I don't know what I want to be yet, but I don't want to be like you."

We'd still spend long lazy days together at our hideout or we'd race each other down the beach before we stopped to collect shells or watch the sun sink behind the rim of the ocean. We were living in a dreamworld then; our life seemed so idyllic on the surface— and then everything began to change.

Chapter Two

IN 1947, AT the start of the Cold War, fear of communism let loose a wave of political oppression in this country that seems almost incomprehensible today. My father became one of the lawyers for the Hollywood Ten, those writers and directors accused of being communists and subpoenaed to appear in front of the House Un-American Activities Committee (HUAC) and testify as to their political beliefs. Daddy believed defending them would be "a piece of cake"—the hearings were unconstitutional, he said. It was not against the law to be a communist.

But a lot of people disagreed with him, especially Senator Joseph McCarthy and J. Edgar Hoover. After Daddy defended the Ten, the FBI began surveying him relentlessly. He lost so many big clients he had to rethink how he was going to support us.

In the next months we moved to New York and Daddy bought the left-wing newspaper *PM*, which he renamed the *New York Star*. He began drinking more and taking pills. Despite his best efforts, the *Star* folded within eight months.

THE REAL NIGHTMARE began shortly after that, on a snowy February 9, 1950, not long after my parents' latest dinner party. We were now living in a rented brownstone on East Fifty-First Street in the heart of Manhattan. My brother and I were upstairs doing our homework. Bart was then at the Collegiate School and at the top of his class. I was at Miss Chapin's and failing almost everything.

Around three a.m. my brother and I were both awakened by a thud. It seemed to have come from the kitchen. We rushed into the upstairs hall and clutched at each other. We heard a scuffling of feet, voices raised. Yanking on our robes, we tiptoed down the two flights of stairs to the first-floor landing. We were just in time to see our father lying inertly on a stretcher and being carried by two attendants out the front door to a waiting ambulance. We couldn't tell whether he was dead or alive. Mama followed, wrapped in her mink coat and smearing lipstick across her mouth. She climbed into the ambulance after him, and it sped off into the night, sirens wailing.

We padded down to the kitchen and questioned the servants—Bernice, our cook, and her husband, Robert, who served as butler/chauffeur. At first they didn't want to tell us anything, but we persisted with anxious questions until finally Bernice admitted that Daddy had taken an overdose of pills. The pills combined with alcohol "could be pretty deadly." Bernice was quoting my mother now, who had pleaded with my father to stop mixing barbiturates with whiskey.

The following day we learned that Daddy had survived the overdose and was recovering at Lenox Hill Hospital. We kept asking to see him and Mama kept telling us he couldn't have visitors. She was trying to protect us from observing anything unpleasant. Only she would watch our father sobbing on the toilet in acute anxiety as he went into withdrawal. He had never experienced such a personal public failure as the closing of the *New York Star*. "He feels humiliated and utterly defeated," she told us.

After two weeks at Lenox Hill, he managed to get more Nembutal through a friend and took another overdose. His stomach was pumped out just in time.

IT WAS ANOTHER month before Daddy pulled himself together. He returned home pale and shaky, insisting he'd kicked the pills. With the support of colleagues he was invited to join the prestigious firm of Poletti, Diamond, Roosevelt, Friedin & Mackay. That lessened his money worries to some extent, but he knew he had to get some big clients to survive in that firm. The next thing I knew, he reeled one in.

I came home from Chapin one afternoon planning to sing along with my new *South Pacific* album, and there was the movie star Montgomery Clift lying on the floor of our living room talking politics with my father.

"Hey, baby," Daddy called out, "you remember Monty Clift."

How could I forget? We'd just seen him in the western *Red River* two nights before.

By now Monty had jumped to his feet and was shaking my hand. I was thinking, *He's as beautiful and mysterious in person as he was on the screen as the cowboy adventurer Matt Garth*. We stood facing each other; his large, dark deep-set eyes glittered under thick black brows. I didn't know how to react, so I bobbed a curtsy. With that Monty bobbed a curtsy back and then let loose with a wild hooting laugh.

I'd never heard such a laugh, gulping and high-pitched, almost faintly hysterical. I heard it a lot for the next couple of weeks, because Monty was in and out of the brownstone talking in spurts to my father—telling us both that he'd just turned down a movie called *Sunset Boulevard*. Then he'd fall into a silence or break into that weird mirthless laugh. I couldn't figure him out, but I couldn't stop looking at him; he was absolutely drop-dead gorgeous. He'd be watching me too and I'd wonder if he thought I was a complete idiot because I was obviously so smitten with him.

He left to star opposite Elizabeth Taylor in *A Place in the Sun*, playing the doomed tragic killer who's sent to the electric chair. Daddy knew the warden at San Quentin, so he arranged for Monty to spend the night in the death house in preparation for his role. When he came back from filming, he visited us again, and I can still see him pacing back and forth around our living room describing what it was like to meet the convicts on Death Row.

Then he disappeared. He'd chain-smoked every time he was with us; the ashtrays were overflowing. I saved one of his cigarette butts. I still have it somewhere, encased in waxed paper.

(At the time, I didn't know that Monty was gay. When I began researching his biography, I discovered he'd always led an agonizingly double life. Those feelings of dislocation, smoldering hostility, and sexual ambiguity are mirrored in all his films, from *The Misfits* to *The Young Lions*. These qualities are part of what's made him a supreme gay icon today. "I dream about him, but I relate to him too," a gay friend said.)

MEETING MONTY WAS one of the few happy interludes during that melancholy spring. Mama wouldn't discuss our father's state of mind, let alone his addictions. He was supposedly okay—except he wasn't. He was starting to medicate himself (later I discovered he obtained his pills on the black market). I could tell the minute his speech slurred or his eyelids drooped, and then I'd start looking for the tranquilizers, uppers, and sleeping pills he kept hidden all over the brownstone. Whenever I found a stash behind the bookcase or inside the liquor cabinet, I'd flush them down the toilet.

Even so, Mama kept telling us, "Everything is all right," in spite of the fact that Daddy still didn't have enough clients, there were too many bills to pay, and he just couldn't stop being dependent on barbiturates, let alone alcohol. But Mama didn't or couldn't deal with what was happening with our father. She evaded our questions; occasionally she told downright lies.

By summer she announced that Bart and I were going to be sent away from home. We guessed she didn't want us to see Daddy screwing up again. I was enrolled at the coeducational International School of Geneva (nicknamed Ecolint). My brother would be attending Deerfield Academy in Massachusetts. He was overjoyed; I protested vehemently. We spent a last melancholy month at Aptos before the place was sold.

THAT FALL I was put on a plane headed for Switzerland. I managed to control myself during the flight, but as soon as I saw the snowcapped Alps I began crying like a maniac. The headmistress of Ecolint, Mlle. Travelletti, who resembled the Wicked Witch of the West right down to her pointed nose and the hairy mole on her chin, greeted me at the airport and drove me into Geneva. I cried all the way. At first she tried to comfort me, but she spoke little English, so it did no good. She ended up taking me to my room and leaving me there to unpack.

I looked out the window at the school buildings that surrounded a gloomy cobblestone court, and I continued to cry. I cried off and on for the next twenty-four hours. My tears didn't cease until Mlle. Travelletti sent me to a hospital. As soon as the nurse left my room I called New York, begging to come home.

My father said no, emphatically. "This is a great opportunity and you must take advantage of it."

I was stunned; I was used to getting what I wanted. I argued weakly, but he wouldn't change his mind. I took his refusal as a betrayal. I'd said something he didn't want to hear. I was disagreeing with him; now he was punishing me.

After I hung up I fell back on the pillows, exhausted from crying.

The windows of my hospital room faced Lake Geneva, with its Jet d'Eau fountain shooting geysers of water into the air, which then plunged back into the lake's shimmering blue surface. But Switzerland's beauty didn't comfort me.

I lay in bed for what seemed like hours feeling lost and abandoned, and then a part of me turned off—a tender, feeling, thinking part of me. I decided I'd never allow myself to be so hurt or in such pain again. And I vowed never to show anyone how I felt about *anything*. It gave people too much power.

I didn't realize at that moment what a big decision this was or how it would affect me. After a while I had a harder and harder time expressing my feelings and became so detached from them that I often didn't know *how* I felt. My second husband would remark on my "coldness." I would assure him "it's just an act." He'd shake his head: "It's too successful."

Maybe, but for a long time I thought it helped me survive.

MEANWHILE, BART WAS happier than he'd ever been in his life. He loved Deerfield. When Mama and Daddy visited him, he'd greeted them with such uncharacteristic exuberance they were surprised. He showed them around, leading them past the classrooms, the lab, and the gym to the seventy-five acres of green playing fields set against the rolling hillsides overlooking the Deerfield River. Once or twice they could hear the sound of a chugging train. The Boston–New Haven railway tracks lay unusually close to the edge of the campus.

Near the end of their walk they were joined by Arthur Mehija, Bart's friend from Town School. Arthur had spent so much time with us that he was almost like a member of our family.

Bart was more forthcoming than usual that afternoon, describing some of his courses and a teacher he especially admired. But he didn't mention he had a new friend named Clark Steuer, who was round and jolly and very, very smart. Arthur had introduced them during the first weeks of the fall semester. The instant they met, they had eyes only for each other and became inseparable.

The friendship between Clark and my brother intensified through the fall and winter. Even so, he and Arthur would always have breakfast together, but as Arthur admitted later, "things weren't as intimate between Bart and me after he met Clark."

One spring afternoon in May, Arthur happened upon the two boys in the locker room of the gym with their arms around each other. They were both naked and had erections. Arthur thought they saw him. He hurried out, shutting the door behind him. "I didn't want to think about what I'd seen," he later told me.

THE FOLLOWING MORNING Arthur went down the hall of his dorm to pick Bart up for breakfast. "It was our routine; we always did that," he said. But Bart wasn't in his room, so Arthur went into Clark's room, "and it was as if someone had ransacked the place . . . Everything was in violent disarray—clothes, books thrown everywhere—windows open, letting in a stiff breeze. I remember thinking how cold the room was."

Arthur hurried down to the dining room. But neither Clark nor Bart was at their regular table. After breakfast the entire student body was called into the assembly hall and there was a brief announcement that Clark Steuer had killed himself. No explanation, no reason.

Apparently, early that very morning—at dawn—Clark had walked across the two sweeping green fields near the school, carrying a small stool with him. He was wearing only his underwear. He hung himself by his necktie from a tree right across from the railroad tracks. A train conductor had sighted the body swinging from the branches.

That same day around noon my brother was hustled out of

Deerfield in a taxi and sent back to New York on the train. He showed up unannounced at the brownstone, my mother told me afterward. "He was in a state of shock. He couldn't speak. He just marched up to his room on the fourth floor and lay on his bed facedown."

MY FATHER PHONED Deerfield immediately, demanding to know why his son had been sent home from the school so abruptly without informing his parents so they could at least have met him at the station. None of the teachers would speak to him, but he finally reached Arthur, who explained exactly what had happened. My father still couldn't understand why Bart had been sent home in the first place. It was as if he was personally being blamed for Clark Steuer's death.

The following morning, Daddy took the train up to Deerfield to confront the headmaster, Frank Boyden, who had also been avoiding him. Boyden was a legendary character, a crusty old despot who had been running the academy with an iron hand since 1902. He'd raised a fortune for the school and had made it more intellectually competitive with Choate and Exeter. Boyden was proud of all that he'd accomplished, and he was not going to let Clark Steuer's suicide tarnish the school's impeccable reputation. After he spoke to my father, he proceeded to hush up the death. (Indeed, when I tried to document the incident decades later, I was told by the school's PR office that a suicide had never occurred at Deerfield, nor had a student named Bart Crum ever attended the academy, although his name was in the school yearbook.)

Daddy repeated to Boyden what he'd asked Arthur. Why was his son removed from the school when he had nothing to do with Clark Steuer's tragic death? Boyden replied, "Your son and Clark had an intense emotional attachment," the last phrase uttered in ominous, accusatory tones. He added that under the circumstances it was better if Bart did not return to the school. "Think about it," he said. Daddy didn't put up any argument. He gathered up his son's books and the clothes he'd left behind, and took the next train to New York.

AT THE TIME I wasn't informed of the terrible incident at Deerfield. In Geneva it was spring and I was barely cracking a book. Instead I necked passionately with some of Ecolint's roughest, wildest students—rich Arab and Egyptian boys whose fathers were oil potentates.

By then I was breaking all sorts of rules, sneaking out of study hall and biking into Geneva after the five p.m. curfew. I started rendezvousing with a mop-headed actor named Raymond whom I'd picked up in a coffee bar in La Vieille Ville. I didn't tell him I was only sixteen; I just made him race me on my bike, ending up on the lawn near the lake.

When Ecolint's headmistress, Mlle. Travelletti, discovered I was meeting Raymond, she flew into a rage because I was a minor. She warned me I'd be expelled if I ever saw him again. Meanwhile I was confined to campus until the semester ended.

That didn't stop me. Through friends, Raymond and I arranged to see each other at dusk in a park behind the school. It just so happened that Ecolint's hefty gym teacher was jogging around the park at that hour. She spotted us kissing behind a tree. I was sent back to New York the following afternoon.

MY PARENTS WERE waiting for me at Idlewild outside customs. After the initial hugs and kisses, Mama asked me, "What in God's name did you do?"

"I don't think I did anything that bad," I retorted sulkily. "I just liked this boy and I wanted to be with him."

I noticed that Daddy seemed preoccupied. He didn't greet me

with the usual "Hey, baby, give your old man a kiss" routine. He grabbed up my suitcases and hurried us into a waiting cab. Once we were speeding back to Manhattan, he started telling me about Bart and all that had happened at Deerfield. He'd been home now for close to a month since his friend's death. "He doesn't talk—won't talk—at all, and he won't do anything except listen to music."

"We are hoping you may be able to reach him," Mama said quietly. "You've always been so close."

Bart had barely communicated to me during our many months of separation. I'd written him a couple of notes—one from London; one from Chamonix, where I'd gone skiing. When he didn't respond, I'd assumed he was caught up with school activities. On his birthday I sent him a box of Swiss chocolates. He'd responded with a scrawled postcard: "I don't like chocolates. Remember?" But again, his silences hadn't bothered me—he never talked much anyway.

Once home we gathered in the kitchen. Daddy brought my brother from his room. He loomed behind our father, looking skinnier and taller than I remembered. Pimples dotted his cheeks. He didn't respond when I attempted to hug him; he just stared vacantly straight ahead.

We proceeded to eat supper in silence, feeling shy and uncomfortable with one another. Nine months had passed since we'd been together as a family. How could we possibly catch up? Were our phones still being tapped? Was Daddy still on pills? Was Mama seeing Saul?

Bart barely touched his food. "Not hungry," he mumbled.

Of course we avoided our pain. We could not, nor did we want to, explain ourselves.

Bart bolted from the table before dessert was served.

After supper Daddy brought up the subject of my expulsion. He thought it was preposterous, but he knew that if it was on my school record, it might be harder for me to get into college, so he subsequently called some high-powered friends in Geneva and the expulsion was expunged from my record.

But I remained in disgrace all that summer. I was not allowed to date; I was coached in math and science, my worst subjects. Most of the time I sat in my room writing in my diary or writing long letters to Raymond in my imperfect French. He'd answer in his even more imperfect English. It was hard to communicate. As the weeks went by, we wrote fewer letters, and then we stopped altogether.

THE WORST PART about being home again was that I seemed to have lost my brother. He had no desire to talk to me or spend time with me. He was no longer my mocking confidant; now he existed in stony silence, rarely leaving his room. I'd bring him his favorite ice cream and he'd refuse to eat it. I'd plead with him to come to the movies, take a walk in Central Park, go off to the American Museum of Natural History—his favorite place was the Planetarium. He'd always shake his head. And when I tried to speak in our private language, he'd clap his hands over his ears.

I was very upset; in the past we'd always helped each other. Now he was resisting me. I felt as if I was starting to lose him.

Mama arranged for Arthur Mehija to make special visits, hoping they'd be a comfort but also hoping that Bart might finally communicate—something, anything. We'd wait while Arthur walked up to the fourth floor; an hour would go by and Arthur would come back down to the living room, shrugging his shoulders. Apparently they barely spoke. Bart would be lying facedown on his bed while Arthur tried to talk to him. Once or twice they played chess.

"But he was practically catatonic," Arthur admitted. "He is going through such agony and shame inside himself."

Soon after Arthur's visits, Mama sought psychiatric help for

Bart. She saw three doctors; she wanted to find someone who would treat her son gently, who wouldn't be judgmental. As usual, she took notes. She shared them with me later, confiding that she'd been brave enough to mention the phrase "homosexual tendencies" in regards to Bart and his friend at Deerfield. That's how delicate a matter it was in those days to suggest that anyone would have the bad luck to be gay. At that point, I certainly didn't want to consider the possibility. I refused to believe that my brother might be gay.

One therapist went off on a rant, saying that homosexuals were "dangerous." Another doctor used the word "unstable." The lack of sensitivity and knowledge about homosexuals was total. Mama told me, "These men were unenlightened and downright ignorant."

Mama knew because Mama had done her homework. In 1948 she'd read and reread two books that had begun to change the public's perception of sexuality. One was *Sexual Behavior in the Human Male* by Dr. Alfred C. Kinsey and his colleagues, a scientific treatise based on thousands of interviews, which revealed that many Americans had a "strong erotic interest in their own sex." The other was a novel called *The City and the Pillar* by a twenty-six-year-old named Gore Vidal. It was the coming-out story of a man who was completely comfortable making love to another man.

Mama underlined passages in Vidal's novel such as "Everybody is by nature bisexual. Nothing is 'right'; only denial of instinct is wrong." She thought a lot about the importance of Vidal's words, but she didn't speak of them to Daddy. My father had a "thing about pansies," as he put it. He felt uncomfortable around them.

THROUGHOUT THAT HOT, muggy summer of 1950, Bart remained in his room listening to music. Mahler's Eighth Symphony would be on full blast, the sound turned on so loud the floors would literally vibrate and the bare empty spaces would resound with choral pronouncements of revelation and redemption while trumpets and trombones blared.

I would tiptoe in and sit next to him.

It was obvious he was still grieving, still caught up in the nightmare of what had happened at Deerfield. I imagined he would finally rage and cry in my arms and explain why his friend had hanged himself. But my brother never moved, and when he finally spoke, his voice was muffled by pillows. "If you care about me at all, you will leave me alone. Go away, please."

I think he would have stayed forever in that room, enveloped by music, but Daddy insisted he leave the house and "get some air." He took us both down to Penn Station the day the Hollywood Ten were sent to prison. "You should see this. It's historical," he said.

I have a vague memory of joining a jostling, respectful crowd of more than a thousand people, some holding signs proclaiming the Ten's innocence. A few people recognized my father and ran over to shake his hand.

When we returned home there was a sedan parked outside with FBI agents in it. Daddy rushed us inside and bolted the door. We peered out a few moments later and the sedan was gone.

BY THE END of the summer it occurred to us that Daddy was spending an awful lot of time at home. Then Mama explained that while we were away in school he'd been asked to leave the Roosevelt firm—no explanation given, but he suspected his politics were the reason. He didn't put up a fight, but after he walked out of his office, he took his third overdose of sleeping pills.

But it hadn't been fatal, Mama rattled on; she obviously thought we were old enough to hear the truth. His stomach had been pumped out and a few days later he was back hustling for new clients and making speeches for Israel.

This last suicide attempt didn't seem to affect him, but it affected

Bart. After listening to Mama tell the story, he ran to the toilet and vomited. It was weird. Daddy was almost radiant and full of crazy energy; I realize now he was probably back on uppers.

My brother, however, never took medication for his depression. So he endured it and it must have been hell.

THAT FALL, BART and I were both enrolled in the same progressive coeducational boarding school in Stockbridge, Massachusetts, set on a rambling estate of nine acres of rolling green hills. I was a senior, he was a junior (Bart had skipped a grade). For the first time in my life I buckled down and studied hard because I did want to go to college and I wanted to prove to my parents that I could achieve academically.

During those months at Stockbridge, Bart and I barely communicated. He'd become involved with a group of rebellious students who seemed disenchanted by everything. Bart followed the lead of a strange boy with a thin, sharp face named Tobias. Late that winter the two of them ran away from the school and were gone for two days, hiding out in Pittsfield where they slept overnight in a movie theatre and then tried to thumb a ride to Boston. When they were brought back to Stockbridge by the police they were sullen and uncommunicative. I tried in vain to get my brother to tell me why he'd worried everybody so, and he just glared at me and then cupped his hand over his ear as if he hadn't heard me and murmured, "Eh wot?"

In the past Bart had always helped me in math and science, in which he excelled. He did coach me while we were at Stockbridge, but he seemed resentful. Then the mood passed. He even seemed briefly happy when I was accepted at Sarah Lawrence. I told him I wouldn't have gotten in if it hadn't been for his help. "That's ridiculous," he said.

*   *   *

EASTER VACATION OF 1951, Bart sank into a deep depression. Mama took him to another psychiatrist. After a couple of sessions with my brother, the doctor met with my parents and told them their son was "clinically depressed" and so despairing he could be suicidal. He rarely spoke in session and often fell asleep. When he did speak, however, he never mentioned his family; he never mentioned having a sister. The doctor concluded that Bart should go to the Austen Riggs Center for more complete evaluation.

My father refused to send Bart to Riggs. "My son is not crazy," he declared. "He will get over this."

As if to prove it, and to get his mind off his troubles, Daddy drove Bart up to see a house in Garrison he had decided to buy as a weekend getaway. It was high on a hill with windows overlooking the sweep of the Hudson River. Bart loved the house and the view. He tramped around the grounds with Daddy and together they discovered, half a mile away, an unfinished castle. It had been built in the early 1900s by a man called Dick. He never had the money to finish it, so it was called "Dick's Folly," but it was famous in the area, taking its place with other historic Gothic castles like Castle Rock, which stands above a steep hill opposite West Point.

Bart was excited about the castle. He told me he and Daddy were going to take sleeping bags and camp out there. I'm almost sure they never did.

Chapter Three

IN EARLY SEPTEMBER, Mama and Daddy drove me up to Sarah Lawrence College. They kissed me goodbye and left, and I was relieved to see them go. Though as I watched them drive away, I experienced the familiar feeling of being abandoned again. I felt the same way I had felt when I'd been sent to Switzerland, but then the feeling passed and I was glad I'd left home and was away from my extremely depressed brother.

I'd been assigned to Westlands, a large Tudor-type dorm building complete with stained-glass windows, which housed the administrative staff and some boarders. It stood at the top of the tree-studded green hills that were part of the campus grounds rising above Bronxville.

I loved the suite I'd been delegated to; it was huge, with a sloping floor and banks of windows that flooded everything with light. I liked my two roommates. They were also freshmen—decent, well-meaning young women who wanted to be friends. For a while they were patient and indulgent with me, but they ended up being exasperated because I could not finish unpacking. For the next three months, my suitcases lay open on the floor, most of my possessions scattered about: movie magazines, my baby pillow, a quilt. As soon as I took off an item of clothing, I'd drop it on the floor, and often I'd just push junk under my bed—old newspapers, candy wrappers, an umbrella. I even left half-drunk cartons of milk on the windowsill to sour.

My lame excuse was that I had no time to clean up my portion of the room. In those first weeks at college I was running around the campus trying to absorb everything. I have a blurred snapshot of me in my black leotard and green jersey, vaulting up the hill to classes. I would often drop notepads and books in my eagerness to attend such and such a lecture or explore the new dance studio at Reisinger Concert Hall or audition for an upcoming play.

Many of my fellow freshmen had vague notions about becoming successful as something—poets, doctors, journalists, painters—but I wanted to be *both* an actress and a writer. The creative ferment at Sarah Lawrence supported our dreams. There were jazz concerts in the student lounge, Norman Dello Joio was rehearsing his opera *The Triumph of St. Joan,* and Joseph Campbell was talking about heroes and myths and telling us to "follow your bliss."

I decided to major in dance. My don was a powerful outspoken woman named Bessie Schönberg, whose kinky hair was yanked into a topknot. Bessie was the head of the dance department at Sarah Lawrence; she'd been at the college since 1938 teaching dance and choreography, and she was a legend in the field. Jerome Robbins used to come up to campus to have lunch with her and so did Merce Cunningham. Bessie had been a member of Martha Graham's original company. She lived and breathed Graham's dictum: It was all about the integrity of the work, the process of work being as important as the work itself.

As we stood doing our warm-ups before class, reflected in the mirrors of the dance studio, she would exhort, "Keep yourselves open and aware! Listen to your urges! Listen to what's motivating you!"

I wanted to lead a life dramatically different from my mother's, who'd virtually given up her career to be in my father's shadow. He called her "his little woman." At our first conference I falteringly told Bessie I hoped to be like Colette, "an actress and a dancer and a novelist and a playwright . . ." (I didn't add, "A woman who believed love and sex were the ultimate experience.")

Bessie smiled. "Your ambitions are very big," she said briskly. "That's all well and good, but first you must learn how to concentrate."

You must learn how to concentrate. I had no idea what she was talking about, but the phrase stuck in my mind. For the next four years I struggled to make sense of my ambitions and tried hard to figure out what the nature of my commitment was.

I WAS DATING indiscriminately, going out with old boyfriends and collecting new ones. Nobody captured my fancy. I felt reckless and longed to be swept off my feet. And then one night, about three weeks after I'd begun classes at Sarah Lawrence, I went with some newfound friends to the favorite student hangout, a bar named the Greasy Spoon. It hung over a hill above the Bronxville railway station, and throughout the night you could hear the whistles and the chugging of trains right below the bar. The train tracks literally cut through the center of Bronxville's Main Street.

That particular evening I was seated at the bar sipping a rum and coke when suddenly a drunken customer pinched my butt—*hard*. I screamed, whereupon a tall, burly young man wearing a beret, who'd been lounging at the far end of the room eyeing me, charged forward and socked the man in the jaw. He toppled over in the sawdust, out like the proverbial light. Everyone in the bar stopped talking and there was dead silence in the place, interrupted by the train whistling below us. With that, my rescuer took off his beret with a sweeping gesture and ambled over to me. "Thank you," I said. "You didn't have to go that far."

"I always go too far," he rumbled back in his gloriously deep basso profundo voice, and put on a playful French accent. "That ees my problem."

I laughed, and then we all watched a waiter drag the knocked-out customer into the men's room. The atmosphere returned to normal; people began drinking and smoking and laughing. Someone put a nickel in the jukebox and Rosemary Clooney sang, "Come-on-a my house . . ."

That's when the young man sat down beside me at the bar and ordered me another rum and coke. He said he liked my outfit. I was wearing a beige cashmere sweater, a cardigan buttoned up the back, and a tartan pleated plaid skirt fastened by a big safety pin. It was the latest fashion. He went on to compliment my hair, which was curly reddish brown. (I thanked God I'd just washed it.) "I'm Jason Bean," he told me. "Who are you?"

"My name is Patricia Bosworth," I said, feeling sort of funny because this wasn't my real name. I mean, Bosworth was my middle name, and I was trying it out as my stage name. My real name was Patricia Crum, but my father had said, "If you become an actress and you get a bad review, critics will say, 'Crummy performance by Patricia Crum,' so take your mother's maiden name."

"Patricia Bosworth," Jason repeated slowly, as if he were tasting something delicious. "I like the sound of it." And then he turned quiet but kept on staring at me and I kept staring back at him because he was like nobody I'd ever met before.

He had shaggy blond hair combed into an absurdly glossy, greasy pompadour. His sleepy bedroom eyes and slow, lazy voice made me feel weak. But I kept on talking, trying to find out who he was. Well, he was taking classes at the Art Students League; he planned to be a painter. When my questions got too personal, such as what does your father do or where do you live, he asked me to the movies. We left the bar and headed to the Cinema Theatre in Bronxville, which was showing *An American in Paris.* The film had just started when we entered the darkened auditorium, the gorgeous Gershwin music enveloping us. "'S wonderful . . . 'S marvelous . . . that you should care for me."

Soon Jason put his arm about my shoulders. Our bodies touched. He smelled of tobacco and BO. I kept waiting for him to kiss me and eventually he did, slobbering wet fierce kisses, his tongue touching mine. His breath tasted sour, but I didn't care. I felt my breasts arching, tensing toward him. My heart pounded. Perspiration streamed down my armpits as his fingers began tickling my crotch.

After the movie was over, we walked out of Bronxville and up the steep hill to campus. The street was dark and calm. We didn't say a word. I felt exhausted, drained; my panties were moist. I wanted to fall back into his embrace and stay there forever. When we reached the wrought-iron gate on the hill, the dormitories loomed up ahead. Only a few lights were on. I'd missed curfew, so I had to climb in with some difficulty through a hole in the fence. Jason chuckled, watching me pulling the bushes aside to make my way. He said he'd be in touch and then disappeared down the hill into the darkness.

THE NEXT DAY he dropped by the student lounge bearing flowers. He was wearing his beret, and he murmured a few words to me in French as a greeting. That did it. He would be my artist lover. I didn't listen when a couple of the other students warned me about Jason. He was well known on campus as a fortune hunter, they said, an operator; he glommed onto girls who came from rich families. "I'm not rich," I would tell them. "My father is actually going broke."

"It doesn't look that way with the kind of clients he has," another student commented.

I started cutting classes; I'd hop on the train to New York, where I'd pick Jason up after his drawing sessions at the Art Students League on West Fifty-Seventh Street. Then he'd take me downtown and introduce me to Greenwich Village, its streets and bars filled with artists and writers. We'd stroll through Washington Square Park hand in hand; there was the sound of guitar music; couples played chess under the great old trees off Bleecker. We went to the San Remo Café and drank whiskey sours; another time we sat in a coffeehouse called Le Figaro and I tasted bitter espresso for the first time. All the while Jason would fill my head with impossible dreams. Next summer we would go to Mexico or Paris, where he would attend art school; he would paint and I would write and act and dance. We never got beyond the talking stage.

So far Jason had painted only one painting (which he'd refused to show me). He sketched a lot and made drawings on a pad, but he admitted he had no idea *what* to paint—just that he *wanted* to paint. His teachers had told him they could teach him only how to draw. This frustrated and angered him, and caused him to drink too much beer. Then he'd sink into a depression and I'd spend too much time trying to cheer him up.

When we weren't in the Village, we would spend hours necking in Jason's brother's car. Long hours kissing and dry-humping. At first I felt awkward and dissatisfied as he gave me lessons as to how to go down on him. He'd say, "Lick it like a lollipop," and I'd hold his swollen penis in my hand and lick it and suck on it until he came in my mouth, and then I would gag because I hated doing that. Sometimes Jason would spank me if I didn't do exactly as he wanted. Once that roused me to orgasm and my entire body shuddered and quivered like a dying bird.

I became absorbed in the physicality of my responses. My belly would heave; the nipples on my breasts would get hard as nails. After a while I decided I loved being dominated. I'd read about being dominated in *True Confessions* magazines; in the beginning, it was thrilling and mindless to surrender to Jason. But I would go only so far. I refused to go all the way, even though he'd tease and paddle me, but I fought him off. I wouldn't put out; I couldn't— didn't—want to surrender to sex, to lose myself totally yet. He would finally give up. I would let my body go limp and he would tell me he loved my body, so white and freckled. "You are so god- damn *hot*."

JUST AFTER THANKSGIVING I brought Jason home to our rented brownstone on East Sixty-Eighth Street. My father was away in Hollywood. Bart was away finishing his senior year at Stockbridge. I knew Mama was home, but she was about to leave for some dinner party. When she heard me call up to her, she answered from the third floor, "Oh, lambie-pie! Why didn't you let me know so I could have something to eat for you? But what a pleasant surprise."

Then I heard her high heels clicking on the stairs and she ap- peared, very blonde, elegant in black lace and fake diamonds. She stopped when she saw Jason. He had not taken off his beret; his jean jacket was paint-smeared.

"Now who are you?" she demanded very grandly, trying to size him up and intimidate him. (I could tell she was thinking, *He is still wearing his beret inside . . . Rude!*) She dared him to answer, and of course he did in his own time and in his lazy, laconic, basso profundo voice.

"I'm Jason Bean. You are Mrs. Bartley Crum." He bowed mock- ingly and they shook hands, but then he held on to her fingers and wouldn't let go. She tried to pull away, but he continued to hold her hand in his big paw, squeezing it and laughing his lazy, seductive chuckle. He often did this with people when he first met them, invariably throwing them off-balance, which both surprised and annoyed them.

"Well, I never!" Mama exclaimed indignantly when he finally released his grip. She gave him an angry look. Then, pausing, she pecked my cheek and swept out, calling over her shoulder, "I think there are leftovers in the fridge."

AS SOON AS we were alone in the brownstone, Jason began wandering around investigating the living room and den, with its floor-to-ceiling shelves that contained hundreds of books from our library in San Francisco.

"Jeez, who reads all this stuff?" he marveled. "You can't tell me your parents have read all these books."

"Yes, they have, and I've read a lot of them too," I told him. I loved books. I'd grown up with books. Mama gave me love sonnets for Valentine's Day; my brother received a biography of Einstein for his birthday. But Jason wasn't listening. He had gone over to the mantel, where a green marble bust of my mother as a young college graduate stared out into the room. "Is this your mom?" I nodded.

"Your folks must be loaded," Jason continued.

"Actually my father has had a lot of trouble earning a living ever since he represented the Hollywood Ten."

"Is he a commie?"

"No, he is left-liberal and a practicing Catholic."

"That doesn't sound too good to me. Me and my brother are gonna vote for Eisenhower."

With that, Jason wandered away and began investigating Daddy's well-stocked bar. The fridge was filled with wine and Jason pulled out a bottle of champagne.

"Shall we?" He grinned.

In the next hour we drank the entire bottle. I began feeling uncomfortable as soon as Jason started kissing me, because I knew that he wanted to go all the way.

I told him to "Please don't!" but I really didn't mean that and he could tell. I was curious about sex. I'd been fantasizing about it for so long. I relaxed my body. Then he was inside me, pushing his penis in and out, and I whimpered that it hurt. He came convulsively. When it was over, I lay there with him heaving by my side. It was not as I'd expected it to be.

All around me were the books from my parents' library. I could recognize their titles upside down—collections of Shaw and Shakespeare, Virginia Woolf and Hemingway. A profound sadness washed over me. Was this what all the excitement was about? Sex hadn't been ecstatic or even arousing. I enjoyed kissing much more, and now I'd lost my virginity. Did I have to go to Church and confess it? I thought about that a lot—but I never went to Confession.

WHILE I WAS putting my clothes on, I heard a noise.

"It's just me, Attepe." I whirled around to see my brother standing in the doorway, pale and skinny in blue striped pajamas. "I didn't know anyone was here," he said in a dull voice.

"Neither did I."

Bart shuffled into the room to observe Jason zipping up his fly and slapping his beret onto his head.

"Why are you wearing a beret in the house?" my brother demanded.

Jason chuckled. "Dunno . . . Guess I feel like it. Say, who are you anyway?"

"Bart."

"Oh—the brother." I had mentioned Bart's depressions, his moodiness, because I was so worried. Now I was terrified Jason would say something inopportune, but he made no comment and I rushed in with, "This is Jason Bean. We met at Sarah Lawrence."

"Tell the truth, baby, you picked me up in a bar. Or maybe I picked you up. Either way we are having ourselves a ball." Jason stuck out his hand and Bart took it. They shook hands, and once again Jason attempted to hold on to his fingers as he had with my mother, but this time it was my brother who squeezed so hard that Jason let go with a yelp. "Jeez! You got some grip, kid. You work out?"

Bart eyed him coolly and shook his head. "Don't call me kid."

"How old are you? I bet no more than thirteen."

"I'm almost sixteen," he answered, then turned to leave. "You better clean up the living room before you go," he told me.

"I will! I will," I cried, and I immediately started picking up the sofa pillows from the floor, the crumpled napkins and overturned empty champagne bottle.

Jason was following me around as I placed the glasses onto a tray. "Don't you guys have maids?" His deep, mellifluous voice was teasing. Bart looked back at me from the doorway, waiting for my answer. His face was stony.

I ran to him. "Please don't tell Mama about this."

"What would I possibly tell her?" He gazed at me with his huge sad eyes and then disappeared up the stairs to his room on the fourth floor.

Now it was late and we had to make the last train to Bronxville, so we ran for a cab to take us to Grand Central. We didn't say much on the trip back. Jason seemed thoughtful. "Your brother is strange," he murmured at one point. "Maybe I should paint him. I like him, and I like few people."

THAT NIGHT, AS we were walking up the steep hill to the college campus Jason proposed to me. We had known each other just six weeks. I hadn't planned to be married yet, but as a Catholic I believed I had committed a mortal sin by giving myself to him, so I *had* to get married. I told him yes. But I felt ambivalent; I wasn't sure I wanted to have someone else define my future for me. Like most girls in the fifties, I had been taught that my ultimate destiny was marriage and a family. Back in the fifties women acquiesced, accommodated. Mama used to quote Clare Boothe Luce: "Women are compromised from the day they are born."

I'd been fantasizing that Jason and I might be able to transform ourselves into an artistic team like Lillian Hellman and Dashiell Hammett, or Simone de Beauvoir and Jean-Paul Sartre. I didn't know these women overlooked the flaws and often exaggerated the achievements of their lovers. I hadn't considered that I might soon find myself belittled, threatened, and subdued.

I told Jason that marriage wasn't going to stop me from finishing college or from pursuing my grandiose dreams of becoming an actress and a writer. He assured me our marriage would in no way affect my plans. But how I would achieve my goals was another question. He had no answers. "You'll figure it out," he said. It was funny; although our life together would turn out to be a disaster, Jason did have a crazy faith in me just the way my father did. That helped to raise my spirits.

THE ONLY PERSON I confided in was Bart. The following weekend I came in on the train from college and burst into his room to tell him that I was getting married. My brother had been lying facedown on his bed listening to Bach. He rolled over and turned off the record player. "Say that again, please. Maybe I didn't hear right."

"I am going to elope tomorrow to Mount Vernon and I want you to be the best man."

My brother's huge, protruding eyes, so like Mama's, grew even bigger. "You've got to be joking," he murmured softly. "I realize you want to get away from home, but this is too extreme."

"I love him!"

"No you don't, you're hot for him."

I wouldn't answer.

"Stupido, moronico, imbecilito . . ." He launched into a scathing monologue in our private language about how I could ruin my life if I married this man, this Jason . . .

"Bean," I finished for him. "How can you possibly know this? You spent only a few minutes with the guy."

"My instincts are always correct about people," my brother answered. "Jason is a faker, a poseur, and he isn't very intelligent. You may be risking your sanity if you marry this—Jason."

I argued back weakly that Jason was an artist and *I* was going to be one too, an actress and a novelist.

With that, my brother broke in sharply. "Your dreams and ambitions are nothing but clichés!"

"We plan to live in Paris next year," I went on, feeling slightly ill.

"On whose money?" Bart fired back.

I didn't have an answer for that. I hadn't thought *anything* out and childishly assumed that all would be well. So far it had been. I had been raised privileged and spoiled rotten, a combination that gives you a weird perspective about life, as well as an unrealistic confidence and sense of entitlement.

My brother told me that eloping was idiotic, foolhardy, that I would regret it immediately, but I wouldn't listen to him. Everything that is so difficult about becoming a woman—the ambivalent nature of choices between career and family, between romance and responsibility, between recklessness and restraint—I didn't consider all these elements that are so much a part of a woman's life. I was virtually unconscious back then. After I got a taste of sex, that's all I thought about. I confused sex with love because not only had I thought I loved Jason but I had somehow convinced myself that he was also the most unique character I'd ever met. Yes, he was scary, but I was turned on by my fear, not put off by it. He was such a mass of contradictions: loving and hateful, smug and doubting, arrogant yet withdrawn, suspicious and yet needy, trusting, boastful and woefully insecure. I saw us as an unconventional couple, Jason in his blue jeans and beret, me in my leotards. We'd agreed we didn't want a traditional wedding with all the trimmings—bridesmaids, reception, lots of gifts. We didn't even want a honeymoon. He would go right on painting; I would continue with college. Hopelessly naive and irresponsible, we didn't talk about how we were going to support ourselves.

At our wedding ceremony, which was performed by a very bored Mount Vernon judge the following week, I decided to forgo the leotards and wore my favorite fuzzy purple angora sweater and a dress embroidered with silken butterflies. That night in the motel room Jason pretended the butterflies were real and he made me stand in front of him while he pulled them off one by one, crushing them in his hand. Then he made fierce love to me and fell fast asleep.

I lay awake most of the night, spending part of it wondering why I'd allowed Jason to pull those silken butterflies off my dress. It was downright creepy. Then I wished Bart had been best man and maybe he would have told Jason to stop—but he couldn't have because he wouldn't have been in the motel room with us. My brother's words rang in my ears: *You are being idiotic, foolhardy . . . You'll regret eloping immediately . . .*

I turned over and lay back on the pillows, gazing at the hulking creature snoozing beside me. *He's my husband!* I said to myself, not quite believing it. *And I'm his wife.* Then I thought, *Maybe I've done the wrong thing. Maybe I should have listened to Bart.* But now it was too late. Now I had to see it through.

Chapter Four

WE TRIED TO keep our marriage secret, living separately for the next week, but then Daddy read about our vows in a New York law journal (all marriages performed in the state are a matter of public record). He called me at college and asked me to come home and explain myself. His voice sounded uncharacteristically cold over the phone. I caught the next train to Manhattan.

When I arrived at the brownstone, my parents were in the living room waiting for me. Mama had her dark glasses on "to hide some of my wrinkles." Daddy did not call out, as he usually did, to say, "Hey, baby, give your old man a kiss." Instead he remained on the sofa, chain-smoking and drinking his first bourbon of the day (it was just after four p.m.).

There they were—my parents. How I loved and feared them at that moment. They were a complicated couple, but in spite of their differences, they had a deep mutual respect for one another. Would Jason and I ever come close to being like them?

No words were spoken for several tense moments. Daddy's expression was drawn and haggard; he was in negotiations for Rita Hayworth's divorce from Prince Aly Khan, so he'd been flying back and forth from Hollywood to New York to Paris. He just gazed at me as if he couldn't believe what I'd done. He let Mama talk since she'd met Jason and had definite opinions on the subject.

She hadn't liked his eyes, she said. Disagreeable eyes, and she thought he'd been terribly rude the night they met. "He wouldn't let go of my hand. It was the damnedest thing," she told my father. "He set out to unnerve me." And then she launched into a series of questions. "Where will you live? How will he support you? What about your college education?" I didn't answer her questions, including the last: "Why did you do this to us? He is a nobody. And what about his family? The name Bean? Is he Protestant or Episcopalian? Is he German or English?"

"Scotch Irish, Mama."

"If he's part Irish he can't be that bad," my father tried to joke (Daddy's middle name was Cavanaugh).

And then Mama added, "You can't possibly love this man!"

"I do love him," I assured them, although I was dimly becoming aware that I knew very little about love.

Next my father spoke—between coughing fits. (He smoked three packs of Pall Malls a day; he was never without a cigarette burning between his nicotine-stained fingers.)

He hoped I realized the seriousness of my actions. "You are too young to be married. You haven't known this boy long enough. You are just a freshman in college. Did you consider any of this?" He finished with, "What were you planning to do about money?"

I answered that I thought he might help us for a while.

"Which is exactly what this Jason person thought," Mama interjected icily. "He took one look at our beautiful brownstone and assumed your father was rich."

"Jason isn't like that," I protested.

Mama shook her head and declared that she thought the marriage should be annulled—immediately.

Daddy seemed to agree, until we had a meeting a couple of days later with my new husband in the office of the president of Sarah Lawrence College.

HAROLD TAYLOR, AT age thirty-two the youngest college president in the country, had called the meeting. A vital, ebullient former philosophy professor from Canada, he had a funny, goofy grin, big white teeth, and rumpled dark hair. He loved to play tennis and drink; he loved to play jazz music on his clarinet. Two of his closest friends were Duke Ellington and the choreographer Agnes de Mille. And he counted Alger Hiss as an intimate.

Dear Harold. Over the next two years I would periodically sneak into his office and pour out my heart to him about my marriage. He was always there for me. After college, we would become friends for the rest of his life.

That morning he gave an impassioned speech directed at me, saying that I had made a choice—a commitment—to being Mrs. Jason Bean. He respected that, wanted to honor it, and as he reminded my parents, I was over eighteen. He hoped they would honor my commitment too.

To my astonishment they agreed (although Daddy whispered in my ear, "You mustn't marry in the Church"), and then the three adults turned to Jason and me to hear what we had to say.

Jason just hung his head; for once he was speechless. He was dressed in an ill-fitting suit he'd borrowed from his brother. We gripped hands. Suddenly the enormity of what we'd done hit me in the pit of my stomach. How *were* we going to support ourselves? I hadn't realized up until that moment that marriage was a responsibility and something quite profound. If this sounds crazy, and I suppose it does, I had never before truly weighed an action of mine. I just plunged into situations, experiences, adventures without ever considering the consequences.

Before the meeting was over, Daddy repeated his request that I finish college; he would pay my tuition, but that was all. "Otherwise you kids are on your own." Then he leaned over and shook Jason's hand. "Good luck, my boy." I believe those were the only words he ever uttered to my husband.

Mama put her arms around me. I relaxed into her embrace, breathing in the delicious fragrance of Joy perfume. I expected her to say something loving and supportive, but instead she whispered in my ear, "Don't you dare get pregnant. If you do, I swear I'll take you to an abortionist myself."

SOON AFTER THE meeting at Harold's office there was a feature in the *Times* and *Herald Tribune* newspapers: "Patricia Crum, daughter of attorney Bartley Crum, elopes in New York." Mama had beautifully engraved cards printed at Tiffany's, which she mailed to all her friends in New York and California. "Mr. and Mrs. Jason Bean at home at 236 East 68th Street," which was of course a lie, since my husband and I never returned to the Sixty-Eighth Street brownstone together as a married couple.

By now I'd moved my books and clothes from my dorm and Jason and I set up "housekeeping" (if you could call it that) in his ninety-five-year-old grandmother's apartment in a fusty old Tudor-style building on Alger Court, a block away from the Bronxville train station.

I hadn't set foot in the place until Jason carried me over the threshold. What I saw was an actual shock to my system. A line of small dreary rooms were all in a row down a long hall connected by a soiled, wrinkled rug. Every piece of furniture in the "front parlor" was either brown or beige: the easy chairs, the falling-down sofa, the three lamps with cracking shades. There was a big, scarred coffee table by the TV set. No books. A pile of ancient *Reader's Digests* stacked inside a dusty glass cabinet along with a Bible. My new home was in stark contrast to the beautiful townhouses and spacious apartments I'd grown up in, but I was too polite to voice my alarm.

Jason explained hurriedly that we were to live in his room, as he led me by the hand to what had once been a maid's room and before that had been used for storage. We were on the ground floor and sharing the space not only with Grandma Bean but with Jason's older brother, Wally, a muscular, flat-faced man with a shaved head. He was a truck driver for Thomas' English muffins. His wife, Faith, worked at a beauty parlor in Mount Vernon. She was plump and monosyllabic.

I also discovered I would have to adjust to living with Grandma's noisy collection of birds. Her aviary, located on the sun porch off our room, was filled with dozens of them (close to a hundred, according to Jason); some in cages, some on perches, all of them chirping and twittering from morning until night. There were parrots and macaws, lovebirds, hummingbirds, and quails, flapping their wings and screeching at one another. Grandma adored her "birdies," as she called them; she was forever rolling around the aviary in her wheelchair, talking to them, laughing with them.

She and Jason took care of them together. "And now you can help me," he said when he brought me to the aviary for the first time to introduce me to his favorite, a green parrot who said, "Hi— hi-hi," whenever anyone came to visit. "You can feed 'em, clean the cages. It gets stinky if we don't do it a couple of times a week. Grandma doesn't have the strength anymore, but now you're here." He patted my butt.

I didn't like birds. I was frightened of them, but I told him I thought they were terrific. He was pleased because he said birds had always been a big part of his life. "I like 'em better than people," he told me jovially. "And you will too. Maybe you'll want a bird of your own someday."

I told him quickly, "Not yet." I had too much to do. My home-work and dance assignments, and the first thing I wanted to do was make our bedroom livable. I bought some pretty plants and a new spread for the lumpy bed as well as some colorful pillows. But there was still the fading wallpaper decorated with brown swans. I wanted to tear it off, but Jason said no.

We tried to figure out how we could possibly exist in such a small space. Jason's two leaky fish tanks took up a lot of room. The water sloshed and gurgled in those glass containers, the fish flickering through their rippling ghostly prisons. They never slept; no matter what time it was, I could always watch them. They kept darting back and forth, circling about the shells Jason had once collected on Cape Cod. It was mesmerizing, but then I'd stop looking at them and wonder how I could get rid of the smell of turpentine. Jason had set up his easel and his paints near the door. And where could I work? I finally had to write my class papers perched on our bed.

Even so, I was ridiculously happy for a couple of weeks. I loved being married, I told myself; I loved being a wife even though Jason was already bossing me around: "Gimme my coffee . . . get me a beer!"

I obediently became his servant. I'd seen Mama serve Daddy his drinks—wasn't serving part of a woman's role? (I forgot that Daddy often brought Mama her breakfast on a tray.) I especially enjoyed sleeping next to Jason's warm, hairy body, whispering confidences to him in the dead of night, our legs entwined. He'd murmur, "You will always be mine," and my heart would melt.

On Valentine's Day he gave me a beautiful card signed "*Je t'adore.*"

But reality soon set in. I began to realize Jason was, to put it mildly, not a very nice person. In fact, he was self-involved, hy-percritical, and bad-tempered. He'd rage at me for not cleaning the toilet; he'd criticize me for being "spoiled rotten" because I'd thrown a dress over the fish tank or left my shoes for him to trip over on the floor.

Until I got married, a maid had always picked up my clothes for me. When an outfit needed pressing, someone did it for me. Sheets and towels were always sent to Madame Paulette's. Now for the first time in my life I was shopping at the A&P and my sister-in-law was teaching me how to use a Laundromat.

Rather than resenting it, I took all of it as a challenge. I felt as if I was on a crazy adventure. Not all of it was pleasant, but I took it as a learning experience. I had a lot to learn, I was realizing. Up till now I'd lived a rarefied existence. Part of me had wanted to escape, wanted a change—wanted to explore a different reality.

I'd been raised to be polite. I didn't like to offend people. So although I found my new family gross and was appalled by the way they lived, in such apathy and squalor, I never told Jason how I felt. I never said anything to anybody. At first I welcomed all the changes in my life.

I did miss my brother. He hadn't contacted me since my marriage. Would we no longer be in touch? I couldn't bear the thought. He'd always been there to focus me and occasionally pass judgment on what I was doing. I shuddered to think what he'd say if he saw me at Alger Court lugging out the garbage or filling water dishes for screeching birds. I could just hear him chuckle and say to me in our secret language, "You are behaving like a character out of Charles Dickens."

OUR MARRIAGE QUICKLY settled into a routine. I would rise at seven and brew a pot of coffee and carry a mug of it in to Jason, who was lolling in bed listening to the radio. Then I would feed the birds as quickly as I could before making breakfast for everybody— everybody meaning Grandma, Wally, and Faith (Jason didn't eat breakfast).

It was best for me to cook since not only did I enjoy cooking but I quickly learned that nobody in the Bean family could cook. Faith was especially relieved when I took over in the kitchen, because she couldn't even boil water and existed solely on junk food.

I had learned to cook when I was a little girl. Cooking was in fact the only thing I knew I could do well, and for a while— don't ask me why—I cooked up a storm for my new family. In the mornings I would alternate pancakes with French toast or scrambled eggs and sausages. For dinner I made fish soups and roast lamb in garlic marinade. I broiled chicken in lemon and olive oil. I baked apple crumb pies and angel cake topped with caramel frosting.

The Beans were impressed, and they weren't easily impressed. They were phlegmatic—"down in the dumps," was the way Faith put it. They all suffered from a low-grade depression and seemed to find joy in nothing. And they weren't especially articulate, either.

I tried not to let their bleak moods get to me. In the beginning these didn't. Mainly because I was so frantically busy. As soon as breakfast was done and the dishes were washed, I was out the door and trudging up the hill to my classes at Sarah Lawrence.

I felt very grown up as I strode around campus. Losing my virginity gave me a brief cachet. Some of my classmates hovered around me whispering, "How does it feel to have an orgasm? Are you wearing a diaphragm? Do you want to get pregnant?" When they reached the questions "Do you get along with your in-laws?" or "Where will you finally be living, in another apartment or a house?" I'd put them off. Some of them even dropped by my new home hoping I'd ask them in, but I never did.

I could never let my friends see the inside of Alger Court. Although I was constantly helping Faith dust, sweep, mop, and vacuum, the place always looked faintly grimy. It was the apartment of a very old lady, and that's what Grandma Bean was. She'd celebrated her ninety-sixth birthday the day I moved in.

LAUREEN MCLAUGHLIN BEAN had been born in St. Louis, Missouri, on January 18, 1857. She rarely spoke and often seemed to be in a trance. She was a tiny thing, almost bald. Most of her hair had fallen out, so she resembled a wizened old man. Her fine dark eyes had sunk so far back in her head I couldn't tell if she could see or not. She had terrible coughing fits. Whenever she stopped coughing, she'd want to see her birds.

We would all take turns wheeling her out to her aviary, a place alive with humming and cheeping and flapping of wings. She'd stay on that porch for hours, greeting her favorites: "Hello, Gypsy!" (her parrot), "Hey, hey, Madame Dominique!" (one of her doves).

Otherwise, she remained in her room, listening to her radio most of the day. She wasn't senile. She must have known her grandsons hoped to be remembered in her will. Grandma Bean owned two apartment houses in Yonkers and a building in St. Louis. "Grandma is loaded," Jason said. He assumed he would inherit the bulk of her estate, but I wasn't so sure.

Relatives kept appearing at the door—long-lost cousins, nephews, aunts. Grandma briefly held court, but she would tire quickly, so nobody stayed very long. Faith said, "They're coming to see if she's ready to croak." But so far, frail as she was, she seemed to be in pretty good health.

Once after a large group of Beans and McLaughlins had left, I helped her get into bed and she murmured to me, "Everyone thinks they're gonna get something from me, but they are mistaken. I won't leave my money to people." It dawned on me that she might leave her money for the care and feeding of her birds. (But I kept that supposition to myself.)

She did seem especially fond of Jason. He flirted with her and wheeled her around and around very fast in her wheelchair because she liked getting dizzy. Every week she scribbled out a check for Jason's expenses and for his classes at the Art Students League. He would promise he was going to paint her portrait. "Like Picasso painted Gertrude Stein."

"Who's that, boy?" she questioned.

SO FAR JASON had painted only one painting, of a bulbous female breast. The painting hung above our bed during our entire marriage. I assumed the breast belonged to a former girlfriend and I kept at him to tell me who, until Wally finally informed me the painting was no more than a picture of a breast that Jason had torn from a *Modern Photography* magazine.

But I couldn't be sure, so I kept on asking. Jason would just chuckle, "Ain't talking," but then he'd brag that he'd slept with maybe a hundred women, "and I'm not counting the whores I picked up on Forty-Second Street or the chorus gal I smoked pot with near the Yonkers Freeway." His heavy-lidded eyes would twinkle merrily because he thought he was making me jealous.

I secretly liked the idea of Jason as grand seducer. Believing he was a great lover intensified our sex life for a while. And believing that I had a kind of sexual power over him made me feel briefly secure. I had a hypnotic sense of fullness and strength from being selfless. I was beginning to realize that female power might best be expressed by giving oneself away with abandon.

Naturally during those first weeks of marriage we made love constantly. Sometimes I'd roll toward him with a kind of stunned sensation as if I'd been drawn to him by some force outside myself. I would look at him and wonder what it was like to be him. I kept trying to find out.

We would kiss and kiss until our mouths grew raw. Then Jason would turn me over facedown. I never told him what I wanted in bed. I would lie there passively. Jason insisted "doggy style" was the best, so I complied obediently—as well as I could—although I hated him ramming into me from behind. Whenever he did this to me, my whole system seemed to reverberate like a gong. Even my teeth throbbed. It was a relief to be turned over on my back and plugged to the brim with him sliding in and out and in and out again.

Then love became a strained searching toward a muffled center. I would begin to feel wanton and fastidious and swooning all at once, and when it was finished, a sharp, brief note of disappointment would fill my being and often I would begin to sob.

Jason would comfort me by offering a lit cigarette and then talking baby talk. "So's oo hurt, li'l baby?" And I'd answer, "No, I's not hurt."

If Jason was in a good mood, he would let me trace my finger around his face, which was square and conventionally handsome: even-featured, thick black brows over his blue eyes, heavy blond pompadour haircut, which he groomed incessantly. He kept a comb by our bed and would get frantic if it was misplaced.

But he believed his nose—perfectly formed, absurdly small— was his best feature. He told me his mother had massaged it daily with expensive creams when he was a baby. "She was afraid I'd get a big schnoz like Dad's. All the Beans have big noses except me."

HE KNEW FEW details of his father's life. "His name was Luther Bean," my sister-in-law Faith told me. "He was in the insurance business and he disappeared when the boys were very young. Wally says he was a handsome devil and had a great many women."

"Dad used to take me to the racetrack when he'd bet on horses," Jason added. "He always had some babe with him. He had a terrible temper—he beat me when he found out I'd stolen stuff from the five-and-dime. He was very restless and had black moods. I take after him. Just before he disappeared, he beat me terrible. Beat me for no reason."

Jason talked about Judith Bean, his mother, only once. There was a single photograph, a snapshot propped on our dresser. Taken when she was very young, a tiny sweet-faced woman with strange eyes and a slightly twisted grin. After she and Luther separated, she'd worked for a time as a nurse for the terminally ill. Then "something happened," and she was now in a state hospital for the criminally insane. As far as Jason knew, she was still there. He and Wally were placed in foster homes. Then Grandma had moved Jason in with her and, shortly after that, Wally, "because she felt sorry for him," Jason said. Jason and his brother didn't get along. "That's because I'm Grandma's favorite and he knows I'm getting her money."

Until Jason told me about his parents, I hadn't realized his childhood was that dark. Did that explain his mood swings? His rages kept increasing day by day, but I was never prepared for them. They seemed to come out of the blue. I kept asking him, "What's the matter?"

He could get upset by the smallest detail: The top sheet on our bed wasn't pulled tightly enough, or when was I going to learn how to iron his shirts the way the Chinaman did in Bronxville?

One afternoon, about a month into the marriage, I forgot to feed the fish and he fell into a depression. He'd been smoking too many Camels, so the bedroom was thick with smoke. He was frowning, pouting. "What's the matter?" I asked, and when he refused to answer, I asked again, and that's when he slapped me across the face. It was the first time I'd ever been hit in my life. My eyes filled with tears. Almost immediately he folded me in his arms and apologized. "Oh baby, baby," he crooned. "I just don't like to talk about myself."

*   *   *

DADDY HAD SLIPPED me a hundred-dollar bill that day in Harold Taylor's office. After it was gone, I asked Jason what we should do. He had walking-around money from Grandma, but it wasn't enough for both of us.

"Ask your father for an allowance," he suggested. He seemed annoyed when I reminded him Daddy had refused to bankroll us.

"That's too bad," my husband drawled. "I told you I wouldn't get a job because I want to spend my free time painting. Guess you'll have to go to work."

"Doing what?"

"You'll think of something." He ruffled my hair affectionately. That was that. Subject closed. I didn't put up any objections.

In retrospect, I realize I was guileless and naive to a fault. And of course Jason used me. But at the time I didn't look at it that way. As far as I was concerned, he had liberated me from conventional wifehood. He was encouraging me to be an artist.

I could be a rule-breaker, I thought; I could dress the way I wanted, in leotards and sandals (no more white gloves). I wouldn't have to create a traditional home, and I could wait to start a family. I would no longer have to attend all those boring cocktail parties Mama wanted me to go to in order to meet "eligible men." By choosing someone my parents disapproved of, I found myself released from all traditional expectations. Although I didn't realize it then, I was part of the first generation to rebel against our mothers and the rules they lived by.

Chapter Five

UNTIL I FIGURED out what I could do to bring in decent money, I waitressed at a local soda fountain in the Bronxville drugstore. It didn't bother me; it was as if I were acting a part. I liked wearing a frilly white apron and tiny hat on my head. I enjoyed reciting the menu to customers: "You can have a terrific hamburger or a peanut butter and jelly sandwich . . . Yes, we have Lipton's tea." I most enjoyed making hot fudge sundaes—they became my specialty. I was also able to indulge my sweet tooth and often gorged (when my boss wasn't looking) on spoonfuls of caramel sauce.

I even coaxed my brother up from New York one afternoon and served him his favorite bacon and cheese sandwich plus a thick chocolate milk shake. He ate without seeming to enjoy it. We hardly spoke.

He was still very depressed. Nothing excited him. About to graduate from Stockbridge, he was already accepted at MIT, but he didn't seem that happy about it.

I waited on another customer, and as I did, I could feel Bart's eyes on me. "You aren't going to make enough money to take off for Europe or Mexico," he told me when I returned to him.

After I got off my shift we walked over to my new home, past the bank and the gas station and the shops, and we stood outside the Tudor-style buildings that made up Alger Court. Bart took in the dying elm trees, the brownish lawn, and the car park that surrounded it. A train roared by and then another. We were just a step away from the station.

"Wouldn't you like to go inside and see my place?"

He shook his head. "Another time."

Another train roared past us, and then another.

"Must keep you awake at night," he murmured.

"Oh, I am so exhausted I fall right to sleep," I lied. "Don't you want to meet the Beans and my sister-in-law?"

"No."

"Jason said he'd like to paint you."

"Not if I have anything to say about it." He grinned briefly. "Gotta get back to New York."

I followed him to the train tracks. "What will you do?"

"Listen to my new Bach albums. Maybe play some chess with Daddy. If Daddy ever comes home."

"How is he?"

My brother shrugged. "'Everything is terrific, everything is marvelous,'" he answered, mimicking what our father said to us when things were especially bad.

"And Mama—will she ever forgive me?"

My brother stared at me. "For what?"

"For marrying Jason."

"She wanted you to marry a prince. Or at the very least a decent man."

"You don't know Jason."

"I don't *want* to know Jason."

"But *if* you knew him—"

"If I knew him any better, I still would not want to spend time with him."

"Why can't you give him a chance?"

"Why do you lie to yourself so?"

"I'm not lying," I lied.

My brother turned away. We could hear the train approaching.

"Shall we go to a movie soon?" I moved toward him. I didn't want him to leave. All the things we used to do together came back to me in a rush—the endless bike trips we took together in California, the days at the beach throwing ourselves into the waves, then coming back and lying in the sand . . . Bart would turn beautifully brown as a nut while I freckled and burned. Once he spent an eternity rubbing my shoulders and arms with suntan oil.

"Stay till the next train," I pleaded. "They come every twenty minutes."

Bart shook his head. "Have to go home now." He paused. "Oh, I'm taking driving lessons. I should get my license soon. Mama is going to let me use the station wagon."

"That's great! She never wanted me to learn—said I was too scattered."

"You aren't, you know."

"What do you mean?"

"You could amount to something if you'd just stop kidding yourself. If you'd stop and think about what you are doing to yourself."

The train was approaching, roaring into the station. Passengers were running past us.

Bart turned. "Bye, Attepe." He darted away before I could embrace him and hopped onto the train. I waved, but he didn't wave back.

IT WAS JASON who suggested I try my luck at modeling. "You're pretty and you're sexy," he insisted, "and it would pay more than waitressing." He took me to the beach on weekends and snapped close-up pictures of me.

So in between my classes—my history seminar, my psych class, and theatre and dance workshops—I started making the rounds of photographers' studios and model agencies. My parents knew Eleanor Lambert and her husband, Seymour Berkson, general manager of International News Service. Eleanor was the first big fashion publicist, promoting American sportswear designers like Claire McCardell and Anne Klein.

Eleanor got me an appointment with Eileen Ford, who with her husband Jerry ran the hottest modeling agency of that time out of their apartment on First Avenue. Eileen was a tough-talking lady with dimples and a poodle haircut; she took one look at my snap-shots and threw them down on her desk dismissively. "You gotta get some decent pictures, kid. But I'm afraid you're too short to be a model. Besides, you don't look like a model."

I'd read enough copies of *Vogue* and *Harper's Bazaar* to know she was right, that I was living in the era of the high fashion model—chic, inaccessible, elegant beauties with high cheekbones who never smiled. Beauties I simply could not compete with.

Luckily, John Robert Powers disagreed with Eileen. He thought I was "fresh-faced" and signed me up. Powers ran the biggest, oldest modeling agency in the country, which specialized in the all-American cover girl, willowy blondes and redheads with white teeth and lithe bodies. Powers bragged he'd discovered Lucille Ball. Her portrait hung in his spacious Park Avenue office. "Lucille made me laugh so much my sides hurt," he told me.

Powers arranged to have me photographed by Ray Solowinski, a young photographer who had a studio on the top of Carnegie Hall. I was very nervous when I walked in. I'd never posed for a pro-fessional before. Maybe that's why Ray decided I should wear my own clothes and not the Powers Girl's uniform of a waist cincher, falsies, a crinoline petticoat, and a shirtwaist dress. Instead I kept on the hooded duffel coat I'd arrived in, and Ray photographed me in that. I felt relaxed and clowned around, even performing part of a dance routine I was choreographing at Sarah Lawrence. The results were some funny, lively images along with a few fashionable ones, since Ray also photographed me looking very snooty in a checked suit and hat.

Powers helped me choose the best ones for my composites, which were then mailed out to hundreds of his clients. I soon began getting jobs.

BY SPRING OF 1952 I was earning quite a bit of money as a model—was it $50 an hour? And I was enjoying it. I'd hang out at "480 Lex," a lively, graceful building officially known as Grand Central Palace. It occupied the block bounded by Park and Lexington from Forty-Sixth to Forty-Seventh Streets. For years it was the city's principal exhibition hall, showing everything from flowers to boats. But by the fifties, 480 Lex belonged to the photographers.

Almost every floor was crammed with them: catalogue photographers, still life photographers, *True Confessions* photographers all clicking away. I did my share of *True Confessions* spreads, once playing a blind girl. I also tried out for the Miss Rheingold beer campaign and "tested" for photographer Paul Hesse.

The Powers Agency was in the adjoining building connected by both an arcade on the main floor and a ramp on the sixth (where Powers was located, so I could walk across the ramp and spend an entire day dropping off my composites). Occasionally I'd stand in the vaulted lobby trying to count the celebrities—Truman Capote, Cecil Beaton, Claudette Colbert—or the great models, such as the ravishing brunette Dovima. They would be going to the eighth floor to be photographed by Irving Penn or Frances McLaughlin-Gill. I never got a booking there. But I dreamt about it.

When I wasn't working I'd drop by 480's noisy coffee shop, sharing gossip with the models I knew, some of whom existed on raw hamburger and codeine to keep thin. These women were older and wiser than me. They were often single mothers or divorced; one was a lesbian. They all loved being independent and having careers, but none of them especially enjoyed modeling. "It's just a way to earn big bucks," one of them told me.

One afternoon I was given a "go-see" slip to take my portfolio to a photographer in a building I'd never heard of. Zeeman or something like that (he had just one name). I marched right over and rang the bell. Nobody answered, so I pushed the door open and walked in.

The studio was filthy, without heat and not much light. There was no secretary, no assistant. I was about to leave when a soft, hoarse voice commanded me to stop. I turned to face an enormous man—over six feet, all bulging muscle and potbelly. He wore a derby hat and baggy khakis, and seemed surprised to see me. "What ya doin' here, girlie?" he demanded. I gave him the go-see slip that the Powers Agency had given me.

"Gimme your portfolio."

I handed it to him. Then, while he glanced at it, I took a look around. There were cameras everywhere—big ones—lights, drop cloths, and piles and piles of newspapers and magazines, packing boxes, clothes on a rack. Junk. Garbage overflowing from a can. Flies buzzing over containers of half-eaten food.

Zeeman explained his specialty was photographing for the "girlie magazines," and did I know that? I shook my head. Then he said he thought he should take some "test shots" of me for a catalogue house he'd started working for. "I'll be photographing lingerie—bras, underpanties—so you have to undress for me."

I told him I didn't have to.

He said it was essential. "Have to see your boobs and ass."

I took my portfolio and backed away from him, tripping on a pile of newspapers.

He followed me. "Don't you want the job, sweetheart?" I didn't answer. I was moving toward the door, but he grabbed me with his paw-like hand, fondling my arm and then sliding his fingers across my breast.

With a swift motion he tore my blouse from shoulder to waist, ripped off my bra and began pinching my nipple, twisting it between dirty fingers. The next thing I knew, he was on top of me, grinding his huge weight onto me. He smelled horrific, like old shit mixed with pee.

I will wake up from this nightmare, I told myself. *I will wake up . . .* (When I eventually reported back to the agency, I would discover that I'd been given the wrong go-see slip.)

Finally I screamed, "I have my period!"

"Oh, fuck," he groaned, and released me. I stumbled out of his studio and ran for the elevator, buttoning my raincoat around me to hide my torn blouse. When I reached Park Avenue, I hailed a cab. I was late for an uptown booking on Seventy-Second Street. I think I cried all the way there.

DIANE AND ALLAN Arbus's studio was in a building off Second Avenue in the East Seventies. They were taking photographs for *Seventeen* and *Mademoiselle* magazines at the time, and they had booked me a lot. I even had dinner with them once in their studio, which they also lived in and which had a flowering tree in the center of the living room.

They were strange, elfin creatures, but they were kind and gracious too, and they asked me questions about my life. Diane in particular took an interest in me; she called me "the child bride." She sympathized with my confusion and self-consciousness about being a wife at such a tender age. She'd married as a teenager too.

That afternoon I stumbled into the Arbus studio out of breath, disheveled, and crying just as a barefoot Diane was emerging from the darkroom. As usual she was wearing the same shirtwaist dress she'd been wearing for weeks. She always wore clothes till they fell apart—"I don't like to think about what I put on," she'd say.

Within minutes I'd babbled everything to her about the fat photographer. She listened, shaking her head.

"Awful, awful . . . sorry you had to go through that. He's a monster and a woman-hater. Thank God you fought back."

With that, she guided me into the dressing room and began helping me with my makeup and expertly twirled my hair into a French twist. I was modeling a line of Judy Bond blouses for her (the photographs would appear in *Charm* magazine). In the distance I could hear Allan setting up the lights and cameras. Diane kept talking.

"You mustn't ever tolerate that sort of behavior, ever. Remember to value your life."

Those words kept resounding in my ears long after I left the Arbus studio and hopped the subway to Grand Central Station.

Value my life. But what exactly was my life? I felt discombobulated. On the one hand, I was a working wife in an era of "housewife heroines," to quote the *Ladies' Home Journal.* I was out in the world earning my living and I enjoyed it. Before I returned to Bronxville I'd usually sit in Chock Full o' Nuts drinking coffee and totaling what I'd earned that day, figuring out whether, after giving Jason cash for some new brushes, I could deposit something into my just-opened savings account.

Then I would take the train and arrive at Alger Court with a sinking feeling in the pit of my stomach. I'd turn into another self, a passive self. I was secretly embarrassed about having a career, afraid I might lose my femininity, so I worked doubly hard as Mrs. Jason Bean to compensate. As soon as I walked in the door I would start performing various housewifely duties: doing the laundry, ironing, or shopping at the A&P if Faith hadn't already done that. Jason and I would feed the miserable birds and clean their cages. And if that was not bad enough, we'd alternate the unpleasant task of emptying Grandma's bedpan.

I'd try to be as quick as possible when it was my turn so I wouldn't have to speak to Grandma, let alone gaze into her wrinkled, wizened, ninety-six-year-old face. I was not her favorite person. She might have responded to me differently if Mama hadn't sneaked up to Alger Court right after Jason and I eloped and tried to persuade her to kick us out of the apartment so Jason would be forced to get a job. I couldn't believe my own mother would suggest such a thing, but when I checked with Daddy, he admitted it was true. He stayed out of it. To my knowledge he never even bothered to meet my in-laws.

Luckily Grandma was usually dozing when I emptied her bedpan. Then I'd tiptoe out of that smelly little room of hers and hurry back to see what Jason was doing. He always maintained he'd been painting for hours, and he'd show me his latest attempts. He was experimenting with form and color. Most of the sketches were done on heavy paper. I did like the way he used colors—mauves, blues, yellows, and greens—with bold structures. Lush coloring, delicate hues, but the work was abstract and, I felt, derivative—in no way was it original—but I said nothing.

He started talking about painting my portrait; indeed, in those early months he made some preliminary sketches that I privately thought were cartoony at best. Sometimes when he was sketching me he'd order, "Get me a beer," and I'd obediently run into the kitchen for a Bud. When I returned, he'd be lounging on the bed in an old paint-splattered shirt and underpants—he loved showing off his legs. Then he'd pull me next to him and give me a wet tongue kiss. As he did, our bodies would be pressed close and I could feel he had an erection. He'd grin and ask me to tell him about my latest booking.

Over these first few months in our marriage I'd graduated to a full-page spread in *Seventeen* magazine promoting Helena Rubinstein lipstick. I was also featured in a Prell shampoo ad that appeared in *Good Housekeeping*. But I was still on the lowest rung of the modeling ladder. I never got much beyond doing catalogue work and on occasion some editorial work in *Glamour* and *Charm*. However, Jason was proud of my small success as a model and wanted to share it with the relatives. Whenever they dropped by, he'd drag me out to the living room to show my portfolio and brag about the assignments I was getting.

Wally and Grandma weren't impressed. They were in fact quite suspicious of me, since after all I was the daughter of "Bartley Crum, a commie lawyer." No matter how much I denied that my father was a communist, none of them believed me. Senator Joseph McCarthy's influence was on the rise; the fear of communists taking over America was extreme. Not only had J. Edgar Hoover's army of FBI agents been haunting our family for years, but in 1951 after Rita Hayworth became my father's client, Hoover stepped up the pressure on him to "name names" in order to prove his patriotism. Apparently, while Rita was still married to Orson Welles, she had lent her name to all sorts of left-wing causes. Hoover had a big fat file on her he marked X, meaning security risk. Now my father had to deal with the FBI on her behalf.

MY THIRTY-YEAR-OLD SISTER-IN-LAW, Faith, advised me to "fuck politics." She was the one member of my new family who not only accepted me as I was but seemed to enjoy my company. We were both huge movie fans. We used to trade back issues of *Photoplay* and *Modern Screen*. Faith loved the idea that I'd actually met Rita

Hayworth and Montgomery Clift. "Tell me everything," she'd beg as I prepared supper in the Alger Court kitchen, the flickering fluorescent lighting casting a ghastly glare on the veal cutlets I was simmering in white wine and butter.

So I'd show her Monty's cigarette butt, which I'd preserved in waxed paper, and I'd assure her that, yes, Rita's favorite nail polish was Revlon's Fire & Ice, and her hair *was* dyed red.

Then I'd ask Faith questions I didn't dare ask anyone else, such as why did I burn and itch so much "down there"?

"Too much screwing," she'd answer promptly. "But it'll let up." Eventually she accompanied me to the drugstore and helped me buy a douche and a saline solution. "Douche, but don't douche too often. You're gonna feel better though." And she was right.

IT WAS EARLY spring. I'd been married about four months when I received the first of many letters from my mother. Mama had refused to see me because she was too angry, according to my father, but she couldn't keep from writing to me. I wasn't surprised. She wrote compulsively, kept a journal, and carried on a correspondence with scores of friends and ex-lovers. It was her way of releasing her pent-up energy and her emotions. The letters were typed on pale blue paper engraved with her initials in red: GBC.

> *Darling girl: Don't think because I am writing you I am still not furious with you. I am livid. WHY ARE YOU THROWING YOUR LIFE AWAY BEFORE YOU HAVE STARTED LIVING YOUR LIFE? WHY ARE YOU TURNING YOUR BACK ON US? & You have been given everything—a beautiful home, beautiful education, a family who adores you . . .*
>
> *When I was your age, I was living in Paris with a French family. I was studying art and attending the Cordon Bleu. I had*

*already met your father and I was in love with him but he wasn't
ready for marriage. Sometimes I think he was never ready for
marriage, but that is the subject of another letter.*

*After I returned to California I became engaged to another
man. It was to make your father jealous. Then I worked for two
years at the* Call Bulletin *as a crime reporter. The happiest years
of my life. That's when I covered the Mail Order Bride Murder
trial in Sonoma and your father came up to visit one weekend
and we decided we'd get married. And I published my one novel,*
Strumpet Wind, *which was based on the trial, and your father
loved my success. He encouraged me to write more books and
I tried and tried and tried and I couldn't. I failed. But I never
blamed your father. It was* ME.

*Your father was the handsomest, dearest, most decent man I
have ever known. He is still the finest man I have ever known. I
had always been attracted to bastards. Men who weren't good for
me. So I understand the attraction you feel for (I cannot call him
your husband). But what you feel is a primitive, sexual, throbbing
hot feeling isn't it? The sex will sour—it always does . . .*

*WAKE UP! HE CAN'T POSSIBLY APPEAL TO YOU
INDEFINITELY IF HE ISN'T BEING FINANCIALLY
RESPONSIBLE.*

*Maybe I should blame myself for your dilemma. After all,
when you were growing up you had me to contend with, and
your mother is a contradictory, troubled woman. I wanted more
than anything to publish more novels. I kept writing them for
years and I failed. My failure made me miserable and resentful
and unfulfilled, and I took it out on you and Bart and didn't pay
enough attention to either one of you. I am sorry.*

*What am I getting at? Above all I don't want you to live a
limited life and Jason, I'm afraid, will limit you. If I thought
Jason was exceptional rather than hopelessly mediocre I wouldn't*

*be carrying on this way. If he was a genius or even a genuine
eccentric I would even applaud your efforts to support him. Does
this make any sense? . . . I am now exhausted so I will close. I
think I will have a massage . . . But please, PLEASE think about
what I have been saying to you. Your loving, concerned Mama*

I didn't answer that letter or the others she sent me. I felt defiant;
I couldn't yet admit to myself that she might be right. But Mama of
course would not be ignored. When I didn't reply, she showed up,
weeks later, at the Powers Agency on my birthday, April 24.

I happened to be there in the lounge collecting my booking slips
when I heard her call, "Lambie-pie, the receptionist said I could
come in here."

That familiar, brisk voice, the way she clipped her words, the
singular pauses—nobody took command of the language the way
she did. Then I saw her standing before me in a bottle-green suit
and bottle-green pie-shaped hat, flaunting her Bette Davis mannerisms, and my eyes filled with tears.

"Well! Aren't you going to kiss your mother?"

She held out her arms and I ran into them.

She enveloped me in a big hug, and I breathed in her wonderful
fragrance. She didn't cry, but I could tell she was fighting tears as well.

"Let me see you." She pushed me away so she could study my
face, thick with pancake, eyebrows drawn on darkly, lipstick bright
on my mouth.

"You look like a chorus girl," she chided. "Do you have to wear
so much makeup when you're modeling?"

I drew away from her. "Yes, I do. The lights are very hot, you
know." I felt self-conscious as her eyes bored into me. "I have to go
to work, Mama," I said.

"Oh, you can't leave now! Please, please, my angel. I want to give
you your birthday present."

With that she handed me a small box from Tiffany's. I opened it. Hidden inside the blue tissue paper was a gold ring with a crest on it. "It's the Bosworth crest," my mother said. "I want you to put on that ring and never take it off. You are a Bosworth, you know."

I obediently put the ring on, and she grabbed my hand. "Let me see," she commanded. "Oh, dear, you are still biting your nails."

"I'm trying not to." I sulked. I was filled with anger, remembering all the times when I'd felt diminished in my mother's impeccably groomed presence. "Goddamn it, Mama, you are treating me like a child!"

"Well, you are a child. You are *my* child, my little girl." She reached out to embrace me, but I turned away. "I have to go to work," I told her, and I picked up my tote bag and marched out of the lounge.

"Wait!" Mama cried. "I still haven't told you what I am about to do."

"*What?* Please tell me very quickly."

"You know how your father is always complaining I spend too much money? I decided I'd earn some myself."

"How?"

"Bloomingdale's has hired me as a food consultant for their Gourmet Shop. I'll be interviewing celebrity chefs."

"That's great, Mama."

"Do you really think so?" She was almost stuttering.

"Yes, I do. You'll be very successful, I'm sure." I moved to go into the Dell studios.

She put her hand on my arm. "It means a great deal to me that you think I can do this," she declared with passionate intensity. "I haven't worked for years, you know. I am not a young woman anymore." She was then fifty-three.

"You're in terrific health and your mind is sharp as a tack," I said. "You are going to be fine. Now I really have to go."

She clung to me. "Don't be a stranger, please." She paused. "Please come to the house. Please? Bart misses you. Your father misses you. I miss you."

"Okay, Mama," I said.

JASON NEVER KNEW, but from then on I periodically did go home. That part of my life, as a daughter and a sister, I couldn't share with him.

One evening I dropped by and discovered that my father had invited Lillian Hellman, the director Herman Shumlin (who'd directed Hellman's *The Little Foxes*), and the composer Marc Blitzstein over for drinks. They were part of what Mama called Daddy's "left-wing buddies." They worked together on the Joint Anti-Fascist Refugee Committee organizing rallies at Madison Square Garden.

But to me they were impressive figures in the Broadway theatre world, a world I dreamed of being part of. I felt shy and self-conscious around them, especially since Daddy always told them, "Patti wants to be an actress," so I just sat and observed.

I was especially in awe of Hellman, a feisty, combative woman— quite homely with an oversize head and a squat body. She dressed elegantly in Balmain, chain-smoked, and rarely stopped talking. That evening she and Shumlin began drinking heavily and shouting at each other. Mama had told me they were lovers. Shumlin had a terrible temper, which he unleashed that night in its full glory.

Hellman seemed keyed up, but this was understandable. Days before, at the Ninety-Second Street Y, she had done the narration for a performance of *Regina*, an opera written by Marc Blitzstein that was based on her play *The Little Foxes*. When it was over the audience had given Lillian a standing ovation, my father explained. Hellman interrupted with "I was so fucking nervous a stagehand gave me a shot of bourbon, and that didn't help, so he gave me another. He had red hair. I wanted to thank him afterward, but I could never find him."

The standing ovation was not just for the opera but for Lillian's statement in front of HUAC, my father argued. He continued, "It was Lillian's letter to the committee that did the trick . . ." and he quoted her now-famous phrase: "I cannot and will not cut my conscience to fit this year's fashion."

"Oh, Bart, for Christ's sake," Hellman roared. "What I really liked was that guy in the press gallery who yelled out, 'Finally someone had the guts to do it.'"

All this time, composer Marc Blitzstein, a slight, dark-haired man, had been listening intently. He was famous for his opera about union busting called *The Cradle Will Rock,* which had been directed by Orson Welles. Late in the evening my brother wandered into the living room. He had heard voices and I suspect Mama had suggested that he meet Blitzstein, since Blitzstein was a musician and Bart loved music so.

My father introduced them and they went off in a corner to talk. After the group left, Bart announced that Blitzstein had invited him to attend his two-week music workshop in the Caribbean. Samuel Barber would be there; so would Leonard Bernstein and Harold Schonberg. My father became agitated. "Well, you can't go. We can't afford to send you," he said. My brother retorted quietly that it was by invitation; Blitzstein was to give him a fellowship. Still, my father argued, it wouldn't be wise. "We don't really know Blitzstein . . . he is not really a friend." This wasn't like my father, who seemed approving of most people, especially his "left-wing buddies." He added that he would have to "think about it. I hope you didn't tell him you were definitely coming," to which my brother answered, "I told him I'd like very much to."

My mother was anxiously listening to all this. Bart's expression was stony. "Just because you don't appreciate classical music," he muttered. And he left the living room.

As soon as he was out of earshot, my father exploded. "I can't let our son be alone with those guys. They're all fairies."

My mother whirled around. "Those 'fairies' happen to be extremely talented musicians. It could be a very rich experience for Bart. Music is the one thing that interests and pleases him now."

"Well, I am not going to allow it," my father told her. He poured himself another drink. That's when Mama began talking about the two books she'd been reading, Kinsey's report and Gore Vidal's *The City and the Pillar*. "It's quite wonderful to read them side by side. My eyes have been opened," she said intensely to my father. "Vidal implies that there is nothing abnormal in having romantic feelings for the same sex."

My father listened but couldn't be swayed on account of his Catholicism. His puritanical repressed temperament was too ingrained. "I'm sorry, Cutsie, but I can't accept what you are saying."

The following morning when Blitzstein phoned to invite my brother to the music workshop, Mama explained that Bart already had other vacation plans. Indeed, he'd been enrolled in a Quaker work camp in Missouri, and he went off tight-lipped. When he returned a couple of weeks later, tanned and very fit, he seemed more depressed than ever. He wouldn't speak to my father for a long time and he confided to me he'd renounced Catholicism. "I'm an atheist now," he told me. "I do not believe in God. I never did. I only pretended to for Daddy's sake."

Chapter Six

JUNE 1952—HOT, STICKY weather in Bronxville. There was no air-conditioning at Alger Court. Jason would wrap ice cubes in a dish towel and he'd rub my naked body with the cloth until my skin felt cool and wet, and then we'd make love. The ice would melt and the sheets would be soaked by the time we fell asleep.

Sometimes we'd escape to New York. As soon as we arrived in the city, we'd climb onto a double-decker bus and ride down Fifth Avenue to the Village. We'd get off at Eighth Street, which was then a marvelous thoroughfare engulfed by swarming crowds often pushing to get into the Art Theater. I saw my first foreign films there with Jason, *The Bicycle Thief* and *Brief Encounter*. Afterward we might drop by the Eighth Street Bookshop and buy some paperbacks—J. D. Salinger, a collection of Fitzgerald short stories. Then we might end the evening at the Five Spot listening to jazz.

But such pleasant interludes were few. Jason was often in an ugly mood because his paintings weren't going well and Grandma was feeling poorly. Once Faith and I had to give her an enema—an experience I tried to forget.

Then brief excitement: I was chosen to be a Camay Beauty Bride.

It would be my biggest break as a model. I was to be paid thousands of dollars and my picture would appear in every women's magazine, including *Ladies' Home Journal* and *McCall's,* for an entire year. John Robert Powers personally congratulated me and my rate went up to $60 an hour. For the next weeks I was fussed over by ad execs and stylists, I was given a new hairdo, and I tried on an endless array of lacy white bridal gowns. Then I posed, clutching a big bouquet of flowers, a diamond sparkling on my hand. My bitten nails were hidden by fake red ones.

I posed for three entire days. Close-ups, profiles, and long shots. I noticed the ad execs huddling. There was a problem. I simply could not muster even the ghost of a smile. The stylist whispered, "You're supposed to look happy. Don't you remember how you felt on your wedding day? Think about that."

I stood there sweating under the hot lights clutching my long white veil. One of my fake red nails popped off and everybody stared at it. How could I explain that I was utterly miserable with my husband and trying to figure out a way to leave him?

Eventually the ad with my woebegone face on it appeared in *Good Housekeeping.* It ran only once in that magazine and then the entire campaign was pulled. I did get paid and was also presented with twelve cartons of Camay soap. I handed that soap out to everyone I knew. Jason used the money to buy a sleek dark green Jag. But he never allowed me to drive the car.

BY NOW I knew I'd made a terrible mistake marrying Jason, but I was too proud to admit it to anyone. Mama sensed I was in a quandary, so she made an appointment for me to see a stately middle-aged therapist named Dr. Aviva, who had a home office in her apartment on Fifth Avenue. I'd go there once a week and try to make sense of my marital problems.

I'd heard that therapy could cure every anxiety, but Dr. Aviva's manner was so unpleasant and chiding that I could barely speak. I can't remember exactly what she said, but I do remember that in our very first session she pronounced me "a baby . . . You are still homesick for your parents," and then she added grimly (after I'd tried to describe my husband), "The language of courtship is very different from the language of marriage . . . You still want romance."

Sometimes she'd bark, "Stop entertaining me and tell me what is bothering you." I had a tendency to make light of what I was going through in my marriage, telling funny stories about the aviary or my cooking sprees instead of zeroing in on the ways Jason mistreated me.

She wanted to know *why* I had married Jason. After much probing I managed to tell her he'd started out as a fantasy figure drawn from movies and novels about Bohemia. "When I first saw him he wore a beret and spoke a few words of French," I told her.

"The cliché dream of the artist!"

"Yes, yes, I know that!" I cried. I'd been swept away by this idiotic fantasy. Hungry for experience, I'd plunged into the dingy chaos of Alger Court without thinking. I existed for my emotions. I didn't consider anything else.

Dr. Aviva would stare at me incredulously as I babbled at her and I'd stare back. I was juggling so many roles in order to survive— wife, student, daughter, sister. Part of me was still a little girl struggling to become a woman. I was a wage earner and proud of that. These roles were preparing me for my future, which I prayed would include my dreams of acting and writing.

Once Dr. Aviva broke in to ask, "Who do you love more than anybody?" and I immediately answered, "My brother." And then I burst into tears. Because until recently Bart had been the one person I could talk to freely, the one person I trusted implicitly, felt at ease with, could be myself with (whatever that was). I had few secrets from him, which was a relief, although I never told him of Jason's abuse. But since Deerfield, Bart and I had no longer been as close, and this upset me terribly. I didn't know what to do about it. I behaved the same way with him as I always had, telling him everything, usually in our private language (which he didn't want to speak anymore). But my brother seemed bored with me now; he didn't want to share as much. We no longer went to the movies or explored the city. He had Tobias.

But I did not mention this to Dr. Aviva.

AUGUST CAME, HUMID and muggy; we'd bought a fan, but it didn't do much good in our tiny room. Late at night, confined in our space and unable to sleep, Jason would turn mean. He'd slap me when he'd discover that I'd forgotten to iron his khakis. He'd slap me harder when I'd refuse to get him a beer. I didn't fight back; I lay on our bed, naked and trembling, feeling totally helpless and caught in a trap.

Nobody talked about domestic violence; even therapists seemed to minimize or virtually ignore the subject. When I attempted to tell Dr. Aviva about Jason's treatment of me, she interrupted to say she'd be away for the rest of August. I burst into tears and begged her to stay in contact. I seemed so upset that after a moment she agreed and scrawled down her address and phone number in Ripton, Vermont.

"But only if it's an emergency. I ordinarily don't do this." Then she rose and ushered me out the door. She had two patients waiting to see her.

I returned home wondering how much longer I could endure my life with Jason. My husband wasn't just flying into rages with me but with his brother too. They had been fighting ever since they were small.

* * *

FAITH AND I were invariably in the kitchen when a fight erupted between them. It was always over something petty—Jason wanted to watch *Mister Peepers*, Wally wanted to watch *What's My Line?*

They would begin by hurling insults at each other: "Nebbish!" "Spastic!" "Cow turd!"

There would be a cry and I would hear Jason yelping in pain. A lamp would go crashing to the floor.

Faith and I would stop what we were doing, run into the living room, and find our two husbands rolling around on the floor pummeling each other viciously, sometimes drawing blood; little puffs of dust would rise from the soiled old Persian rug.

Faith would bellow at the top of her lungs, "Stop it, you guys—or I'm gonna tell Grandma!"

But there would be no need for that, because by now Grandma was rolling herself into the living room in her wheelchair, and she'd glide around the fighting men, poking at them sharply with her cane.

Only then would they stop. Sweating and petrified, they would clamber to their feet and apologize: "Oh, jeez, Grandma, you know, just kiddin' 'n' horsin' around." And they would chuckle and try to kiss her.

Grandma would wave her cane at them and go gliding down the hall to her bedroom.

Afterward I'd help Jason back to our room, and I'd bathe his scratched bloody face and make sure his precious nose hadn't been broken.

I didn't cook supper for the rest of the family those nights. They had to fend for themselves. We'd sneak out for a hamburger, and then crawl into bed and cuddle and Jason would hold me tight, vowing eternal love.

"I'm so crazy about you, baby," he'd murmur. "Promise you'll never leave me. Never, never?"

Even though I felt trapped and totally alone, I'd promise.

JASON AND I fought too, over my continued refusal to ask my father to support us. "I can't understand why you don't," Jason would say. He would point to one of the tabloids that featured a photograph of Daddy, and under it a caption about the million-dollar settlement he hoped to get for Rita Hayworth.

We had our ugliest fight going into New York on the train. We kept bickering ("No, I won't ask my father"; "Oh yes you will—") . . . By the time we reached Grand Central and climbed into a cab, I began to insist that *he* earn some money. Then he started slapping me.

And in between whups he let loose with a crazy monologue: "You don't listen!" (Whup!) "You never listen!" (Whup! Whup!) "Why don't you listen? Because you are spoiled rotten." (Whup! Whup! Whup!) "Why should I work just because everybody else works? Did Picasso have a job?" (Whup!) "I will never be a shitty white-collar worker. Painters are supposed to paint. You'll ruin me if you keep pestering me to get a job!" (Whup!) "You are driving me nuts." (Whup!) And then he began shaking me. "If you didn't have enough confidence in me, why did you marry me?"

Throughout I was screaming at the cabdriver to stop the cab, but Jason ordered him to drive on. I kept sobbing and pleading with the driver to let me out. He refused. "He's the boss, lady," he told me, nodding at my husband.

It was a nightmare. Then I remembered what Diane Arbus had told me. *It's your life. You don't have to be a victim, you know.* We had just ground to a stop at Vanderbilt Avenue and Forty-Third Street when I decided I'd had enough. I found myself vaulting out of the cab and diving into traffic. I breathed in exhaust fumes and sewer stink coming up from the grates. I crazily thought, *I could compose a dance*, as I moved in and out of the lines of trucks and buses. In the background I could hear Jason screaming, "Come back, you little bitch!" which made me run even faster. I ran and ran until my heart constricted and I was panting and streaming perspiration. I ran until I came to the Port Authority Bus Terminal and I bought a ticket to Ripton, Vermont. It was the boldest action I'd ever taken. When I sank back on the seat of the bus and it rumbled out onto Ninth Avenue I breathed a sigh of relief. At least I had done *something* for myself.

Chapter Seven

EXHAUSTED, I SLEPT all the way to Ripton. I had Dr. Aviva's address. When the bus let me off, I walked from the stop down a dirt road. Her cottage was nearby and surprisingly modest, white shingles with green shutters. I'd imagined she lived in a bigger place, a farm or an estate. I knocked on the door. She opened it and stared at me in annoyance and surprise. She seemed a bit breathless as she pulled a kimono about her ample bosom. Did I see a male figure hovering behind her?

"What are you doing here, Patti?" she demanded.

"I need to talk to you," I began urgently. "It's my husband—he's been hitting me . . . and I . . . You said if it was an emergency . . ."

She interrupted. "I am on vacation now. I'll speak to you about this in September."

"I'm sorry, but please help me. I just didn't know what to do . . ."

She shut the door in my face.

I stood in the dusty road, sun beating down on my back. Now what? I was in the wilds of Vermont. I didn't know a soul. I began to sob. Then I started to walk. I walked and walked, past farms and stretches of cropland until I came to a crossroads with high old poplar trees and an inn. There were cars and trucks parked outside and men running in and out carrying lights and cameras. The next thing I knew, I was in the lobby of the inn—a comfortable, rustic place with low leather chairs and potted plants. In front of me was a reception desk and a rather attractive middle-aged man, bearded, wearing what looked like a safari jacket and corduroy pants. He was conferring with the receptionist. He had a foreign accent. As soon as he saw me, he regarded me with interest and concern. I guess I looked pretty forlorn; my face was streaked with tears and I was disheveled.

"Are you all right?"

"Nooo!" I wailed.

Without another word he took me in his arms. Within minutes I had told him everything—my escape from my brutish husband, the trip to Vermont to consult my doctor, her rejection.

"You poor kid."

"And to top it off, I have no more money," I choked out.

There was a long silence, and then the man gently cupped my face in his hands and studied me with great intensity. He had large brown tired eyes. I guessed he must be in his fifties—old enough to be my father.

"It will be okay . . . It will be okay," he said. "I will see to that."

I stared at him. Who was this man with the gentle voice and an accent I couldn't place?

He put his hands on my shoulders.

"Have you ever heard of Robert Frost?"

"Of course I have. He's a great poet."

"Well, I happen to be making a documentary about this great poet. Today, this afternoon, we are filming him at his farm. I will take you with me. You will forget your troubles, and then we will come back to the inn for dinner and we can decide what you should do. Now how does that sound?"

I didn't answer.

"By the way, my name is Bela Kornitzer. I have made many documentaries on President Truman and Roosevelt."

"I'm . . . Patricia Bosworth." (I just couldn't say Patricia Bean.)

We shook hands.

THE SUN WAS flooding the lush green meadow outside Frost's farm. While Bela set up the cameras and recording devices, he had me sit next to Frost and keep him company. The great poet had soft white hair and a ruddy, heavily lined face. He was then seventy-eight years old and had won four Pulitzers for poetry that defined rural life in America.

At first he seemed crotchety with me beside him, a total stranger. But he warmed up when I told him I was from San Francisco too. He'd been born in the Bay Area in 1874, and he remembered the sound of the foghorns and the great fire of 1906, which had destroyed most of the city.

Then Bela turned the cameras on and began the interview. He asked Frost questions about his inspirations—"Shakespeare, myths, and Bible stories," he said. He'd had twenty years of rejection before any of his poems were published, twenty years of writing about stone walls and brown earth and blue butterflies, and nobody cared. He'd been a farmer and a teacher; he'd raised five children. He'd bought his first farm for a thousand dollars. Then he recited a poem, "Fire and Ice."

After the filming was finished, we shook hands, and then he said to me, "You should take life seriously, girl." It was over too soon.

That evening Bela invited me for supper at the inn; the dining room was half empty. He ordered for us, mulligatawny stew—an Indian dish, he said. He asked for a bottle of red wine and then lit a cigarette and gave it to me, and then he began talking to me very softly about luck and chance and how it was an accident that we'd met but we would now be good friends. He said he'd remember this evening for the rest of his life, and I said I would too. *Take a good look at this room*, I reminded myself, *the paneled walls, the ivy plants, the middle-aged waitress who took our order and wore a hairnet.* There was slow, soft music coming from the bar, just bits and pieces: "*Night and day, you are the one . . .*"

I told him who my father was, and it turned out they'd met in London in 1946 when Daddy was on a mission for President Truman. "I was trying to make a documentary about Albert Einstein," Bela said. And then he switched the subject to his own life in Budapest. He'd begun as a journalist, he told me. When the Communists took over Hungary, they'd charged him with seditious writing. In 1947 he sought exile in the United States. With fellow Hungarian Joseph Pulitzer's support, Bela was able to write his books and film his documentaries.

Bela did not want to hear about my husband, but I told him our story anyway and he shook his head. "Your marriage will be over soon," he predicted, "and then it will be as if it had never happened."

Near the end of the evening he took my hand and read my palm. "You will be married three times and you will live to be very old." (He pointed to my lifeline.)

"Will I be happy?"

He shrugged. "I have no idea. You will be restless, impatient . . . You will have many lovers." He laughed. "I will not be one of them."

At the door of my hotel room, he kissed my hand very formally and then he gave me his card. "We will always be in touch," he said, and then he guided me into the room, patted my shoulder, and disappeared down the hall.

The next morning I caught the bus back to New York. I kept turning over Bela's card in my hand as if it was a talisman: *Bela Kornitzer, documentary filmmaker.*

*   *   *

WHEN I RETURNED to New York from Vermont I didn't go back to Jason. Instead I camped out at Sarah Lawrence, sharing Marcia Haynes's room. Bela and I stayed in touch; he'd leave messages at the Powers Agency for me. I'd call him back and report how I was doing. Whenever I got depressed, I would remember my afternoon with him and Robert Frost. Until I met Bela, I'd been so caught up in my unsettling life with Jason I'd forgotten how surprising and beautiful the world could be.

Jason and I hadn't even spoken, but I knew he felt terrible. Marcia had been in touch with him. Apparently he'd phoned her hysterically after I disappeared into the traffic on Vanderbilt Avenue. She assured him I was okay; that I'd consulted my doctor in Vermont and now I was staying on campus with her. I needed time to think, to take stock of what had been happening to us these past six months. Miraculously Jason accepted my decision and this was a relief. But would I ever be able to figure out what I wanted to do? My life seemed to be in total chaos. Guilt, resentment, exhaustion overwhelmed me.

My parents felt I still needed outside help. Since I refused to continue with Dr. Aviva, Mama arranged to have me see an even more prestigious analyst named Sandor Rado, a round jolly man with a thick Austrian accent who happened to be one of Freud's closest disciples. I suppose you could call me his patient—I saw him off and on for many years—but I never felt like one with him. It certainly wasn't a formal analysis. Or maybe it was and he was so clever I didn't notice. I did know I had a very difficult time trying to confront what was bothering me. I couldn't move beyond certain ancient grievances (such as my mother's controlling attitude toward me). There were other conflicts inside that I couldn't resolve, let alone articulate (like whether or not I wanted to return to Jason).

I did talk about Jason with Marcia, who was urging me to go back to him and give him another chance.

Marcia and her boyfriend Gene Hill had been the only friends who'd ever gotten to know Jason. My husband tolerated few people, but he genuinely liked them. We'd often spend evenings together drinking in Gene's Village apartment on Bank Street. Gene kidded Jason about his arrogance but always encouraged his dreams of becoming a painter.

I HAD STARTED to keep a journal. It was one of the first assignments from my new writing teacher, the poet Jane Cooper. I bought a loose-leaf lined notebook and filled it with tiny scribbles.

An early entry from September 18, 1952:

> *I am in Marcia's room. She has prepared chicken soup for us on a hot plate and she is knitting Gene a sweater. She is so comforting, my friend—she is always there for me—she grounds me . . . I wish I could stay with her forever, if only so I could figure her out. She is very beautiful, but she is also dour and melancholy, and she does not express emotion in interpersonal conversations the way most of us do. Her gaze floats . . . takes me in all sorts of directions, except when she is speaking about Gene. She is totally obsessed with pleasing Gene and worried he doesn't really love her. I have watched her turn inside-out for him . . . and I think this is not right . . .* Have I made the same mistakes with Jason? *Gene is as taciturn as Marcia, but he doesn't appreciate Marcia's extravagant devotion. He assumes she should be doing for him, serving him, polishing his shoes, sewing buttons on his shirts . . . mixing him martinis . . . Her life is not her own . . .*

Another entry, a couple of weeks later, was decorated with a sullen photograph of me as a model looking very apprehensive and captioned:

> *Married eight months . . . Now separated from Jason, who I don't want to go back to—yet. But do I ever want to go back? I feel very far away from him and Alger Court . . . far away and very sad.*

In the meantime I had returned to my classes with enthusiasm. I loved my writing assignments with Jane Cooper, and dance class offered me a real emotional release for all my pent-up feelings. I began choreographing pieces under Bessie's guidance, among them a duet with my own reflection in the mirror. Bessie quickly recognized it as a rip-off of Gene Kelly's memorable number in *Cover Girl*. She spoke to me bluntly: "You can begin by imitation, but unless you transform your work into something uniquely your own, forget it!"

I STAYED AWAY from Jason for close to six weeks, refusing to see him or talk to him. In the meantime Bessie organized a dance workshop at Reisinger's, the big new theatre on campus. I was performing a solo set to a poem by e. e. cummings, "Your Little Voice (Over the Wires)," which I recited as I danced. As I recited the words in a tremulous voice, I felt that I was growing larger and more important to myself.

Marcia had invited Jason and he showed up in the audience, along with my father. I could hear Daddy coughing and laughing. I thought I could hear sparse applause as I took my curtain call, dripping with perspiration. Both men came backstage to congratulate me. I took one look at Jason and felt weak in the knees. I still loved him in spite of everything. He stared at me very hard.

Then there was an uncomfortable silence. Daddy didn't speak to Jason, but he hugged me and said, "You were wonderful, my darling!" Then he quickly made his excuses. "Late meeting back in New York City, kiddies." He ran off to his hired Carey Cadillac limousine outside the theatre.

As soon as he'd gone, Jason grabbed me and kissed my cheeks, my nose, my lips. His strong arms felt good as his kisses rained down on me. He wouldn't let me go.

"You coming home, baby? Please, you coming home? I have a

job . . . I am making some money." He held me close. "Oh, God, I have missed you, missed you." There were tears in his eyes. "I love you, I really do love you."

With some trepidation I agreed to go back with him to Alger Court that night. Once in the bedroom we began to kiss frantically, moaning, gripping each other, tearing off our clothes. The fish tanks were still gurgling in the background and I could hear the birds chirping on the sun porch. We ended up making love on the floor.

Jason was working for Wally delivering trays of Thomas' English muffins to supermarkets and diners all over Westchester. He complained about it, but he knew that if he didn't earn some money, I might leave him for good, and so our life went on for a while longer. It was not the same. I stopped cooking elaborate meals for the family; we existed on takeout and frozen foods. I was more intent on my college classes and I'd started auditioning for TV shows and commercials.

On weekends we'd hop in the Jag and zoom over to Bear Mountain State Park, lie on the grass, drink cheap wine, and try to plan our future. Jason wanted to go to Europe; I wanted to move from Alger Court before we did anything else. "We have no privacy," I told Jason. I wanted to create a home.

Jason hedged. He agreed we should move, but not quite yet. I knew he didn't want to lose access to Grandma and her estate.

In the meantime we would talk until it got dark and then we'd drive back to Bronxville, fall into bed, make love. Jason consumed me all over again with his tawny hairy body, fucking me deep and hard, rocking me back and forth in his arms, holding me down while he tickled my nipples with his fingers until I moaned. I hated myself for feeling so consumed by him. I disliked the man, and yet I stayed with him. Something bound us together. Years later a tough old movie star, Shelley Winters, told me, "When the sex gets better and hotter so you can't get enough of it, you deceive yourself into thinking your marriage is getting better, when in reality the rest of your marriage is full of shit."

BY THIS TIME I was starting to view our marriage as a kind of bizarre adventure. I never knew what to expect. I certainly never expected to meet Jason's mother, who had been incarcerated in a loony bin for decades. But not long after Jason and I reconciled, Mrs. Bean suddenly appeared at our door. She looked almost the same as she did in the photograph on our dresser—same twisted little smile.

It was midafternoon. Jason had returned from his job driving the Thomas' English muffin truck. He had just grabbed a beer from the fridge and the bell rang.

There she was, Judith Bean, standing in the doorway in a thin cloth coat carrying what looked like a cardboard suitcase.

"Mom?" Jason stood and stared.

"I'm back." She smiled sweetly and put her suitcase down. "I'm back just for a little while . . ."

Jason pulled me next to him. "Mom, I want you to meet my wife, Patti . . ."

Judith Bean shook my hand very solemnly. "I'm glad my son has married such a pretty little girl."

"Mom . . . Mom . . ." I could tell Jason didn't know how to handle the situation. "Listen," he said, "Mom, did you just leave . . . the hospital, I mean."

Judith Bean stood up very straight. "I walked out. I wanted to see you before I die," she said. "I wish you'd visited me. Why didn't you visit me?"

Jason hung his head. "Dunno, Mom. I guess . . . we may have been told not to."

Judith Bean surveyed the room. "Where's Grandma?"

"She's probably sleeping," I said. "I can wake her."

Jason held my arm. "Don't do that, baby."

"I'm hungry," Judith Bean announced.

"I'll fix you something," I said.

"That would be nice."

I hurried into the kitchen and made my mother-in-law a peanut butter sandwich. There was coffee in the pot.

I brought everything out on a tray. Judith Bean was perched on the sofa staring into space. She wolfed down the sandwich and gulped the coffee, and then after wiping her mouth, she looked at us with burning eyes.

"Don't you want to know *why* I came to see you, Jason?" she asked.

"Yeah, Mom, sure I do."

With that, Judith Bean jumped from her perch and declared, "Because I am going to kill myself right now, and I want you to watch me." Before we could do anything, she had zipped through the door and onto the street and was jogging toward the train station.

We ran after her, but she was an amazing little runner for a sixty-five-year-old crazy lady. Lying down on the train tracks, she gripped the rails. It took all Jason's strength and mine to pull her off. By this time she was yelling like a banshee. "No, let me go, I want to die! I want to die, *please*!" A crowd gathered. Wally appeared, still in his Thomas' English muffin overalls.

"Oh my Gawd . . . Mom!" He knelt beside her writhing body. Jason was continuing to hold her down. "Call an ambulance, call the police!" he ordered to me.

In another hour Judith Bean was taken to a hospital in a straitjacket and eventually was driven back to the state hospital.

She escaped one more time. Once more we raced with her to the train station, and once more she lay down on the tracks and pleaded with us to let her die in peace. "I long to be crushed and obliterated—nothing left of me," she cried.

Jason let out a great sob and folded his mother into his arms. "Oh, Mom, oh, Mom," he moaned. He loved his mother. He seemed to relate to her torment. He was very shaken by the experience.

I momentarily felt sympathy for my husband. He'd never had a childhood. But even after this shared experience, our life together didn't change.

Chapter Eight

ONE EARLY EVENING, Jason returned from work cradling a dying bird in his hand. Was it a starling, a blue jay, a baby hawk? Even Grandma didn't know, but Jason was determined to nurse the bird back to health. I remember how carefully he fed it with an eyedropper, murmuring sweet nothings to it as the bird lay inertly on the living room couch that first night. Television was forgotten, supper left unprepared—until Grandma started complaining and I heated up a can of soup for her—but Jason was utterly absorbed with this bird.

Grandma didn't approve. All at once she spoke, in a hoarse, croaking voice, more than she'd spoken during our entire marriage. She told Jason he could not keep the bird uncaged; she was worried the bird might be carrying a disease. She ordered him to put it in the aviary with the other birds or get rid of it. Wally backed her up and so did Faith. I said nothing. Thus ensued a raucous argument. It ended with Jason storming out of the living room, shouting, "The bird is gonna be with us!"

HE CALLED THE bird "Lucky," and from then on Lucky remained in our cramped bedroom as Jason nursed him back to health. He did keep his job, but he stopped painting.

I'd come home from class or a modeling assignment and find our room in a mess, pillows on the floor, shades drawn, the dusty bureau heaped with racing forms and an amber beer mug filled with pennies.

Jason would be lying on our bed wearing only his underpants, with Lucky on his stomach. He'd be feeding the bird, petting it.

"He knows me, the little bugger." He'd grin. Jason had always preferred birds to humans because, as he put it, "They don't talk back."

AS SOON AS the bird got well, Jason allowed it to flap around our room uncaged. I began suffering from insomnia, afraid that Lucky might peck my eyes out as I slept. I took to snitching some of Daddy's Nembutals whenever I went home for a visit.

Weeks went by. Finally I had to know. "How long are you going to keep Lucky?" I asked Jason one night.

"What do you mean? He's gonna stay here," Jason answered belligerently. "He likes it here, don't you, boy?" and he'd kiss the bird's beak and urge me to do the same.

I would draw back whenever Lucky's claws gripped my flesh, whenever his wings beat against my skin. I couldn't communicate with him the way Jason did, chirping and twittering at him tenderly. Lucky actually would peep back.

"Birds are amazing creatures, free and beautiful and brave. They fly all over the world. Birds are nicer than people."

"I guess they're nicer than your fish," I'd answer. "You don't pay any attention to your fish anymore."

We would both stare at the fish, swimming rather disconsolately around in their murky tank. "Tank needs cleaning," I'd say.

"So? That's your job," Jason would reply coldly. "Clean it, baby." And he'd go back to allowing Lucky to chew on his finger.

*   *   *

NONE OF MY classmates except Marcia knew about the strange realities of my marriage: the bird that flapped around our sagging bed; my ninety-six-year-old grandmother-in-law who ranted about my "commie poppa"; my sadistic, narcissistic, self-involved husband whom I couldn't break away from. For a while a rumor circulated on campus that my parents had disinherited me because I'd married someone they disapproved of. Hence my need to earn a living. I angrily denied the rumor.

I did keep up a frantic pace running up the hill to campus in an effort to get to class promptly, sometimes stumbling, almost falling as I slipped into a seat. I was invariably late or rushing off to another modeling assignment or audition. Being a model did have some compensations. Like going off on a Caribbean weekend for a location shoot for bathing suits. Or lunches al fresco at photographer Milton Greene's penthouse studio high above Lexington Avenue overlooking Grand Central. The debonair, skinny Fred Astaire and the equally dashing Cary Grant were being photographed by Milton for some *Life* magazine spread. I was there for a less impressive booking, but I was able to watch them pose and then nibble at some delicious repast.

ONE NIGHT I escaped for dinner and the theatre with my mother. Once we were together it was as if we'd never been apart. I forgot about being Mrs. Jason Bean. I was Patricia Bosworth Crum, college student/aspiring actress/model. We talked about subjects that interested Mama, such as her job at "Bloomie's." She was reading "everything by Rebecca West"—*Black Lamb and Grey Falcon* and her account of the Nuremberg trials; Mama had bought a new hat at Lilly Daché; she'd just invented a marvelous new soup, cold tomato with a topping of curried mayonnaise.

Then we went to see William Inge's new play *Picnic*, directed by Joshua Logan. The show really affected me. It was set in a small

Kansas town on Labor Day weekend in the communal backyard of two middle-aged widows, Flo and Helen, who live in adjoining houses along with one of their boarders, a spinster schoolteacher desperate for marriage. Nothing ever happens to them until Hal, a sexy, mysterious drifter, appears in their midst. His animal vitality upsets everybody, especially Flo's young daughters—Madge, who's bored by her beauty, and Millie, a bookish tomboy played with agitated intensity by twenty-five-year-old Kim Stanley. Her performance was so close to the bone I found myself almost hyperventilating. I liked the young, skinny Paul Newman too, and Janice Rule as Madge, especially in the scene where she and the drifter (played by Ralph Meeker) dance seductively in the yard and you know she will sacrifice a wealthy marriage (to Newman) for the excitement the drifter promises. She does run away with him, and all the other women want to run away with him too.

By the end of the show I panicked, realizing that Jason would wonder where I was. As soon as I put Mama in a cab I called him from a pay phone in Times Square and said I was on my way home. When I reached Alger Court, my heart was thudding. I knew that as soon as I admitted I'd been to the theatre with my mother Jason would be angry. But I had to keep seeing my mother and my father too. They were both reminders that I wasn't Jason's prisoner. Until I married, I'd taken the intense, complicated world I'd exiled myself from for granted. I needed to be reminded that this other world of privilege and beauty and opportunity was still available to me. Yes, there was pain and darkness in it too, but I could take the good parts and create a beautiful world for myself. It was part of the reason I could go on living.

I did not want to share my parents' world with Jason, but then they had never invited us as a couple to the brownstone on East Sixty-Eighth Street anyway. That was their way of rejecting him. As far as they were concerned, he didn't exist. That must have hurt him.

I was in the midst of describing how *Picnic* had moved me when Jason hit me square in the face. While I began crying, he watched me coldly. "Your mother isn't good for you," he said. "She's feeding you lies about me."

"No, she isn't," I sobbed. "She doesn't like you because she doesn't know you."

"She doesn't *want* to know me."

It was true, but I couldn't admit that to him.

We undressed in silence and crawled into bed. Lying next to him was excruciating. I felt so helpless. I'd learned too late that I was married to a bully. And to make matters worse, I'd returned to our relationship of my own free will. By staying with this man I was helping sustain and excuse the abuse.

I SAW MY brother now and then, but it was always an effort. He didn't want to see anyone. His spirits and psyche had not improved in the last year. He had graduated with honors at Stockbridge and gone on to MIT. But he had lasted there only a couple of months. It had been a painful experience for him. He could do the work, that was no problem, but he could not make any friends. He felt totally isolated and alone. He came home and explained quietly to my parents that he no longer wanted to be at his dream school. My father suggested he take the year off to just relax, figure out what the next step might be. He got him a part-time job at the *Daily News* as a copyboy. Bart didn't last there more than six weeks.

Now he was home again, "rattling around in the brownstone," as he called it. He was going to movies and seeing his best friend Tobias. He was thinking of going to Reed College in Oregon in the fall.

"It's smaller, it's supposed to be very good . . ." Tobias had enrolled there. I disliked Tobias. He had a sallow face and shifty eyes;

he lisped. I thought he was like a character out of a horror movie. I told my brother that.

Bart was indignant. "Tobias has had a hard life, harder than you will ever have. He knows a lot of stuff about people that I don't know."

"Like what?"

"Stuff that you wouldn't understand."

"Try me."

My brother gazed at me pityingly. "If you leave Jason, maybe I'll tell you why Tobias and I are friends."

Bart and I would usually end up at the Bronxville Drugstore sipping lemon cokes. I noticed he was still speaking in dull, flat tones; his face was expressionless. He had acne dotting his cheeks. We would sit in silence, and then I would ask him what was the matter, using our private language. He wouldn't react, and when I'd repeat the sentence he'd scoff, "Stop talking like that. We are too old for that now."

He would admit he was enjoying driving the station wagon to the Cloisters or to Garrison by himself. It was quiet up there. He'd catch me up on what was going on at home. Mama was planning events in Bloomie's Gourmet Shop. Daddy was still working on the Rita Hayworth case.

Overall, our parents were leading pretty separate lives. "But that's par for the course, isn't it?" my brother said quietly. We finished our lemon cokes and I walked him over to the train station.

And then out of the blue he asked me, "Was it worth it? Is sex that great?"

I FELT so foolish and helpless; I had gone past the phase of thinking my life with Jason would ever get any better. So I simply withdrew from the experience of being a wife and began to devise a method that allowed me to live with myself and with him, despite all the confusion and pain.

We were both busy with various jobs. Jason had started to paint again with his sporadic gusto, and then there was his obsession above all with his damn bird.

"Ships passing in the night," he used to say to me as I'd follow him to the bathroom for my nightly shower. We weren't communicating much, except in bed, and that was passionate but wordless. I was still frightened of his temper, but I'd lost all respect for him. "The thrill was gone," as Wally would say.

I kept everything bottled up and never told Jason what I thought of him. But after—was it now sixteen months?—I stopped being committed to the relationship. From then on I felt like a hypocrite for pretending I cared when I didn't. Instead I began trying to figure out a way of getting out of the marriage gracefully.

During those last months I saw my father more often for lunch. He was insisting on it. And I was grateful. I'd missed our long heart-to-heart talks (mostly dream talk about my future; Daddy was a fantasist who painted a rosy picture: "You will be on Broadway and in the movies . . . You will be very, very successful. I feel it in my bones."). How could I live up to such expectations? I would tell my father to please tone down his hopes for me, that I was bound to disappoint him. I wanted to do everything I dreamed of doing, but I was worried I wouldn't be good enough.

We always ate lunch at 21; it was Daddy's "club." He knew the waiters and most of the clientele—Hollywood agents, politicians, old soldiers' wives like Mrs. Douglas MacArthur, who would sit next to us in the A section of the restaurant. The tables nearby always overflowed with Washington lobbyists, real estate brokers from Tel Aviv, gossip columnists like Earl Wilson and Leonard Lyons, and sometimes Ed Sullivan and Bill Paley. Once Earl Warren, who had been in high school with my father, came over to chat. Everyone would greet Daddy with affection.

My father would get a sad expression on his face whenever someone from California dropped by our table. He missed San Francisco terribly, he told me; he never should have left, but he could never go back "now that I am under a cloud," he said. "I was too old to move to New York and take over a newspaper that had no advertising, a left-wing paper at the height of the Red Scare. What was I thinking?"

He'd order corned beef hash but often not touch it. All he'd do was drink. There was a terrible deliberateness about the way he doused himself with whiskey in 1953. He said he felt sick that Adlai Stevenson had lost the election and he was disgusted by Eisenhower's refusal to take on Joe McCarthy: "He says he doesn't want to get down in the dirt with him—why not? He is president, he is the most powerful man in the world. McCarthy is scum . . ."

My father would drink and drink and then he'd let me take a sip from his glass. I'd keep the glass for a while to keep him from getting too drunk. Was he being absentminded or did this mean he accepted me as a grown-up? This seemed to be my cue to describe what was happening in my life (leaving out the mental and physical abuse I was still occasionally receiving from my husband).

I'd tell him we'd moved to a funny attic apartment in Fleetwood. I did not say we'd been kicked out of Alger Court by the Bean family after Lucky had chewed up Faith's plants and nipped her on the arm. Actually, Wally had put our belongings on the street. I came home from college and saw my suitcases and books in a pile on the lawn and Jason lounging in the Jag with an embarrassed smirk on his face.

I'd tell Daddy that Jason was applying for an art scholarship, that he'd begun several paintings. I did not say we had gotten into violent shouting matches because he was still threatening to quit his job. He was now sorting mail in the Bronxville post office.

By the end of the meal I would be describing the TV commercials I'd gotten, the auditions I'd been going on, and Daddy's face would light up. "Jesus, my darling, you are making headway." His voice was growing slurred. I would ask him to stop drinking for a minute. He would shake his head impatiently. "Am cold sober," he'd maintain.

Then after several cups of black coffee and numerous cigarettes, he no longer seemed drunk. "So how are you, baby?" he'd ask. "You can tell your old man."

"I'm okay," I'd lie.

"Well, you don't look okay. You look like hell. Skin and bone and your clothes are a mess. Wrinkled. There's a spot on your blouse. I know I sound like Mama, but you should at least be well groomed. What exactly is going on?"

Well . . . Jason is . . . difficult."

"How so?"

"Temperamental . . . moody."

"Does he abuse you?"

I didn't answer. I didn't want him to know.

He didn't press it, but his silence put me on the defensive.

"I'm trying to work something out."

"Work out *what*?" My father's voice rose impatiently. "What's there to work out?" He took a deep breath. "Oh, I know, he's an artist and he is trying to find himself." His tone grew mocking. "But so far nothing is happening for him, right? So he is probably taking it out on you. Am I correct?"

I nodded.

"I'm not asking you to leave him, but I just hope he realizes what he's got in you."

I made a grimace.

"Don't underestimate yourself. And don't feel guilty if you decide to get out of the situation. You are not trapped. You are independent financially, don't you realize that? You could just walk out."

"I know, I know."

"No, you don't know yet. But something will trigger it. Or something will trigger you into an even stronger commitment. But you must remember it is not the worst thing in the world to admit you've made a mistake."

I WOULD COME back from a lunch with my father exhausted, hungover, depressed. Jason would often be in an ugly mood after sorting mail for eight hours. He was going to quit, he'd threaten—he couldn't keep up with this boring routine. I'd say I'd leave him if he did. We'd glower at each other. He didn't hit me any longer, but I was always on guard and my body remained very tense even when we made love.

We saw very few people. Every so often Marcia and Gene dropped by for supper. I'd cook pasta on a hot plate in our bathroom, which served as a makeshift kitchen when a board was placed over the tub.

DURING THOSE BALMY spring weeks of 1953 we kept the windows open in the apartment. We were directly over a parking lot, so there was the frequent sound of car doors slamming and tires churning in the thick soft gravel far below.

I was staying up late at night reading for my Great Books course, which I was taking with the Scottish poet Alastair Reid. Novels had acquired a new value for me. I'd often stay awake till dawn, my brain ringing with fatigue as I escaped into the works of Tolstoy and Gustave Flaubert.

Sometimes Jason would call me to come out and look at his paintings. He would be standing in front of his easel, frowning. A gooseneck lamp glared down at the canvas. Blobs of color, dribbles of green and gold, a mishmash of symbols, a cross and the Star of David—I didn't know what to make of his work, so I would say nothing except "It's coming along, hon." And he'd grin tiredly. Above us, Lucky swooped and flapped.

BY EARLY JUNE, Lucky had grown fat. Uncaged, he flew around and around the apartment. Occasionally he'd shit on our bed or the couch or peck at my arm. I hated that bird. I told Jason repeatedly he must be kept in his cage, but Jason said no. "Lucky likes to be free."

One afternoon I came home early from classes. As usual the place was a mess. I set about cleaning everything, stuffing dirty laundry into a pillowcase and sweeping beer cans and Coke bottles and candy wrappers into a heap. It was hot (we had no air conditioning), so I opened the window to let in some air. I did not see Lucky fly away. In fact I didn't notice he was gone until Jason came home laden with groceries from the A&P. I was already busy doing some homework in the living room.

"Hi, hon," Jason called out in his creamy mellifluous voice. "Bought us some steaks on sale." I could hear him moving around the kitchen/bathroom, which was outside in the hall, and then he came into the living room. "Where's Lucky?"

"Don't know, hon."

Jason ran into the small bedroom at the back of the apartment. "Lucky boy?" He started to cheep. Lucky didn't cheep back. After a few minutes Jason let loose a groan, "Lucky is gone!" He ran back into the living room and faced me. He seemed very agitated.

"Have you looked in the bathroom?"

"No!" He vaulted out of the apartment and into the kitchen/bathroom in the hall. He returned within seconds. "Not there either," he said. Then he noticed the wide-open window. "Oh my

God," he cried. "He must have flown away!" With that he stuck his head out the window and yelled, "Lucky! Lucky! Lucky!"

I joined him at the window. The sky was leaden—gray, empty. We waited a couple of minutes. Below us the lot glittered with parked cars.

"I'm sorry," I murmured, touching my husband's arm. "I'm so sorry."

"Sorry? I loved that bird." His voice was hoarse. "I loved Lucky."

"I'll buy you another," I offered lamely.

"You'll *what*?" Jason whirled around and grabbed me by the shoulders, shaking me hard. "You did this on purpose—you opened the fucking window and shooed the poor little fellow out!"

His hands gripped my shoulders painfully.

"Stop—you're hurting me!"

"You did it on purpose," he repeated angrily. His face was growing very red.

I struggled to break free. "No I didn't, Jason, honestly . . ."

"Oh yes you did, yes, you did." And with that my husband put his hands on my throat and began choking me.

Jason's fingers were very strong pressing against my windpipe. I struggled, I pounded my fists against his chest. I felt as if I were in a bad movie. I twisted and turned in his grasp, and after a moment I managed to kick him hard in the shins and break free. I stumbled into the hall and began calling for help.

I could hear myself calling "Help!" in a soft weak voice. I was so terrified I could hardly get the words out. Since we were on the top floor of the building, in an attic apartment that cost $50 a month, there were no other apartments on our floor.

Jason came after me and grabbed at me, and this time I kicked him even harder and managed to dart over to the fire stairs. I raced down the twelve flights and through the park surrounding our apartment complex. I couldn't tell whether he was coming after me or not. I didn't dare look back.

It was humid out. The drenching heat made me break out in a terrible sweat. I ran past the supermarket and the Laundromat and into a drugstore. A blast of freezing air-conditioning hit my face. I slipped into a phone booth and thanked God I had some change in my jeans.

I dialed the family brownstone. Miraculously my brother picked up the phone. "Please, please come and get me," I sobbed. "Jason is trying to kill me."

"Where are you?" Bart's voice was very calm.

I told him where I was. He ordered me to stay put—"Hide in the phone booth if necessary." He would pick me up in the car as soon as he could get Mama to give him the keys.

And that's how it happened. That's how my marriage ended—with Bart picking me up outside the drugstore in Fleetwood forty-five minutes after I'd phoned him. I threw myself into the front seat and we were off. We said nothing to each other until we were speeding along the Cross County Parkway. I remember my brother sat very straight behind the wheel. He drove with great confidence and élan. He had just gotten his license.

I started to tell him about Lucky's flying out the window and Jason's choking me. Bart shook his head and gave a brief chuckle. "I don't want to hear about it. You were almost murdered before you woke up. Your husband is such a jerk. But I guess I don't need to tell you that."

We drove home the rest of the way in silence.

MY PARENTS HAD stationed themselves at the front door. As soon as she saw me, Mama wrapped me in her arms. "The electric chair is too good for him. He should be imprisoned for life!" she exclaimed.

"Oh, no," I cried. "I wouldn't want him arrested."

"For God's sake, Patti, are you blind?" Mama interjected angrily. "He tried to kill you."

"No, no, he hadn't meant to hurt me," I insisted, although in truth Jason had been victimizing me for months. He *did* abuse me, but since it didn't happen too often, I kept excusing it and him, telling myself it couldn't be that serious.

Late that night Jason came to the brownstone, pounding on the door. Bart and Daddy had to hold my arms to keep me from letting him in. Jason called out, "Patti, Patteeeee! Come back!" I was sobbing hysterically.

But I didn't want to go back to him. And yet somehow I wanted things to end "nicely" between us, which wasn't possible.

The following morning, my parents sat me down in the dining room, and over coffee, Daddy advised me not to press charges. He was deadly calm. "You must never see or speak to this man again. Leave him the car, the furniture. Don't go back for your clothes. I will arrange for your divorce in Reno, baby. It will be taken care of."

THAT AFTERNOON I had an emergency session with Dr. Rado. The scary ending of my marriage had made me aware that I had a lot to learn about myself before I ever entered into another relationship. Again I found myself excusing Jason's appalling behavior.

Dr. Rado retorted dryly, "The will to deny the event is stronger than the will to proclaim it."

We talked back and forth some more. There were moments when I heard myself sounding coldly realistic, but mostly I waxed sentimental. Near the end of the session I blurted out, "I think I still love him in spite of everything."

Rado shook his head. "Your adult self sees the logic in ending this marriage, but your romantic side doesn't. You want it both ways. Can't be done."

When he said that, I started to cry. "Will I ever grow up?" I wailed.

Rado smiled and lit another cigarette. "Let's hope."

YEARS LATER I would wonder why I'd allowed myself to become such a victim. It was a question I'd never addressed during the marriage itself; I was too ashamed to tell anyone how severely Jason was abusing me physically and psychologically. I kept myself frantically busy so I wouldn't have to think (one woman friend joked with me about 1950s love relationships, "It was all about *feeling* and not about *thinking*!") and Jason's behavior was insidious—he would slap me but then make love to me later, leading me to think he would stop. I now know that this is a classic pattern of abuse, but at the time I wasn't aware of it.

I would relive the traumatic memory of the near strangling for years; I kept seeing Jason's Adam's apple moving up and down like some bulbous growth as he encircled my throat with his hands. I had nightmares of Lucky swooping down at me, bigger and fatter, his claws digging into me and pecking me violently.

What bothers me to this day is that at the start of our "romance" I'd failed to detect that there was anything the matter with Jason (although early on his hair-trigger temper had unnerved me). I didn't bother to ask him tough questions about his family or explore the warnings from students who knew him and said he could be a bully, that he was self-centered and a con artist. And then there was the voice of my brother, whom I'd always listened to in the past. Why didn't I hear him?

When I finally described the abuse in my marriage to Rado, he theorized the following: that the violence had excited me to some extent, that the fights were something I'd never witnessed growing up, that it was a relief to hear arguments and problems brought out into the open even if they were accompanied by bloody fists. Rado may have been correct, but he didn't know that my assumptions about a world of safety, security, and peace of mind had been shattered early on, long before I entered the grubby confines of Alger Court.

Part Two

Focusing

Chapter Nine

Daddy had booked me in a place in Reno called Shangri-la—The Divorcees' Retreat. Mama objected, "It sounds seedy," but Daddy insisted several of his clients had been happy there. Even so, I had a funny feeling as soon as I arrived in Reno and told the taxi driver where I wanted to go. He looked at me as if I was crazy. "Shangri-la? Jesus, girlie, you aren't the type to go there."

I refused to answer, so he gunned the motor and we were off. After we left the city limits we began bumping along a blackened highway that cut through the desert. All I could see were sun-blasted hills and sand. We passed an abandoned mine and a burnt-out shell of an automobile rusting on a sandy hill. Once a speeding truck hurtled past us. We drove for what seemed like hours until we came to a dip in a desert valley at the foot of the Sierra Nevada mountains. Just ahead I could see a series of bungalows that looked as if they were made out of driftwood; they were half surrounding a murky swimming pool, and nearby was a jam-packed parking lot.

The minute I left the cab, the heat overwhelmed me. It was deliriously hot (the cabdriver had said the temperature was over 115°). I had to walk past a surly dog growling at me and pulling on a leash. I felt almost giddy from the heat as I registered in the office while a bored receptionist with peroxided hair stared at me in silence and then handed me my key.

My room was so small and crammed with furniture I could barely turn around in it. The shades were drawn and lights blazed in two standing lamps. Overhead a fan whirred, but the air was stifling and smelled of mothballs. I took a cold bath, which made me feel better, and then I wandered out to the dining room, where I joined two middle-aged women with deep tans and expensive jewelry and a man who resembled an aging Clark Gable complete with a pencil mustache and cigarette holder. No introductions. There was a discussion about snakebites, and someone had seen a coyote near the swimming pool. Did I have a car? "You better have a car or you'll be stuck in this godforsaken place for six weeks and then what're ya gonna do?" The final question to me was "How old are you?" I admitted to being twenty. "Jailbait." Clark Gable chuckled. "You look like a goddamn virgin." They wandered off.

Supper was on the table. I tried to eat the tuna casserole and the fruit salad, but I skipped dessert and fled to my room. I just could not stay at Shangri-la. I waited until most of the guests had departed for Reno and gambling, then called my father from the pay phone in the hall. Sobbing that I couldn't stand Shangri-la, I described the place, the people.

Daddy understood. "I'd been misinformed, baby. I thought it would be nice . . . I will arrange for something else right away. Give me twenty-four hours."

I WAS AWARE that I was slipping right back into being "Daddy's girl." I'd programmed myself to depend on him from the time that I was little, fervently believing, often wrongly, that he would be able to solve all my problems. (Forgetting that while I was married, I'd been forced to solve a great many problems on my own, I didn't give myself credit for my growing independence.) As time went on,

Daddy helped me less and less. But I would continue to turn to him when I was in trouble until he died.

WITHIN TWENTY-FOUR HOURS I was whisked back to Reno and moved to a lovely old shingled house high on a bluff overlooking the Truckee River. The house belonged to a woman named, believe it or not, Reno Thatcher. She was the widow of Judge George Thatcher. He'd been one of the most respected legal minds in Nevada. He and my father had conferred on various cases over the years.

Reno was a warm, good-natured lady who liked to wear silk print dresses and jangly bracelets. After setting me up in my bedroom, she took me out onto a breezy porch, where we drank iced tea and she attempted to comfort me.

"You're awful tired, aren't you, sweetheart?" I nodded, unable to get my words out. "Take a nice cool bath and then go to sleep."

I did. For the next couple of days I slept and slept. When I woke up, Reno would bring me a sandwich and a glass of milk on a tray. I'd eat as much as I could and then fall back on the pillows again.

I hadn't realized how exhausted I was from being on the go the past fifteen months—to classes and modeling work and taking care of Jason and being petrified of Jason (which was extremely tiring in and of itself).

My body relaxed when Reno took me swimming at Lake Tahoe five days later. As I splashed around in the cool, crystal-clear waters, the Sierra Nevadas surrounding the blue pool that was the lake, I thought of a time long ago when Mama had thrown Bart and me into Lake Tahoe when we were on vacation as kids. We'd learned to swim before we could read; we swam like fish throughout our childhoods.

After a week of sleeping and swimming I felt ready to face life again. Then Reno sat me down on that breezy porch and told me,

"You have close to six weeks here. You should do something constructive. Take typing lessons and a course in Spanish at the University of Nevada." I registered for classes at the university, a short walk from Reno's house.

Those classes kept me busy; I tried not to think about myself, but I did think about Jason. For a while I missed him terribly. I had an almost physical ache in my body. "Was it just about sex?" I wrote in my journal. I knew sex was an expression of love, a part of love. What I hadn't realized was that sex could transform a relationship. It had created a bond between Jason and me as well as an actual craving on my part. Physical intimacy creates huge needs. I hadn't been aware that sex could deepen love and love could deepen sex, even when love was on the way out. But what was it in me that also needed to get hurt and punished? Did it have to do with low self-esteem? I didn't understand.

It wasn't until decades later that I came to terms with the fact that I'd been in an abusive marriage; then I wondered whether I'd married Jason because I'd had this powerful urge to leave home, leave my parents, and strike out on my own. This urge had been more powerful than the sense I had inside myself that Jason was scary.

I remember seeking out a friend from Chapin who'd also had "abuse issues," as she put it. She had married young, as I had; for years she'd endured whips and chains—much more violence than I'd ever experienced. She gave the man three children before she finally had the courage to divorce him.

"It goes on like that with so many women, especially of our generation," she said. "Nobody ever gave us any information about what we were doing to ourselves. We did not speak of such things; we simply went along with the abuse."

While I was in Reno I tried in vain to figure myself out. "Will I continue to stumble through life?" I scribbled in my journal. "Make lousy decisions? Love the wrong men? I have disappointed and angered my parents. My brother thinks I'm a fool. I want to change. I want to keep my independence. But I long for romantic love and I'm determined to have it."

TIME PASSED WITH agonizing slowness. The Nevada heat was punctuated by thunderstorms and fires—fires in the hills, houses going up in flames. The air often smelled of smoke and burning wood. I would rise before seven, put on a sleeveless dress and sandals, and run down to class by eight a.m. In those six weeks I learned how to type and mastered the rudiments of Spanish, but I spoke to none of the other students, all of whom were kids. They didn't speak to me either. Near the end of the term I discovered that most of them were from various parts of the country; many of them were getting divorced and, like me, too ashamed to admit it.

The university had no air-conditioning. By early afternoon the buildings shut down. I'd wander through the deserted campus, cheap sunglasses from the drugstore hiding my face. I'd usually have a hamburger and a Coke, and then I'd escape into a movie theatre. I'd sit in the blessedly cool darkness watching the latest hits of that summer.

One film stands out for me: *Roman Holiday*, a delicious fairy tale of a movie that introduced the radiant Audrey Hepburn to the world. What a beguiling, captivating presence she was. Elegant, gentle, gamine—half tomboy, half regal lady—she was perfection playing Ann, a Central European princess on an official tour of Rome. She's so bored being a princess that she escapes from her palace one night and has her first experiences of freedom with a cynical American reporter played by craggy Gregory Peck. It was a real Cinderella-style romantic comedy and I sat through it twice.

My favorite sequence: Audrey, perched behind Gregory Peck

on his Vespa, arms tight about his waist as they zoom around the Eternal City. She's just impulsively had her long hair cut off (what a liberating gesture), and she is reveling in it. Mama had always overseen my hairdos, often accompanying me to the beauty parlor, sitting next to me, bugging me. Audrey's enjoyment with her new image and her just-found independence was infectious. I was ready to cut my hair off too.

I'D LEAVE THE movies feeling lonely. Some nights I'd go to Mapes Hotel and Casino to play the slot machines. The Mapes was one of the most popular tourist attractions in Reno, open twenty-four hours a day and packed with gamblers, miners, call girls, and gangsters. If a circus was in town there were transvestites and midgets at the casino too.

One evening a muscular sandy-haired marine joined me at the slot machines. We fell into a conversation. He was polite and soft-spoken, with a wariness that attracted me. We went for coffee. His name was Lou. He was thirty-two and divorced. His ex-wife was a showgirl—she and their two kids lived in a trailer outside Las Vegas. At first I didn't want to tell him why I was in Reno, but he kept pressing me. He couldn't believe I was twenty. "You look about thirteen," he joked. He said he'd been stationed in Tokyo for a couple of years and now he was working as an engineer at the nuclear testing site in Yucca Flats deep in the Nevada desert. He was one of twenty thousand people on the site—soldiers, scientists, researchers, a few journalists.

J. Robert Oppenheimer was overseeing the routine test explosions, and Lou said they were frightening to behold. There would be brighter-than-the-sun flashes of light through the desert air and the earth would tremble and shake, and then the fallout from the explosions would drift into southern Utah. Yucca Flats was the ideal area—flat, not very populated, good weather conditions—

meaning that the wind would blow the fallout away from concentrated areas of people.

I recalled my father talking worriedly about the intensity of the arms race between the United States and the Soviet Union. Ultimately there would be hundreds of tests done at Yucca Flats, many underground. It was the height of the Cold War.

Daddy came to Reno once—something about Rita Hayworth's divorce proceedings—and after he'd finished his business, we had dinner at the Mapes Hotel and I told him about the atomic bomb testing at Yucca Flats. And about Lou. "Are you behaving yourself, baby?" That was all he wanted to know. I assured him I was.

I FANTASIZED ABOUT making love with Lou; I imagined he knew much more about sex than I did. He sometimes looked at me as if he could see what I was wearing under my sundress. And then he kissed me—the first man to kiss me since Jason—and it had been one of the most passionate, heartfelt kisses I'd ever experienced. I tried to kiss him back, but he drew away.

"You're a greedy little thing, aren't you?" he murmured, chuckling. "You're spoiled too. You aren't used to being turned down. Am I right?"

I nodded, fighting back tears. I'd always been the most popular girl in spin the bottle at Ecolint. I was used to being fawned over and desired.

"You want everything too fast. Slow down." He cupped my face in his hands. "It might have been different if you were staying here. If you were staying here, I'd do more than kiss you. We both know that."

I was aroused. For a couple of minutes I tried to figure out ways of staying longer in Reno, but I decided against it. I did not see Lou again after that night of the single kiss. But I often thought about him.

*   *   *

I SPENT ALL of August in Garrison with Mama and Bart, but he was in the woods most of the time shooting at those tin cans. He'd return to the house in the evenings sullen and preoccupied. Mama would ply him with corn soufflé and all his other favorite dishes. But he'd leave most of his food on his plate.

"What's the matter, Boofie?" she'd ask him. (Boofie was her nickname for him, short for beautiful.)

"Nothing, Mother," he'd answer in the weary ironic tone he'd picked up from his best friend, Tobias. Tobias visited us once, only for a day—such a dark, creepy presence. But Bart seemed fascinated by him. He took Tobias to see the castle. They were gone for what seemed like hours.

Mama was worried. "I can't reach him—I don't know what to do!" she'd say. As usual, Daddy wasn't around, so she talked long distance to him about Bart. They realized he was chronically depressed, but neither one of them had a clue as to how to help him.

Mama distracted herself, either by exercising or by lying under a sun lamp until she turned nut brown. She'd appear in my room and demand, "Don't I still have the body of a young girl?" I'd look at her thighs and stomach, flat as a teenager's, and I'd say, "Yes, Mama, you do." She'd drag me out into the hall and have me stand next to her in front of a full-length mirror, where we would study our reflections in the glass: Mama sleek and tanned, wrapped in an emerald-green towel; me disheveled in cutoff jeans and T-shirt. She'd cry, "Oh God! Why do you insist on looking like a slob when you could be really beautiful? Hiding behind your dirty hair and freckles is an image of my own lost perfection!"

She'd leave me to contemplate my face. How often did I return to that mirror? Constantly. Because I couldn't figure out who I was. Only weeks before, I'd been a wife and a workingwoman, sleeping every night with an unpredictable man; now I was back home with my parents, feeling like a beautiful spoiled child who didn't have a serious thought in her head.

My brother was the only person who could make sense of me. We had one of our last conversations in Garrison lying on the grassy hill overlooking the sweep of the Hudson River. I was being especially silly, describing an inane rendezvous I planned to keep with some nameless Yalie at the Biltmore Hotel. "He is so outrageous," I was telling my brother. "I barely know him. He's pockmarked, he likes to make scenes, and I am wildly attracted to him."

"Shut up," Bart ordered. "Shut up. Shut up. Why don't you think slowly and carefully about something for a change? You're too impulsive; you're giving yourself away. But . . ." He stopped and gazed at me with his huge, sorrowful eyes. "You may be saved by your imagination and your conscience, I pray to God."

He paused and grinned slightly. "If I believed in God."

I WOULD SPEND only one more afternoon with my brother in early September just before he left for college in Oregon. He said he was looking forward to going to Reed because his friend Tobias was going to be there. Bart was skinnier than ever and very tan. He said he'd been playing a lot of tennis. He'd just had his photograph taken for his first passport and he gave me a copy, a mournful close-up of his face.

"Are you planning to take a trip?" I teased him.

"Never can tell," he murmured.

Chapter Ten

DADDY RETURNED FROM Bart's funeral gray-faced. He told us a Mass of the Angels had been said in downtown Sacramento at the Cathedral of the Blessed Sacrament. All the relatives had been standing with him next to the coffin dressed in black—Aunts Rosie, Maggie, and Kate, and Daddy's mother, Mo. He added that everyone wondered why we weren't there and he'd tried to explain we were too prostrate with grief. I winced when he said that. Bart was buried in the family plot in the Sacramento Historic City Cemetery.

After the ceremony, Daddy flew to Portland and spoke with the president of Reed, who expressed his deep regrets. "Your son was a fine student and a decent, good boy. We have no explanation."

Bart's landlady had said essentially the same thing. Apparently he'd done his laundry just before he shot himself. His khakis and T-shirts were folded neatly on the bed next to his slumped bloody body.

After recounting this, my father broke down, and Gene and Marcia, who'd dropped by, ran to him. Gene poured him a stiff drink. We were all in a state of shock. Mama stood off by herself, arms folded, face impassive. Then she announced in a clear, cold voice, "Bart was murdered. I am certain of it. He would never take his life." She insisted that Daddy call in the FBI to investigate, an ironic request given the fact they were pressuring my father night and day to name names.

I slipped out of the living room while they were still talking and ran up to Bart's room. I lay down on his bed, moaning, "Why, why, why?" in our private language. I soon hated that question because so many people asked me the same question about Bart. I'd think back on our last conversations—usually so brief—about how he was feeling, what he was planning to do at Reed, what excited him, interested him. He'd always refer to Tobias this, Tobias that. How could this strange, depressing friend give him so much? What was his secret?

The next time Tobias was in New York, I begged to see him. He was reluctant. He kept arguing, "I don't have anything to say." "You are the only person in the world Bart liked to be with," I pleaded, to which Tobias replied, "He always said you exaggerated, and you're exaggerating now."

We met at Schrafft's, the one on Fifth Avenue near Lord & Taylor, where the light was dim on the paneled walls. I could smell the fragrance of cinnamon toast. I ordered Bart's favorite dessert, angel food cake with caramel sauce (then was unable to eat it). Tobias ordered tea. He hadn't changed since the Stockbridge school. Same thin, sharp face, pasty blemished skin with blackheads on one cheek. His clothes were rumpled.

We did not bother with small talk but got straight to the point.

"Did you see him the last day of his life?" I asked.

No, Tobias had not seen him on the last day of his life. He'd seen him the day before.

And had he said anything?

"Yes. He told me he thought he was worthless."

"Did you try to make him feel better?" I asked him. "What did you say?"

"I didn't know what to say," Tobias replied. He added that my brother had been depressed ever since the terrible incident at Deerfield.

Had he ever spoken about it? I asked tensely.

Tobias nodded. Apparently the morning of the tragedy Bart had wakened at dawn, sensing something was not quite right. He'd dressed quickly, then tiptoed into Clark Steuer's room; Clark's bed hadn't been slept in. Clothes were strewn about; the windows were open. Bart had run out into the large green field near his dorm. He often did that in the early morning so he could watch the trains; the engineer usually waved at him, he said. Not that morning. After the train chugged by, Bart saw Clark hanging from a tree. He tried to get him down, but the body was too heavy, so he ran back to the school.

As soon as Bart reported the incident to some passing teachers in the hall, everybody got hysterical. There was a huddled conference between Headmaster Boynton and some of the senior faculty, and then, without any explanation, Bart was driven to the station and sent home. The next thing he knew, he was standing at the front door of our house at 236 East Sixty-Eighth Street, ringing the bell. He was in a state of shock and couldn't even speak. Tobias added grimly, "Bart never recovered from the way he'd been treated at Deerfield; it was as if he had caused Clark's death."

"Did he ever tell you anything about Clark Steuer?" I wondered. "Did he ever speculate as to why Clark had killed himself?"

For once Tobias didn't have an answer. He hung his head.

"Did he ever speak about Clark?" I pressed.

"No," Tobias answered finally in an irritable tone of voice. Then he blurted, "I didn't know his name until you said it. Clark Steuer . . ."

We stared at each other. Bart had been secretive about many things.

After a long pause Tobias exploded, "In the end, your parents were to blame for what happened to Bart. They always paid more attention to you. You were the favorite."

"No, I wasn't," I insisted. "My parents loved him so much. They were worried about him."

"They were easier on you, admit it."

"Bart was the brilliant one. He used to help me with my homework."

"He hated doing that," Tobias told me. "You were always praised. He never was."

"I was a lousy student."

"Bart said you were lazy and boy crazy. He didn't like that husband of yours. Nobody did." Tobias smirked. "Bart said your father would make you sing for guests and Bart said you sang off-key, but your father was always praising you. Your brother felt unloved. He once told me, 'I was an unwanted child.'"

"That's not true either," I argued. "Mama adored Bart—she doted on him. She wanted more children, but she couldn't have them. But oh, she loved Bart."

"Bart said she had temper tantrums, usually directed at him."

"Not true!" I cried. "They were directed at both of us, at all of us—Daddy too, but Daddy was always away. Mama had unfocused rage."

Tobias railed on. "Bart was disappointed in your father. He was never there for him. He didn't pay attention. Bart wanted a car. Needed a car at Reed to get around. He was living in a room miles off campus. He'd have to thumb rides to get to a class. Your father visited Bart two days before he shot himself. Bart asked him to please buy him a car. Your father said no. That was the last straw."

I didn't want to hear any more. It was too awful. Tobias was looking at me very hard.

"Did you know he loved Salinger?" he asked.

I shook my head.

"I introduced him to Salinger," Tobias said smugly. "As soon as he read *Catcher in the Rye,* he started feeling better. He had found a kindred spirit. Salinger didn't like phonies. Bart couldn't tolerate them either. He thought your husband was a phony. He was glad you divorced him."

I put money down on the table. "I've heard enough." I was close to tears.

Tobias put his hand on mine. It was icy cold. "I was just getting started."

I pulled my hand away.

"I created an entire Holden Caulfield day for Bart and me. We did everything Holden did—went skating in Rockefeller Center, toured the porn shops on Times Square. He tried to pay for a prostitute, but the girl thought Bart was too young."

I wanted to scream. What a vile person Tobias was, and Bart had spent his last months almost exclusively in his company.

He didn't fight me when I paid the check. I rose to go, feeling ill.

"Wouldn't you like to know how our Holden Caulfield day ended?" Tobias insisted.

I shook my head, but he continued in his lisping voice. "Bart had been very depressed that day. Very depressed. I thought I could shock him out of his depression by taking him to a freak show. Hubert's Museum—the midgets, the bearded lady, the man who trained seals, the half-man half-woman. 'They all look so bored,' your brother said. We ended up at Grant's and we ate clams and french fries and two swishy men tried to pick us up, to no avail."

"Bart remained depressed, didn't he?"

"Yes," Tobias answered. "I couldn't figure out why."

*   *   *

AFTER I SPOKE to Tobias I couldn't shake my own depression or my grief. Now I knew my brother had not only seen his friend hanging from a tree on the Deerfield campus but tried unsuccessfully to cut him down. I could only imagine what it must have been like for him when hours before they'd had their arms tight around each other. Bart had been grieving for so long he'd decided life was worthless.

I returned to college and was living on campus in a tiny room. One night, very late, Jason phoned me. When I heard his deep, rich voice, my heart started beating so fast I couldn't catch my breath.

"Baby? I am so sorry about your brother." He sounded as if he meant it.

I couldn't answer.

"Are you okay?" he asked.

I managed to get out the words "Yes. I'm okay."

"Okay, then . . . g'bye." He hung up and I never heard from him again. But his call unnerved me. I hadn't thought about him in a while. Just hearing his voice unloosed memories of the birds, the cramped space where we'd made love over and over. Was he still living in Alger Court? Did he have a new girlfriend? How was his painting going? I didn't dwell on the ugly stuff and I felt no anger, just sadness. But I had a hard time sleeping.

SO FROM THEN on, throughout that spring, I'd stay awake half the night staring at the ceiling. Sometimes I crashed in other dorms. I'd curl up on a couch and fall into a doze, and then I'd jerk awake and start talking to my brother.

"Why did you do it?" I'd whisper into the dark.

No answer.

Long pause, and then I'd add, "It must have been hideously painful."

Just for a second and then relief.

"Relief from what?"

Despair.

"What happened at Deerfield?"

A lot. Meaning, can't explain attraction. Can't explain a need.

"Do you understand what you've done to me?"

It always comes back to you.

"And Mama."

She lives in a dream world. Who would want to murder me except me?

"Daddy is devastated."

Daddy is Daddy, but I forgive him.

"Do you forgive me?"

For what?

I had started to cry. "For not being there, for not being able to help you."

Nothing would have helped.

"Oh God! How can I go on?"

You'll be fine. Hide behind your facade.

WHICH IS WHAT I'd do. In the morning the students would wander into the living room from various bedrooms on the first and second floors; some would be in their pajamas. They'd move past me to fetch coffee in the kitchen and I'd sit up and exclaim, "Hi!" They'd nod politely, but few of them spoke to me. None of them were my friends, although by now everyone on campus knew my brother had killed himself. But no one mentioned it, so I think whenever I crashed in a dorm, I was the object of some discomfort, because I was a reminder that something terrible had happened, which no one could deal with. I felt very isolated by this kind of generalized dismissal, but then I didn't want to talk about Bart either.

After a while I'd jump up and run to the library. I'd sit in the stacks, comforted by the walls of books, and just stare into space.

Then I'd run to the ladies' room, splash some cold water on my face, yank my hair into a neater ponytail and sprint up the hill.

I escaped into work. Between classes I got my first professional acting job playing a teenager on a fifteen-minute TV soap opera called *Concerning Miss Marlowe*, which was telecast out of a tiny NBC studio atop Grand Central Station. I'd switched my major from dance to writing, so now between everything else I was doing I was also pouring energy into notes for a novel I called *Four Flights Up*. I also sketched out a story about Jason and the bird, and I started a special notebook, filling it with questions I was asking myself about art, politics, and my chaotic ambitions. I couldn't figure out why I was in such a frenzy of activity. I would sometimes be so tired I would be overcome with dizziness. Every so often I would vomit and then collapse into bed and sleep for hours.

I would subsequently discover that most suicide survivors are workaholics, insomniacs, alcoholics, druggies, driven restless super-achievers brimming over with guilt and sadness. For a long time I spoke to no one about my brother, holding the memory of his death inside, where it festered. As I grew older, I discovered that two of my closest friends were also suicide survivors. Tony Lukas, the brilliant prizewinning author of *Common Ground*, whose mother had taken her life when he was a small boy, and Judy Collins, the legendary folk singer, whose son locked himself in his car and asphyxiated himself, leaving a tape for his mother to play. Sharing my agony with them helped. "You never get over it," Tony told me. "You just get used to it." But Tony didn't. He ultimately killed himself too.

Back in 1954 I was so filled with anger and melancholy I could hardly contain myself. My writing teacher, the poet Jane Cooper, had given me Tennyson's "In Memoriam" to read; she thought it might comfort me and some of the lines did. Grief, according to Tennyson, can be passionate: "The blood creeps, and the nerves prick / And tingle; and the heart is sick."

The tumultuous politics of the time, particularly the Army/McCarthy hearings, helped take my mind off my troubles. And once a week I visited Dr. Rado to pour out my woes. He told me restlessness was part of grief. "Grieving is necessary. Mourning is necessary too."

I told him I felt as if I'd been struck dumb. I walked around like a zombie. I wanted to cry but I couldn't, and I had a hard time articulating my thoughts.

Rado nodded and explained that my emotions—my pain—were buried inside me as if inside an iceberg. "It may take a lifetime to unmelt." Then he said very gently, "Don't be too hard on yourself." He went on to give me Freud's opinion of suicide. "We have no adequate means of approaching the problem of suicide." Rado felt it was an almost impossible subject to begin with. "It's all about how much you value life." Then he retreated into silence and lit another cigarette and I lay on the couch wishing I could tell him everything I was experiencing—the vomiting and dizziness, the huge anger. But in those days when extreme privacy was the norm, I found it almost impossible to speak intimately even to a therapist.

IN JANUARY 1955 Mama decided to move from the Sixty-Eighth Street brownstone. "Too many memories of Bart," she said. She decided to rent a double duplex in a house on East Fortieth Street off Lexington in the Murray Hill district. "There are two bedrooms in the back duplex for you and Marcia [who was living with us at the time], and one bedroom for me and your father in the front one." (Daddy ultimately slept on a pullout couch in the living room, but he seemed to like that.)

After we moved, Marcia and I took turns helping Mama unpack the vast collections of books and china and silver, the piles of pale linen tablecloths and napkins, the candelabra, the jade elephant from Gump's. The one box I didn't want to open was the one marked "Bart Crum—Possessions from Reed," so Mama did. The contents revealed the ivory chess set Granddad had given him, a dog-eared paperback of *Catcher in the Rye,* empty notebooks, pencils, and his .22 rifle hidden inside the ragged blue blanket he'd had since he was a baby.

Mama unwrapped the gun slowly, almost lovingly.

"You're not going to keep that thing, are you?" I murmured.

"Of course I am!" she exclaimed and cradled the gun to her bosom. "It was the last thing he touched—*if* he touched it at all. I don't believe he killed himself. I believe he was murdered or it was a grotesque accident."

Marcia and I didn't argue with her. What was the point? She'd refused to read the FBI reports.

Mama kept Bart's .22 rifle in her closet until she died. Then I threw it in the trash.

Chapter Eleven

D URING MY SENIOR year at Sarah Lawrence I had a big class load, but I spent most of my free time trying to get jobs in the theatre. The 1955–1956 Broadway season would be rich in quality and quantity, so much so there was a jam-up of out-of-town tryouts in New Haven and Boston. Musicals like *Pipe Dream, Most Happy Fella, Silk Stockings*; Edward G. Robinson in *Middle of the Night*; Julie Harris in *The Lark*; Enid Bagnold's *The Chalk Garden*; Bert Lahr in Beckett's ruthless cartoon *Waiting for Godot*. The list was dizzying, made more so because my parents— especially my father—were making sure I saw every one of those shows.

I now had an agent named Bret Adams, a genial young man who liked to wear bow ties and whose office was in a West Side brownstone. Bret had seen me in a Prell shampoo TV commercial, washing one side of my hair with an inferior shampoo, then singing the praises of Prell as I lathered the other side with—you guessed it—Prell.

"You were so convincing and cute!" he enthused. He began sending me up for TV shows and Broadway plays, but I didn't get anything. Bret blamed the way I dressed. "You look like a bum," he'd say whenever I'd show up at his office, wearing my uniform of skirt over leotards and the ragged duffel coat I'd bought when I was in Geneva. Later he would call me a beatnik.

One day at a TV soap audition I sat next to a platinum blonde wrapped in a black cape. She was bragging to anyone who'd listen that she'd just been accepted as a member of the Actors Studio, having auditioned five times. She had written the audition piece and, she added proudly, her partner had been none other than James Dean. I'd just seen *East of Eden* and was struck by the way Dean's body language flowed into the turbulent life of his character as he sits on top of a hurtling train, hunched over in adolescent agony. I would never forget that image of him.

"Jimmy's going to be a big star," the actress continued. She went on to say that they'd rehearsed their audition material in Central Park. "We'd stop total strangers and ask them to watch our scene. We rewrote and rehearsed our lines in bars and in taxis."

"What's the Actors Studio?" I asked. She was about to answer when the casting director called out her name and she darted away, sweeping her cape about her.

I SOON LEARNED that the Actors Studio, described as "a workshop for professional actors," had been founded in 1947 by Group Theatre members Elia Kazan, Bobby Lewis, and Cheryl Crawford. Their overall purpose: to smash theatrical traditions and to challenge "acting that looked like acting." Kazan in particular had envisioned a private place where he could nurture a generation of actors in such a way that they would be able to create complicated inner lives for their characters. Young actors needed a radically different performance style to dig out the hidden meanings in the emotionally charged plays that were being written by Tennessee Williams and Arthur Miller. Kazan had already been testing his approach of "turning psychology into behavior" on Marlon Brando when he directed him in *A Streetcar Named Desire*. The result, Camille Paglia wrote, was that "Marlon Brando mumbling and muttering and flashing with bolts of barbaric energy, freed theatrical emotion from its enslavement by words."

By the mid-fifties the Studio had created a revolution in performance; it resulted in a distinctive acting style that stood for a kind of hyperintense American realism.

Hundreds of actors auditioned to get into the Studio every year. Few were accepted. I spoke to one actor who'd auditioned seventeen times before he got in; he also said auditioning for the Studio was the most terrifying experience of his life. Maybe it was because there was so much at stake. Anyone who made it to the finals would be judged by master teacher Lee Strasberg, Broadway producer Crawford, and of course Kazan. This genius director had discovered not only Brando but also James Dean. With their quicksilver intensity and eroticism, these two actors were heralding a revolution in American acting; they would soon become supreme icons of American culture. They were both members of the Actors Studio.

IN LATE MARCH 1955 I noted in my journal, "I've decided to audition for the Actors Studio. Very scary move. I will probably fail. But why not try?" The very next time I came to New York I went directly from bustling Times Square to a battered white former Greek Revival church on West Forty-Fourth Street in the heart of Hell's Kitchen; the building faced the Hudson River and was surrounded by dilapidated brownstones and tenements on all sides.

A bespectacled young director, John Stix, who was also Kazan's assistant, happened to be in the Studio's shabby back office. He told me what to expect. There were few rules. Anyone over eighteen could audition. No monologues—you have to have a partner. Don't do Shakespeare or the classics, and no scene longer than five minutes. If you pass your preliminary audition, you will be in the finals.

He gave me a look. "You should try something very simple like *Ah, Wilderness!* or maybe a piece of a Salinger short story." He went on to say that the Studio was looking for a unique special energy, and he added, "Yes, a certain commercial viability—but you don't have to be that accomplished. We are looking for actors who have something original about them—something different." I signed up and thanked him for his suggestions. "I'll be watching out for you," he said. "I happen to be one of the judges for the preliminary auditions, so I'll be holding the clock."

My partner for the Studio auditions was a polite, good-looking young actor named Richard (Rick) Morse. He and his brother Bobby, also an actor, lived in a shabby, chilly walk-up on West Fifty-Seventh Street, which they shared with an old Russian ballet coach. That's where we rehearsed night and day. Every so often Bobby, who was then working at a car wash, would come home in dirty white coveralls and flop down on the couch to watch us. (Bobby went on to become a big Broadway star in musicals like *How to Succeed in Business Without Really Trying*. More recently, he appeared in the TV show *Mad Men*. I'll never forget his beguiling, gap-toothed smile.)

I had no idea how to act, but that didn't bother Rick. He taught me some basic rules such as "You have to connect to me, talk to me, really talk to me when you act." After we read a couple of plays together, he gave me a few questions to ask myself about the character I was playing: Who am I? Where am I? What do I want? What's in my way? And what do I do when I get what I want? (These were also questions I should have been asking myself!)

Rick spent hours teaching me how to listen and respond. "Don't act it! Don't act it!" he'd exclaim when I'd fake an emotion. He showed me how to make an entrance and where to put my hands. ("At your sides or gently clasped. A sure sign of an actor who doesn't know what he's doing is how he uses his hands.") It was a crash course in acting, and I'll forever be grateful to dear Rick, whom I developed a crush on but he would have none of it. "Never get romantically involved with the actor you're working with," he warned me. "It is inevitably disaster." How I wish I'd listened to him.

We passed our preliminary audition on the first try, but we were asked to bring in different material for the final. We returned three separate times with different scenes; nobody liked our selections. Then John Stix suggested we do the soda fountain scene from Thornton Wilder's *Our Town*. It's about two teenagers, Emily and George, who are in love but unable to come out and say it as they sip soft drinks at the corner drugstore. We brought in the scene and the judges pronounced it "perfect for you."

For the next three months we rehearsed and rehearsed, and in between rehearsals I'd take the train back to Sarah Lawrence and attend classes. I managed to squeeze in some modeling and I also had a small part in a low-budget movie called *Four Boys and a Gun* with James Franciscus; I played his befuddled, very pregnant wife.

I never seemed to stop. My friends on campus marveled at my energy and my cheerfulness. When I look at photographs of myself during this period, I am usually smiling. What an act I was perfecting. I'd learned to hide my grief and my feelings of profound loss behind an inane grin.

So I was smiling when I graduated from Sarah Lawrence, and smiling when my parents took me, along with Marcia and Gene, to celebrate with a lavish dinner at 21. We drank a great deal of wine, and then I couldn't go to sleep.

The next night, the night of my final audition, I stopped smiling. I was quaking with fear. Perspiration streamed from my armpits as I dressed in my "costume," a simple gingham dress, my hair in a ponytail. Rick made me drink hot tea with milk to settle my stomach, and he held my hand all the way to West Forty-Fourth Street.

We arrived at the Studio at 8:45 on the dot. We'd been told to be on time.

The downstairs area was deathly quiet—both front room and back, where the kitchen was. Couples stood in corners by the stove and near a watercooler; everybody was smoking or mumbling lines. They all glared at us as we came in the door.

"I feel like we're about to go to the electric chair," Rick tried to joke.

Our names were checked off on a list by a good-looking man with black hair curling long on his neck. "I'm Marty Fried," he told us in a soft, hoarse voice. "I'll help you set up—for *Our Town*—you need two chairs and a table, right?"

Rick nodded. We followed him up the steep stairs to the theatre entrance. "Wait here and then go in as soon as your names are called." Within seconds two young actors burst out the door and pushed past us down the stairs, one of them moaning, "You forgot your first fucking line. How could you possibly forget your first fucking line?"

Then a disembodied voice called out, "Patricia Bosworth and Richard Morse. You're next."

Somehow we made our way into the theatre, a brick-walled room so dark we could hardly see. Marty appeared out of nowhere, setting up two chairs behind a table—our soda fountain—and then he disappeared to train a spotlight on us. Now we were blinded.

"What are you gonna do for us, kid?" a voice demanded brusquely.

"*Our Town*," I managed to stutter.

"Good. Go ahead."

We had five minutes to prove we were talented. I can remember only this: I was in the middle of my favorite speech, when Emily tells George she loves him: "I always thought about you as one of the chief people I thought about . . ." and the same brusque male voice called out, "Stop! Time's up!"

Rick started to leave, but I remained in my chair and then began to sob helplessly.

"Stop crying," the brusque voice continued impatiently.

But I couldn't stop. I heard myself wailing, thinking back to the months of rehearsal, the pressure, the loss of sleep coupled with the fact that Rick had never kissed me and that I could never share any of this with my brother. I had worked so hard. I had struggled. Now the audition was over and I had failed.

I put my head down on the table and blubbered uncontrollably.

With that, a stocky, ruggedly built figure leapt out of the darkness and yanked me to my feet. I recognized the scowling face from news photographs. It was Elia Kazan.

"Stop crying, kid, for Christ's sake!" He took me by the arm and literally dragged me out of the theatre. "Stop crying," he repeated. And then he whispered in softer tones, "You passed," and then loudly again, "Now get the hell out of here!"

I stumbled down the stairs. I was still crying, but now I was crying tears of joy. Rick was waiting outside of the Studio; he ran over and put his arms around me and I nestled against his chest.

"Oh God, Rick," I sobbed. "Kazan told me I passed. I passed the audition." I waited for him to react.

"What about me?" he asked very quietly. "Didn't he say anything about me?"

I had to admit no.

We knew the auditions ended at eleven p.m.; the voting among the judges took place immediately. All the auditioners who passed would receive a phone call that night no matter how late the hour. I went home to tell my parents the news. My father hugged me and said I would never forget this night. I never did. Around two a.m. I received the news I already knew: I was now a lifetime member of the Actors Studio. I was one of six who'd been accepted out of the five hundred people to audition.

But Rick's telephone didn't ring. The Studio had not invited him to be a member, even though he was a far better, more accomplished actor than I was. It wasn't fair. Rick was very philosophical about it. "I am not the Studio type," he explained to me when we met for coffee later that same week. Was I?

Chapter Twelve

USK HAD FALLEN. The heavens were a deep dark blue, and as I trudged up from the subway, teetering a bit in my high heels, I could hear music streaming down West Twelfth Street. It was floating from the open windows of Broadway choreographer Valerie Bettis's townhouse. She was hosting the Studio's annual spring party, and as a new member, I'd been invited. I'd bought an expensive dress for the occasion, an off-white silk Jax shift.

I stood for a while watching the guests arrive by limo and cab and on foot. They would walk up the steps in twos and threes, laughing and talking, and when the door opened, light would bloom on their faces and I would recognize Shelley Winters or Mike Wallace or Jack Paar. I was nervous about going in but I had been invited, after all, so eventually I pushed my way up the stairs and into the edge of an enormous double living room just in time to see a barefoot Marilyn Monroe, in a skintight black dress, undulating across the floor opposite Paul Newman, lithe and sinewy in khakis and a T-shirt. They didn't dance very long, maybe three minutes, but what a hot, pulsing three minutes it was. A small crowd gathered as they kept time to the jubilant tune of Harry Belafonte's trademark "Banana Boat Song." (His phrase "DAYOOOH, DAY-HAH-

HAY-HOWWW" had taken the nation by storm.) When the two broke apart, there was a spatter of applause; Marilyn giggled and Newman bowed and then moved past me through the crowd to grab a beer from a bar.

The room was alive with people I recognized but didn't know. Everybody I'd ever read about and admired was passing before my awestruck gaze: Norman Mailer (who I noticed had big ears), Henry Fonda (who I'd just seen in *The Caine Mutiny Court-Martial*), Julie Andrews, Truman Capote, the great anguished clown Bert Lahr. I felt raw and unqualified to be with such shimmering, achieving creatures.

"Hello, Patti." Leonard Lyons, a tiny natty man in a pinstriped suit, approached me. Lyons was the gossip columnist for the *New York Post*. I'd had lunch with him and Daddy a couple of times at 21. Lyons wrote about the arts in his column "The Lyons Den," but he also wrote a lot about politics. He often referred to my father's problems with the blacklist.

"You can help me count the celebrities," Lyons said. We posted ourselves by the bar and I reeled off the names while Lyons jotted them down on a pad. "Comden and Green, Garson Kanin, Ruth Gordon, Jed Harris, Gwen Verdon, Tennessee Williams, William Inge, Eli Wallach, Anne Jackson, Betsy von Furstenberg, Farley Granger." Many of them strolled by with a few mumbled hellos to the gossip columnist. "Hi there, Lenny . . . say hello to Sylvia for me." Sylvia was his wife, who rarely appeared in public with him.

"Why won't anyone talk to me?" I asked Lyons finally.

"Stars prefer the company of stars."

"Are stars starstruck?"

"We're all starstruck." He put his pad in his pocket and started to move on. "Gotta go." I watched him disappear into the crowd. He would continue to make his rounds all over Manhattan, picking up tidbits of gossip. Before he was through (around four a.m.) he would have stopped at the Latin Quarter, the Stork Club, El Morocco, the Copa, Billy Rose's Diamond Horseshoe, maybe ending up at Nick's in the Village.

Meanwhile the party continued to churn around me. At midnight I did recognize somebody else I knew slightly: Marty Fried, the good-looking man with thick black hair who'd helped Rick and me set up our Studio audition.

"Hello!" I shouted through the din. My voice sounded unnaturally loud across the swarm of celebrities undulating around me. "Hello there!"

Marty turned. As I got closer, he gave a chuckle of recognition. "I thought you might be here," he said in his soft, hoarse voice. Then he turned to the people with him. "This kid just passed her final audition at the Studio. Congratulations, Patricia Bosworth."

Everybody laughed. Marty offered me a cigarette and lit it for me and I proceeded to inhale deeply and then blow a plume of smoke in the air. The tobacco burned my lungs and chest. I tried not to cough.

"Are you okay?" Marty asked. "You don't have to smoke, you know."

"I love to smoke," I lied.

"Are you having a good time tonight?" Marty asked.

I could feel his black eyes studying me. "I don't know anybody," I admitted.

"I'll show you around," he said, and he did for the next hour. He introduced me to Cheryl Crawford, a tall stately woman with a mannish haircut who was one of the founders of the Studio with Kazan as well as a successful Broadway producer (her latest hit was *Brigadoon*). I would soon discover she was one of the kindest, gentlest souls in the business. I met Julie Harris. Red-haired and freckle-faced, she was smoking a cigarette and staring dreamily into a tiny cup of espresso. All I could think of when I saw her was her performance as the unconventional tomboy Frankie in *The Member of the Wedding*. Oh, how she'd burrowed into that strange little character who dreams of having a thousand friends.

"I can't breathe anymore," she cries out. "I want to tear up the entire world!"

I had the impulse to repeat those lines to her; they had meant so much to me when I first heard them. But we barely exchanged a word because she was pulled out of her reverie by a lanky, sallow-skinned man named Jay Julian.

"He's her ex-husband," Marty whispered. "Big-time lawyer."

After circling the room a couple of times, we ended up on a deserted couch. The party was starting to thin out. I could see the contours of the double living room, hung with gilt mirrors and lit by many candles. We walked to the open windows and looked down into a big garden. Chinese lanterns glowed and rocked back and forth in the trees.

We remained by the window talking. Marty told me he wanted to be an actor and that he was Lee Strasberg's driver. In return for free acting lessons, he chauffeured Lee all over New York in his medallion cab.

Around two a.m. the party ended. Marty left me. "I'll see you later," he promised. I decided I'd better go home. As I was walking into the front hall I saw Lee Strasberg shrugging into a black overcoat. He'd been surrounded by a group of adoring young actors when we were briefly introduced and he had barely looked me in the eye, but now he said gruffly, "Darling, do you want a lift?"

And he gestured to a cab outside—presumably Marty's—idling on the curb.

"Oh, thank you, Mr. Strasberg."

"Call me Lee, darling."

"Lee."

We walked without speaking again into the street. Lee got in front with Marty, who gave me a wink.

I slid into the backseat, where I found Marilyn Monroe huddled in a corner dreamily puffing on a cigarette. Her bleached blond hair was tousled; she seemed to be wearing no makeup. I noticed there was dirt under her fingernails, but I couldn't stop looking at her. We were about to pull away from the curb when a voice cried out, "Hey Lee, goin' my way?" and Harry Belafonte hopped in beside me. We drove uptown in silence.

I knew Marilyn was aware I was looking at her. She was used to being looked at, and she wasn't self-conscious. She had a mysterious indefinable quality that made her a star and separated her from everyone else. At the moment she appeared to be floating in another world as she puffed delicately on her cigarette and blew the smoke softly out of her mouth. The newspapers were full of stories about her—how she'd left Hollywood and come to New York to be a "serious actress," how Lee was coaching her at his apartment and letting her observe sessions at the Studio.

It was muggy in the cab. A spring rain was falling, pelting down; lightning flashed as Marty drove through puddles in the street. Still no one spoke. After a while Lee rolled down the window and moist cool air whooshed in. Marilyn gave a sigh and shrugged out of her coat. That's when I noticed the pearls. She was wearing a necklace of what looked like vintage pearls; they were lustrous and creamy and matched her skin, which seemed almost iridescent. She positively glowed.

"Those are gorgeous pearls, Miss Monroe," I said.

"Yeah." Marilyn fingered the pearls absently. "The emperor gave them to me."

"The emperor?" Harry Belafonte asked.

"Hirohito of Japan. When Joe and I were on our honeymoon in Tokyo, he gave them to me in a private ceremony." Her voice trailed off as if she'd lost interest in the subject. She had, we knew, lost interest in Joe DiMaggio. They were about to be divorced after a marriage that had lasted only nine months. Lately she'd been telling her friend, the Hollywood gossip columnist Sidney Skolsky, that she was going to marry Arthur Miller.

"Darling?" Lee murmured tenderly from the front seat.

"Yeah, Lee?"

He turned and stared at her with adoring eyes. "How *wonderful*, darling." His voice was full of feeling. (Marty told me afterward that Lee so rarely responded to anyone in an overt way that it was thrilling to see him react.)

Silence once more. Then we reached our destination, the Strasberg apartment on Central Park West. Lee stepped out of the cab and waited for Marilyn to get out; then the two of them disappeared into the ornate lobby. She was spending the night, as she often did, with the Strasberg family; daughter Susan gave up her bedroom for her and slept on the couch. Marilyn was between apartments; she was lonely and had a hard time sleeping. The Strasberg apartment had become her refuge, a second home. Her psychiatrist, Marianne Kris, lived in the building too. Marilyn saw her five times a week, and afterward she would go back to Lee's apartment for a coaching session.

We continued to drive over to West Seventy-Fourth and Riverside. Belafonte vaulted out of the cab.

"Night. Thanks, Marty." And he was gone.

"Harry's apartment is twenty-one rooms," Marty told me—then added, "Come on, sit up front with me. I'll drive you home."

He chauffeured me over to East Fortieth Street and parked. Then we talked till dawn, mostly about his relationship to Lee.

"I'm like his surrogate son," he said. "I was an orphan brought up in a foster home. Lee and his family sort of adopted me after I began driving them all over New York in my cab. We got along—I didn't talk if Lee didn't want to talk. After a while Lee started to depend on me, take me here, take me there." He knew Marty longed to be an actor, "so he invited me into his classes for free. Now I'm on call for Lee twenty-four hours a day—which means I am on call for Marilyn too."

"It sounds as if your life isn't your own," I kidded him.

"That's not true. I have a life separate from them," he insisted. "Lemme take you to dinner in Chinatown tomorrow night." And then he kissed me. It was a very nice kiss.

"I like you," I said.

"I like you too." He grinned. "I'll pick you up at here at seven."

BUT IT WAS never to be. The following night he phoned apologetically and said he had to drive Marilyn to Roxbury to see Arthur Miller. From then on, Marty kept on making dates and breaking them.

Then I ran into him one morning at the Actors Studio. "What's been going on?" I demanded. I'd liked him—he was funny, he was sexy, and we'd been attracted to each other.

He looked at me helplessly. "I've been teaching Marilyn how to drive," he admitted. "It's . . . taking longer than I thought it would. She's nervous . . . she's forgetful."

"But she's Marilyn Monroe," I kidded him. "That's okay."

"It's not okay. I like you."

"I like you too. So let's be friends."

Marty guided me over the years as I struggled to gain a foothold in the toxic celebrity-laden world of the Actors Studio and the Broadway theatre as well. And he once did take me to dinner in Chinatown.

A FEW DAYS after the party, the director Arthur Penn phoned. He'd noticed me at the party, he said, and thought I'd be right for a part in a play he was directing at the Westport Country Playhouse, the most prestigious pre-Broadway tryout theatre in the country as well as one of the top theatres on the summer circuit. Arthur Penn was one of the most successful directors of live TV in New York; he'd done countless shows on *The Philco Television Playhouse*, *The United States Steel Hour*, *Playhouse 90*, etc. It was said he was an actor's director like Mike Nichols; he loved to experiment and improvise, to share his discoveries.

We met at his basement apartment on West Eleventh Street. The one room was like a monk's cell—a single cot, two chairs, and a desk; books and scripts were piled on the floor. When I arrived, Arthur was pacing about; he couldn't seem to stand still. A short, compact man with curly hair, immaculately dressed in khakis, a white shirt, and tennis shoes, he peppered me with edgy questions: "Where were you born? How old are you? Where'd you go to college? Who'd you study with—Sandy Meisner or Stella Adler?"

I had to admit I'd never studied acting. I'd just gotten into the Studio. When he pressed me, I confessed I'd never acted professionally on a stage. "But I was on a live TV soap for a summer—*Concerning Miss Marlowe* on NBC."

"Good experience, live TV."

I agreed it was.

Then he told me about the play, *Blue Denim*. It was written by friends of his, James Leo Herlihy and William Noble. The play was about a fifteen-year-old girl named Janet who gets pregnant by her boyfriend. They are both thrown into a panic; she must get an abortion. She can't tell her parents, so she relies on a mutual friend, another classmate who maintains he knows a doctor who can help.

"The subject of abortion is taboo in this country," Arthur said. "It's a crime, it's a sin, so the play will be controversial." (Indeed, when it was performed, the word "abortion" was used only once, and when *Blue Denim* was made into a film, it was excised from the script entirely.)

"It's an emotional story," Arthur went on. "A very contemporary story. These kids are alienated from their families. They go through something very traumatic together, but they can't talk to their parents. I relate to that. I had a very traumatic adolescence."

He did not elaborate. Then he asked, "What about your growing up? Was it peaches and cream?" His tone was sarcastic. I ignored the question.

In the end Arthur asked me to read one speech from the play, Janet's monologue when she discovers she's pregnant. I'd had plenty of experience talking to myself in my bedroom to my fantasy husband. I read the monologue imagining I'd just come from the gynecologist's office. I actually felt slightly sickened and empty inside. I knew when I finished that I had sounded pretty good.

Arthur nodded. "Not bad . . . Think you can do it?"

"Absolutely!" I exclaimed, although I had no idea whether I could do it or not. Arthur told me he'd be arranging for me to audition for the playwright and the producers and handed me the script.

As soon as I returned to Fortieth Street I shut myself up in my bedroom and festooned the script with notes. I composed a character sketch of Janet, trying to imagine what it felt like to be pregnant. I researched morning sickness. I remembered a classmate at Sarah Lawrence, a Chinese girl on scholarship, who had gone to some nameless abortionist in New Jersey. Her boyfriend drove her there in a rainstorm. Their car broke down. The abortion itself was botched. My classmate suffered terribly. She came back to Sarah Lawrence white-faced and bleeding. She had a miscarriage in her bathroom and was rushed to the infirmary. Weeks later she told everybody her ugly story. "I have never felt such pain," she said.

*　*　*

I AUDITIONED FOR *Blue Denim* at the Helen Hayes Theatre on Broadway. As I entered the shadowy backstage area, I counted six other actresses waiting in the wings to read. They were all recognizable to me, experienced "ingenues" with many shows to their credit. They looked at me curiously as I took my place at the end of the line of wooden chairs. Sitting there, I pretended I was waiting to see an abortionist, hoping that would put me in the mood.

When my name was called I felt my knees buckling, but I managed to walk out on stage in a straight line. Ahead of me, beyond the footlights, loomed the theatre itself, which seemed big as a football field, with rows and rows of empty seats. The house lights were half lit, so I could see Arthur Penn in his uniform of white shirt and khakis, deep in conversation with two people I didn't recognize. They were introduced as playwright James Leo Herlihy, a tall shambling man with a handsome ruined face, and producer Lyn Austin, dark-haired with a thin mouth.

When I finished reading with the stage manager, who spoke his lines in a meaningless monotone and looked at me as if I was the worst actress he'd ever encountered, they said, "Thank you!" and then called, "Next?"

I was called back to audition three more times. Each time I read more of the script with Burt Brinckerhoff, who had already been cast as Arthur the boyfriend. Burt was very polite with me and superserious, in blue jeans and a T-shirt.

At the final audition I gave the penultimate speech—discovering I was pregnant. I'd been up half the night working. I gave it my all. When it was over, Herlihy ran up to the footlights to shake my hand and say I'd read the scene exactly as it should be read.

I ended up winning the role of Janet and felt briefly elated.

The rest of the cast was excellent: Katherine Squire played my mother (she would play my mother in three other shows). A member of the Actors Studio, she had a stern, prim quality. She seemed perfect for the part, as did Burt and Mark Rydell, who had soft blue eyes and a tough-guy manner. (He would go on to direct movies like the Oscar-winning *On Golden Pond*.) Back then he seemed to inhabit the role of Ernie, the friend who insists he knows the perfect abortionist but who in the end, we find out, is lying.

THE CAST SPENT the first day of rehearsals for *Blue Denim* listening to Arthur lecture us about how we were living in an era of conformity; he seemed to be talking too much, maybe because he had never directed a play before. He was as nervous as I was. We went on to have a couple of table readings and then we did some improvisations.

Once we were on our feet, Arthur would hover around Burt and me as we were playing a scene, cupping his hands and zeroing in on our faces as if with a camera. I could feel his breath on my cheek as he murmured, "Where are you going with this character, Patti? I don't think you know where the fuck you are going."

He was right. I didn't know what I was doing. For a while I existed on sheer nerve as rehearsals continued, with Arthur hammering at me that I wasn't revealing anything. He couldn't hear me, he said; I had no emotion. I'd return home at night in a panic and close myself off in my room. I'd sit on a chair, rocking back and forth. I believed I had talent, but I had to come to terms with the fact that I had no craft, no technique yet. *Face it*, I told myself grimly, *I've never acted on a professional stage before*. But other young actresses had faced this challenge. I willed myself to get better, to concentrate more.

Arthur kept badgering me and I remained terrified that I'd be fired, but I wasn't. However, he didn't let up on his criticisms even after we'd arrived at Westport for the last days of rehearsal before we opened. He singled me out the afternoon Lawrence Langner watched a run-through. The distinguished, white-haired Langner was head of the Theatre Guild and ran the Westport Playhouse.

From the first day of rehearsal, I'd been kidded by the cast about the way I reacted to their constant use of the word "fuck."

"Fucking good weather," Mark would say, and then Burt would add, "We have fucking good bagels here but fucking bad coffee." They'd watch my disapproving expression and start chanting "fuck fuck fuck" and then the rest of the cast would howl with laughter (except for Katherine Squire—she didn't like to hear the word "fuck" either).

I'd explain I'd grown up in a family that never used dirty words. I'd say things like "Please, I hate those words" or "It's unnecessary," which made them say "fuck" all the more.

The afternoon of the dress rehearsal I was in the midst of a very emotional scene with Burt when Arthur stopped us.

"You aren't going to play Janet that way opening night, are you, Patti?" he asked in scathing tones.

"Well, I thought I was on the right track," I answered in a tiny voice.

"Right track?" Arthur chuckled mockingly. "Jesus fucking Christ."

"Oh, Arthur," I blurted. "I wish you wouldn't use that word."

"What word?"'

"You know . . ."

"You mean *fuck*?" he bellowed. "You mean F-U-C-K?"

I nodded, wondering how much longer this was going to go on. Meanwhile the rest of the cast had gathered in the wings to watch as Arthur marched over and took me in his arms as he would a lover.

"I feel so sorry for you," he crooned. "You will never be another Kim Stanley. I am so sorry." And he did seem genuinely sorry as he battered me with his criticisms.

Then he released me and we stood facing each other. "Now then," he said ominously, "I am going to give you a little test. I am going to lock you in this closet." And with that he dragged me, protesting, into the prop closet right offstage. "You will stay in this closet until you scream 'fuck fuck fuck' and then I will let you out and you will do this scene with Burt with all the emotion you've built up inside you. Do you understand?"

I didn't say anything. I couldn't. I let my body go limp and allowed myself to be crammed into the closet, along with a ladder, a pail, and a broom. The lock clicked.

It was pitch-black and smelly; the broom prickled against my legs. I have claustrophobia, so of course I screamed and cried and pounded on the door. A couple of minutes later Arthur unlocked the door and I burst onto the stage screaming, "FUUCCCCK-KKK!"

The closet experience became the abortionist's office, and shaking and sobbing, I imagined the terror of having my womb scraped. Burt and I played the scene to a fare-thee-well and we repeated it on opening night.

How had I done it? I'm not quite sure, except I've always had an unshakable faith in make-believe. My imagination was going a mile a minute. I made believe I *was* Janet: being examined by the abortionist, my legs splayed apart on those hideous stirrups, rubbery fingers up my vagina and rectum, the whole ghastly experience. Looking back on it, I'd been so involved with my personal misery that it had threatened to take over my present. Maybe I'd needed Arthur's brutal treatment to shake me awake. Now I felt strangely confident and I could concentrate on the work. I received terrific reviews for my performance as Janet, and for the entire run I was able to build and build on what I'd created for the character.

It was an exciting time. Every night my dressing room would

be filled with friends. I basked in the compliments I was getting. Arthur, however, never praised my work and chose to ignore me.

Mama was in Europe, but Daddy sat through the show three times, maintaining, "You just get better and better."

The entire cast had been living in a rustic old house right on Compo Beach. At the closing night party we roasted hot dogs over a fire near the bay. Mark Rydell and I sat on a blanket and drank bottle after bottle of cold beer while he assured me I'd developed during rehearsal and by opening night "you'd created a genuine character and it came out of yourself and what you went through with Arthur. Arthur Penn is a sadist. He's like Kazan—but Kazan is more subtle and not as mean. But both directors will do anything short of murder to get actors to do what they want with a part."

"Yes!" I cried. "Arthur is a fucking bastard."

We both burst out laughing. From then on, my conversations were peppered with expletives.

I WENT ON with my career. Arthur and I did not speak to each other again until 1966, when I happened to attend one of the first screenings of his landmark film *Bonnie and Clyde*. Everything critics say about the movie is true. Arthur's revolutionary treatment of sex and violence transformed the film industry. The story was loosely based on two minor gangsters of the 1930s, played by Warren Beatty and Faye Dunaway. In Arthur's hands it became something dangerous and innovative; I remember distinctly how the audience at our screening gasped when a comic bank robbery climaxed with Clyde shooting the bank teller in the face. There was stunned silence at the end of the movie when the outlaw couple died in a torrent of bullets, their bodies twitching in slow motion, blood spattering everywhere.

People left the screening in silence. Arthur was standing off in a corner by himself.

"Hello, Arthur," I said cheerily. "Fucking great movie." He stared at me.

I was older now; I wore glasses; my hair was cropped short. Did he recognize me?

He looked at me oddly. "I beg your pardon?"

My voice grew a touch louder. "I said great fucking movie, Arthur."

He gave a step back. "Oh." He nodded, smiling slightly. "Oh yeah . . . Patti . . . Thanks."

AFTER MY SUCCESS in *Blue Denim* I expected to be working again immediately, since my agent could now get me into most producers' offices. I auditioned for every upcoming Broadway show, but to my great disappointment, I wasn't cast in any of them. I longed to be given a chance to play high-strung, defiant young women. Instead I would appear on *The Philco Television Playhouse* as a flirty teenager in a two-piece bathing suit mouthing inanities.

I fell into a depression. When I wasn't working I began to sleep all day. I'd wake up in the late afternoon and stagger down to the back deck of my parents' duplex. Daddy was often there by himself drinking. He could see I was blue. I couldn't tell him I thought I was failing as an actress. When I'd complain I was getting nowhere, he'd say I was being ridiculous. He had such confidence in me. He wouldn't allow me to be negative. And then he'd change the subject by saying silly things like "Can you make love with a straight face?" Then we'd barbecue a steak and polish off an entire bottle of red wine.

We spent a lot of time on that deck, Daddy and I. It became our favorite place. It was full of cool green shadows from overhanging trees and it had a big awning. Daddy was in a better mood. His career was on the upswing. Rita Hayworth was keeping him busy; he was now advising her on movie roles. He thought she should play the dancer Isadora Duncan.

The main change in his life, though, was that the political climate was quite different from what it had been when he was defending the Hollywood Ten. The FBI was no longer pressuring him; he was sure our phones were no longer being tapped. There was a lessening of public interest in the hunting down of communists. The Korean War had ended, and in 1954 the Senate had voted to condemn the tactics of Senator Joe McCarthy. By 1955, HUAC was in a weakened condition, although committee members were planning four days of scrutinizing the entertainment industry in New York and there were plans to subpoena Arthur Miller.

ALL THAT SUMMER Mama was away. She spent the next three months traveling in Europe. After making the disruptive move from the Sixty-Eighth Street brownstone to the Fortieth Street double duplex, she disappeared and spent the next three months traveling. We'd read her letters out loud—long enthusiastic, bubbly, funny letters about the people she was meeting, the recipes she was collecting, the sights she was seeing. She would try and phone us, but the connections were always very bad.

Daddy seemed genuinely pleased she was having a good time. "She needed to get away," he said.

By August, Gene and Marcia were married. We gave them a champagne reception at the apartment. Now we were totally alone. We'd wander around the two duplexes feeling lost.

"Which living room shall we use tonight?" my father would ask. His eyes would brighten; his cheerful smile never let up, even as some secret anxiety etched new lines around his mouth. He wanted me to believe everything was within my reach. "So you are having a quiet time for the moment. Why don't you enjoy yourself with your various men?" I would nod, although the suggestion irritated me. I didn't like him monitoring my comings and goings.

Whenever I came home with a date he'd be up offering us drinks and we'd have to sit and talk with him. I didn't like living at home. I wanted my own place, but I didn't have enough money. I was determined to move. I asked my father to lend me $1,000. He refused.

"Mama and I need you!" he'd exclaim, so I stayed for a while longer.

He thought it was wonderful that I was going out with so many eligible bachelors, like the genial ad executive Rib Smith. But I introduced my father to only a few of the men that I was seeing. Secretly I was going through a strange phase of sex without intimacy.

My phone rang nonstop, because I was divorced and considered a "hot property." Supposedly I knew what I was doing in the sack; that's what a Wall Street broker mumbled as he crawled on top of me. Except I didn't know what I was doing, or more to the point I didn't know what I wanted sexually, nor did I know the questions to ask. Jason's "me Tarzan, you Jane" approach had left little to the imagination. I lay there and took a lot of pounding. It turned me on, but not for long. It took me a while to find pleasure and harmony with a man.

Today it's said that women own their sexuality and can have sex on their own terms. I don't know if that's true, but back in the late 1950s, just before the sexual revolution and the advent of the Pill, women bargained with sex for love and money, or they were too repressed and ignorant beyond belief—especially about their bodies. I for one was totally disconnected from my emotions. So many sad lost nights reaching out to so many sad lost men. The estates attorney who was so boring I had to stop seeing him, even though he gave me great orgasms. The musician who chewed speed gum and was constantly tripping out. He brought me to the only orgy I've ever gone to. It was held in an apartment on Central Park West with many bedrooms. I refused to participate. As I was leaving, I ran into a man dressed in priest's robes. I was told he was George Plimpton.

Eventually I confessed some of my escapades to Marcia. She was appalled. "Haven't you any self-respect? What are you trying to prove?"

I reminded her that we'd both read Mary McCarthy's *The Company She Keeps* our last year in college. It was a book all our friends were reading—our mothers too. Mama had given it to me and festooned the most notorious story, "The Man in the Brooks Brothers Suit," with paper clips. In that story Margaret Sargeant (aka McCarthy) gets drunk on a train and proceeds to have rough sex with an overweight stranger. It was shocking; it was daring. A feminist before feminism, McCarthy seemed out to prove you could have a casual relationship with a man, a one-night stand where love didn't enter the equation. Casual sex could be energizing, couldn't it? Liberating even? And you were not supposed to feel guilty.

"But as a Catholic I bet you feel guilty as hell," Marcia exclaimed.

I had to admit I did. I still felt tied up in emotional knots.

"As well you should, and let's hope you don't get crabs or gonorrhea."

"Oh my God."

"Well, you didn't know any of these men, did you? Weren't most of them virtual strangers?"

I admitted most of them were.

"Grow up, for God's sake! How old are you now—almost twenty-three? You should settle down and get married."

"I've already been married."

"Okay, okay, but why don't you go back to that Rib Smith, the ad guy? Gene really likes him and Rib liked you. You just brushed him off."

"He was sort of boring."

"You don't know him enough to say he is boring. He is decent and hardworking—"

"And boring."

Marcia rolled her eyes. "You will never be satisfied with an ordinary man; he has to be weird and strange."

I was getting tired of our conversation. "I'll give Rib a call. I can take him to a cocktail party I've been invited to."

So I did, and I had a better time than I'd expected.

RIB WAS A tall, good-natured account executive from Young & Rubicam. Typical *Mad Men* type—chain-smoking, martinis for lunch, very popular with the models and actresses he was hiring for commercials. Then he started to date me and he stopped playing around. We'd have long drunken dinners at P. J. Clarke's, where he'd try to persuade me to give up my career and live with him. He'd start fulminating about "the inner-directed man and the outer-directed man" (popular phrase of the time), and he kept urging me to read David Riesman's *The Lonely Crowd*. I had no interest. I was too busy finishing Mary McCarthy's *Memories of a Catholic Girlhood*.

Rib's family had a big home out in Douglaston, Long Island, right on the water. He kept his boat in their dock. We went sailing on it late that summer, all the way up to the Cape. By the time we reached our destination—Wellfleet—I was rosy with sunburn. We visited Gene and Marcia, who were honeymooning in a shack on the dunes. We went swimming in the bay, and then at dusk we roasted lobsters on an open fire, along with fresh corn and potatoes. Endless bottles of white wine were consumed; we sang Russian war songs, vowed eternal friendship, then passed out. I enjoyed myself. Rib was so likable and affectionate. Sometimes he'd pick me up and whirl me around in his arms. He wanted to take care of me. That felt good.

A week later we sailed back to New York and holed up in Rib's cramped one-room apartment on East Forty-Ninth Street overlooking Second Avenue. He made gentle love to me over and over, and then he asked me to marry him. But I said no. It was too soon; I wasn't ready to commit. I wanted to be "free" and didn't want to be "possessed," but I didn't know that being free and unpossessed could tear the heart out of intimacy. I didn't know that being free meant taking chances with my life. I hadn't counted on what it would cost. The price was losing someone quite precious.

Even so, we continued to see each other for the next couple of years, although it wasn't the same. We also saw other people.

Chapter Thirteen

THAT FALL I began attending sessions at the Actors Studio. It took me a while to adjust to the manic energy of the place. Elia Kazan affectionately called the Studio "a zoo." Open 24/7, it was a place where every member seemed to be working on personal projects and competing for rehearsal space.

Every Tuesday and Friday at eleven the theatre was crowded with show business luminaries as well as members sitting in on sessions so they could observe performers challenging themselves in front of master teacher Lee Strasberg. In the next decade I would watch Lee coddling, haranguing, and inspiring the most gifted actors in the history of Broadway and film—including Al Pacino, who in his first scene performed a terrific stunt, moving from a monologue in *The Iceman Cometh* to a soliloquy in *Hamlet*.

I was also witness to some high-pitched arguments and equally high-pitched romances. In an era known for repression and loyalty oaths, the Studio's attitude was decidedly male chauvinist piggish to an alarming degree. "The actresses are here to be fucked; the actors get all the praise and attention," I was informed bluntly, even though in point of fact the female members who were there when I was, like future Oscar winners Anne Bancroft, Lee Grant, Estelle

Parsons, Ellen Burstyn, and Jane Fonda, were as talented if not more so than their male counterparts.

There was a time early on when I was goosed as soon as I walked in the door and felt a tongue in my ear, then was almost suffocated by bear hugs. The tongue belonged to Harry Guardino, the bear hugs and goosing were courtesy of Tony Franciosa and Ben Gazzara respectively. They were a trio of sexy Italian actors about to open on Broadway in *A Hatful of Rain*, which had been developed entirely at the Studio through improvisations. Harry, Tony, and Ben were all genial male chauvinist pigs and they expected me to be available to them, as many other young Studio actresses were. But I'd tell them to "Fuck off!" in my newly learned language of the jungle. I was starting to be aware that my body was mine and nobody else's and I could choose those I fooled around with. Even so, the atmosphere was so alive and seductive I'd succumb to it myself every so often at a late-night rehearsal—usually with actors I didn't want to be seen with in broad daylight.

ONE MORNING I came face-to-face with Kazan. At that point he was the hottest director in America, having just won six Oscars for *On the Waterfront*. He was lounging in the kitchen just before session started, his dark angry eyes zeroing in on everybody like an X-ray; he literally charged the air with his huge positive energy. He was wearing his uniform of khakis, an old work shirt, and scuffed boots. I noticed many of the actors milling around him wore similar outfits; they were in his thrall. Then he saw me and we exchanged looks. His gaze was so riveting I turned away. Did he remember me from my audition? Might he be considering me for a part?

Marty had already mentioned that Studio members Karl Malden, Mildred Dunnock, Rip Torn, and Eli Wallach were set to play in Tennessee Williams's black comedy *Baby Doll*, which Kazan was directing, plus he was in preproduction for *A Face in the*

Crowd, a movie about the evils of television, which Budd Schulberg had written. Patricia Neal and Tony Franciosa had been promised major roles. It was obvious that the actors in that room were hoping Kazan would be choosing some of them for the roles still open. He often didn't audition you; he just talked to you, took you for coffee, to figure out what made you tick.

"He psyches you out," Marty told me. "He likes it if you're ambitious."

"Hey, kid!" Kazan called out to me in his rough voice. "Hey kid, come over here."

Conversation ceased as I crossed the kitchen. "Good morning, Mr. Kazan," I murmured, fighting my urge to curtsy. I was now close enough to see he hadn't shaved.

"Mr. Kazan?" He mocked. "Polite."

He continued to study me. My heart was pounding so loud I was sure he could hear it. Then after a minute he commented, "You got strong hands."

I looked down at them, embarrassed. He had singled out my worst feature. They were big, ungainly, freckled. I waited, hoping he'd say more, but he lapsed into a silence. I would soon learn he didn't talk that much. He once told me, "If you can't say what's on your mind in the time it takes to soft-boil an egg it isn't worth saying."

"You wait," Marty had predicted. "Before session starts, every actor will be sucking up to Kazan, hoping and praying he will give them a break." They included Actors Studio members who hated his guts for naming names in front of HUAC in 1952. "He betrayed friends to save his career," Marty said.

Kazan maintained he'd given his testimony because he loathed "communist goals," and the revelations of what the Soviet Union had been doing to its writers. The death camps, the Nazi-Soviet Pact, the suppression of so many millions of people, horrified him.

But he did admit that "anyone who informs on other people is doing something disturbing; it doesn't sit well on anyone's conscience to inform."

Only a few sympathized with Kazan. There had even been a tumultuous meeting where there was an almost unanimous demand that the Studio take a public stand against him. Kazan had retaliated by saying he had never asked anyone to state *their* political beliefs to him. What he'd done was private; everybody's politics were private. The membership pulled back, but Kazan didn't show his face at the Studio for over a year until tempers cooled.

Nobody knew at that time that naming names would become the defining event of his life—for some, the indefensible event. He certainly had no idea his name would forever be associated with the betrayal of friends. He would remain haunted by this one act in spite of his overwhelming success, his gigantic genuine accomplishments as an artist.

I WOULD DISCOVER that Kazan and Strasberg did not get along, although they never revealed their complicated feelings to the membership. Kazan had been Lee's student in the early days of the Group Theatre. Then Kazan surpassed Lee in every conceivable way artistically. Some felt that when Kazan stopped running the Studio to concentrate on his flourishing career, he'd handed over the directorship of the place to Lee out of guilt.

Cold, inscrutable, Lee ruled the Studio with an iron hand. Everybody was afraid of him. Be that as it may, he was a remarkable teacher—he taught me how to depend on my instincts and imagination. He taught me how to *dig*.

He believed the actor was noble. He gave us all dignity and he was fascinated by the creative process: writing, directing, and of course acting. Everything he talked about (and he was a rambling, discursive talker)—music, painting, politics, philosophy, theatre, sex, psychology—related to "the human experience" that lay at the heart of the creative one.

He gave credit to Konstantin Stanislavski for revolutionizing acting some decades earlier with his work at the Moscow Art Theatre. Lee took Stanislavski's personal exercises for the actor and developed them into his own Method. Where Stanislavski focused on realistically portraying a scene, Lee urged actors to access their private pain. The aim was to release the emotions and create genuine characters. The most important tenet: relaxation. Everything flowed from that. It was hard for me to ever relax, onstage or off, so I didn't work in session right away. For a while I'd sit in the back row of the theatre taking notes, jotting down everything I saw— and I saw plenty.

Such as watching Paul Newman attempt to play Petruchio in *Taming of the Shrew* as a preening, gum-chewing narcissist. Or trying to figure out what Jane Fonda was doing in her "private moment" pacing around a chair and then squatting over it. Later I figured out that she was confronting her bulimia, since she could often be heard vomiting in the ladies' john.

"Behavior, behavior," Lee would singsong. "You have to learn how to behave truthfully onstage." Behaving truthfully wasn't easy. It was easier to fake, but then you could never fool Lee.

I ALWAYS THOUGHT he was best when suggesting character details to the greatest talents, the most experienced actors at the Studio.

"Lee knows what you need to open up your instrument," Geraldine Page told me. She was an amazingly gifted character actress; offstage she frequently resembled a bag lady in soiled, wrinkled dresses, her pockets jangling with keys. But onstage she could be incandescent, as she had been in her first hit, playing the spinster Alma Winemiller in Tennessee Williams's *Summer and Smoke*. In that play she'd had a jittery reality, a way of delivering her lines with pauses, and then she'd change her voice from booms to whispers. She constantly fluttered her hands. Her mannerisms got in the way of her acting.

One morning I watched, fascinated, as Lee guided Gerry in a scene. "He knew what I needed to undo in my acting," Gerry said.

She had taken on Jean Giraudoux's *Electra*, playing the part of Clytemnestra. Lee told Gerry to perform the monologue in the balcony of the theatre.

"Do the monologue standing," he said. And then he had someone tie her arms to a pillar. "So you can't move, darling. You just speak in a loud clear voice."

Gerry proceeded to do just that, and at such an exalted pitch we were all on the edge of our seats. Her mannerisms dropped away; she was getting to the core of the character.

Kazan was there that day in session. He was so impressed he cast her as the flamboyant fading movie star "Princess" in *Sweet Bird of Youth*.

I WAS STILL taking notes when a scene came up that featured twenty-six-year-old Steve McQueen, another new member. I had been watching him for weeks, staring at him, daring him to stare back. He was lithe and tanned and bursting out of his skin with animal magnetism. In T-shirt and jeans he made boyishness magically attractive.

Steve and his ex-girlfriend Peggy Feury did a scene in bed, rolling around laughing and softly grunting under the covers, that seemed to go on forever and ever. No words were spoken; passionate wet kisses were exchanged, so passionate in fact that Peggy was drooling at one point and Steve gently wiped the drool from her chin.

Lee finally stopped it. "I can't see what you are doing," he told them as they emerged from the sheets. "What were you doing?"

Peggy, a slender, determined blonde, snapped back, "Preparing. We hadn't gotten to the dialogue yet," and then she pulled the sheets around her. It looked as if she was half nude. There was laughter from the audience and Lee's stone face cracked into a tiny smile. Peggy was a favorite, such a steady relaxed presence onstage that he often used her as an example of someone who knew how to work moment to moment (Peggy would later become a legendary coach to Hollywood stars like Anjelica Huston).

"So, Steve? What have you got to say?"

Steve shrugged and then grinned. "I wish you hadn't stopped us. We were having a great time."

More laughter. Lee glared. "We are supposed to be working here." End of laughter. "Obviously I can't comment on anything. I ask you to bring in the scene again, but next time do the preparation offstage."

Steve ambled over and collapsed on a chair. I began staring at him and he stared back, mocking me, daring me to come over. Already he exuded the casual star-actor quality—assured, cocky; he was going places, about to replace Ben Gazzara in *Hatful of Rain*.

We continued to stare at each other.

"Be the aggressor for once, you idiot," I said to myself. Most of the time men chose me. I took a deep breath and sauntered over, although I felt like running.

"You wanna go out with me, don't you?" he challenged.

"Yes!!" I found myself almost shouting. Several members who'd overheard our exchange chuckled.

"Okay, Patsy."

"My name is Patricia."

"Too formal. Pat, then." He rose slowly to his feet and gave a yawn and a stretch so that his T-shirt hiked up and I caught a glimpse of his tanned flat belly. "Come on, I'll take you for a ride on my bike."

As we walked down the stairs from the theatre, I watched Steve's taut muscles bulging, practically undulating, as he moved. He reminded me of a graceful tomcat on the prowl. Members were crowding the shabby front office and flowing into the kitchen; many of the women watched enviously as we moved out onto the street.

Steve's motorcycle was parked right on Forty-Fourth Street and Ninth Avenue. He climbed on and revved up the motor. I clambered up and sat behind him, wrapping my arms loosely around his waist.

"Get a good grip, sweetie, or you'll fall on your little ass." I tightened my hold on him and looked down. I was straddling his buttocks; I could feel the muscles tightening in his thighs as he revved up the motor some more. Then we were zooming off into the bright afternoon, careening up Tenth Avenue past crumbling tenements and bars and then around and past Columbus Circle. We ended up in Central Park. Steve parked the cycle on the grass and then vaulted over to a vendor, bringing back two hot dogs and two Cokes. It was a crisp fall afternoon.

We didn't say anything; Steve wolfed down the food. "Fuck, I was hungry," he mumbled, wiping some mustard off his mouth.

What could I say? I was with a man I'd had a crush on for weeks. It was too good to be true. I remember only fragments of what we talked about. I asked about his life. He was born in Beech Grove, Indiana; his father was a stunt pilot who'd abandoned him and his mother when he was a child. Steve had been in reform school and then the Navy. He'd had all sorts of odd jobs: oil rigger, towel boy in a brothel.

I think he asked me a couple of questions, but then he got right to the point. "I have to level with you, Pat. I'm in love with someone— Neile Adams. She's a dancer in *Pajama Game*. So we can't do it. I don't want to screw around . . ."

"Okay," I said, although my heart sank. "I understand, but why did you bother taking me for a ride on your bike then?"

Steve gave a short laugh. "I thought if I didn't you'd piss in your pants."

It was my turn to laugh. "Did I really look that intense?"

"Yeah. You bugged me. So now you won't give me the eye anymore, will ya?"

"I promise."

DECADES LATER, WHEN I was a journalist and Steve was number one at the box office, I interviewed him in New Orleans where he was filming a picture called *The Reivers*. He'd already done *Bullitt*, *The Cincinnati Kid*, and *The Thomas Crown Affair,* and he was the highest-paid star in the world. It was a coup for me since he wasn't giving interviews. I found him pacing around his hotel suite's bar when I came in. As soon as he saw me, he ran over and enveloped me in a hug. "How ya doin'?"

For the next few minutes we got caught up. I filled him in on my life; he asked after mutual friends. He told me he'd been reading some of my articles in the *Times* and *New York* magazine.

"Maybe you shoulda been doin' this all along."

"Maybe."

He was smoking one cigarette after another and belting down drinks. He looked trim and in good shape, but when he took off his dark glasses, he seemed tired. I tried to get started on the interview.

"Oh, okay," he drawled. He flopped down on the couch and then jumped up again and began pacing. The phone rang continuously, but he refused to answer it, and finally with a volley of cursing, "Shit! Fuck! Fart!" he pulled the phone from the wall. I was startled by the violence of the act. Then I noticed some white powder on the coffee table; he'd been snorting cocaine.

"Listen," he said. "Did we ever fuck?"

"No, we didn't," I answered. "Don't you remember? You told me you were in love with Neile Adams—the woman you married and the mother of your children . . ."

"Oh, yeah, yeah, sure." He shook his head. Suddenly he looked old and forlorn. "There have been so many . . ."

WHEN I AGREED to do my first scene at the Studio from Clifford Odets's *Night Music,* it was with another new member, Bob Heller, a rambunctious fellow who'd started off as a stand-up comic in the Catskills. Good-natured and funny, he ended up being another confidant of mine, like Marty Fried. I grew to depend on Bob for advice about everything from my agonizingly short-lived romances to who was the best agent in town.

Years later I asked Bob, "What was I like as an actress? Tell me the truth."

He answered, "You were accessible," and then he added, "You reminded me of a flower. A lovely bright yellow flower." He went on to say, "You treated me like a brother."

I may have, but I never told him about Bart or his suicide, or my marriage to Jason, for that matter.

"I knew nothing about you," Bob said. "Except," he went on, "you were the loneliest girl I'd ever met."

I'd forgotten how lonely I was. At the Studio I'd been sur-rounded by people, but the minute I left the place I felt so solitary, so alone. Often after a session I'd wander the streets of the city aim-lessly. Arthur Storch, a wonderful Studio actor who later became a gifted director, told me he'd developed a crush on me but was too shy to ask me out. Instead he stalked me as I wandered around Manhattan. He said I spent a great deal of time looking at myself in department store windows.

*   *   *

BOB AND I performed *Night Music* twice. We were not very good. As the courageous society girl Fay, I couldn't project; my voice seemed lodged in my throat. And Bob playing Steve, the rash, uncontrollable Greek American, was all over the place onstage. Lee was surprisingly gentle. He suggested we try something "closer to your own life experience."

As we walked up the aisle I recognized Kazan in the audience. He'd created the role of Steve in the original production of *Night Music* on Broadway. I ran out of the Studio confused, my body aching with tension. I was stumbling up West Forty-Fourth Street when a figure came up behind me and put his arm around me. It was Kazan.

"Aw, kid," he said, his voice sounding sympathetic. We walked up toward Ninth Avenue.

"You weren't so bad," he went on. "You were sure as hell human as far as I was concerned. I believed you were fucking scared. You were vulnerable, but you were tentative about it. Know what I mean?"

I nodded.

"If you'd *experienced* being scared, if you'd 'used' it—you woulda been home free."

I nodded again. I was beginning to understand, I thought.

We continued to walk. "I was in *Night Music* when I was in the Group," Kazan said. "Last play I did." He paused. "But you knew that, didn't you? You knew I'd come because I'd be curious." He chuckled briefly.

I admitted that my partner Bob Heller and I both thought it had been a good idea. "We did hope you might want to see it again."

"And I did."

I waited, expecting he'd say something about our performances, but instead he confided, "I wasn't a very good actor. I was too angry all the time—except in *Waiting for Lefty*, the anger worked for that part." He stopped. "Gotta go to a meeting."

He darted away but called out, "Keep at it. Just keep working. That is the secret to everything. Keep working at it."

I HAD FEW encounters with Kazan after that; he was at the peak of his career and exceedingly busy, but every so often we would bump into each other at the Studio. He somehow sensed that I needed support and encouragement and would give it to me in the form of a brusque word of advice, or he might suggest a book to read or a piece of music to listen to.

Our conversations lasted only a couple of minutes, but I treasured every one of them. They invariably took place on West Forty-Fourth Street—both of us either coming or going to the Studio. Once we walked an entire block together from Eighth to Ninth Avenue, his arm around my shoulders. "Someday you'll run sessions at the Studio, Pat," he said to me. And eventually I did.

I found myself fascinated by Kazan's Jekyll and Hyde qualities. He seemed so generous and kind to me and many other Studio members, but he was a notorious philanderer. Everyone seemed to accept that about him.

"Fuck him and you may get cast in one of his shows. It's not a guarantee, but it usually works," a hard-bitten actress advised me.

Had it worked for her? I wondered.

"What do you think?" she retorted.

I had the feeling it hadn't.

But then I was tested myself. Kazan's office called me to audition for the part of Heavenly in *Sweet Bird of Youth*. It was the kind of part I was usually up for, the pure virginal type. I wanted desperately to work for Kazan, so I was thrilled to be called and I read four times, once with Paul Newman, who would be playing the male lead.

When I finished the fourth reading, Kazan sprinted up to the footlights. "Nice," he told me. "Very nice. Pat—it's Pat, isn't it?"

I nodded.

He looked hard into my face. "Tell me something," he murmured. "Why are you so sad?"

The question startled me. *Yes, I am sad*, I said inside myself, *but I won't tell you why.* "This is the way I am."

Kazan was continuing to study me. "Just wondered," he said, and he turned away. "Guy!" He called to his assistant, Guy Thomajan, a rather sinister man with bent shoulders and swarthy skin who was hovering nearby, holding a clipboard. He darted close and Kazan spoke to him so softly I couldn't hear.

I assumed I'd been dismissed, so I called out good-bye and walked into the backstage area to pick up my jacket and tote bag. Straight ahead I noticed a row of actresses waiting nervously to audition. A few smiled weakly at me as if to say, "You got through it."

I was almost out of the theatre when I heard Guy calling after me. "Wait up, Bosworth. Kazan will see you for dinner tonight at Downey's. Seven p.m. sharp."

I turned to face him. I was well aware of what that meant. Dinner and a quick roll in the hay.

"I'm busy," I countered, and then I added lamely, "I have a boyfriend."

"What's that got to do with it?" Guy demanded.

"Nothing, I suppose."

"Don't you want this part?" Guy asked.

I thought for a moment. "Not that much."

"Okay, okay, that'll be all," Guy retorted, dismissing me with a wave of his hand, and then he turned on his heel and called out to the next actress waiting in the wings.

I WALKED PARTWAY through Shubert Alley and then stopped and gazed back at the Morosco Theatre, where Kazan was auditioning. I almost cried out to Guy, "I changed my mind—I'll meet Mr.

Kazan at seven on the dot!" but I didn't. Instead I dashed through ongoing traffic onto the opposite curb, pausing in front of Sardi's, but I didn't go in. I stood looking at my reflection in the restaurant window.

What was the matter with me? For the past three years I'd been screwing around indiscriminately, mostly with a bunch of mediocrities, and yet when confronted with going to bed with a genius—Elia Kazan—I was suddenly a paragon of virtue, a Goody-Two-Shoes holding on to my dignity and my body as if they were treasures. Something in me was starting to change. Was I beginning to wake up and take myself seriously? Perhaps. I did know I didn't want to have a one-night stand with Elia Kazan. In my journal I'd described him as "probably an animal—a charismatic animal—crude, surly, secretive, sly, bold, self-involved, and virtually unattainable, which makes him more desirable to *moi*." But what I really wanted from this complicated, brilliant man was to be his friend and colleague. I wanted him to affirm me as an artist. I knew it would probably take a long time, and it did. The affirmation took thirty years.

IT HAPPENED IN 1978. By then I'd become a biographer. I'd written a book about Montgomery Clift and had interviewed Kazan for it; now I wanted his imprimatur. I remember going to his house on West Sixty-Ninth Street carrying the manuscript, heart in my mouth, and ringing the doorbell.

Kazan answered it himself. He had the same angry eyes, the same bristling energy. He knew why I was there. He took the envelope, snapping, "If I don't like it, I'm gonna tell you, Pat." Then he shut the door.

A couple of weeks later he phoned me. "It's good," he told me. "It's very good."

It was the beginning of our friendship.

A couple of years later I rented a cheap office in Times Square, which happened to be on the same floor as Kazan's space. By then he was in the process of writing his mammoth autobiography, which would encompass his remarkable career in theatre and film, as well as his tempestuous private life and, last but not least, his decision to cooperate with HUAC and name names. Coincidentally I was in the process of writing about my father's informing; the FBI had forced him to prove his patriotism by betraying his colleagues and I felt ashamed.

I remember confessing all this to Kazan as I stood in the doorway of his office while he sprawled on a battered couch, smoking a cigar. "Your father's decision to name names has nothing to do with *your* feelings," he said. "Or whether or not you thought it was right or wrong." He paused a moment and went on to say, "Betrayal is ugly. Unforgivable. It haunts you forever. You have to learn to live with a terrible no-win decision and go on. I say you write about it," he ordered, "and then *you* go on and stop mooning about it."

He added he was discovering in writing his autobiography that "we all live on three levels at once. The future is part of the present and the past, and our past always affects our present and future. By juggling all three, you find the tension in the story."

I DIDN'T KNOW it, but I was living that way while I was a young actress at the Studio, existing in the high-pressure present tense of that place. Then I'd attempt to do a sense-memory exercise from my past with an imaginary object—in my case, the little soot-blackened china horse statue saved from the fire in the nursery. It was one of my most treasured objects, and it proved to be my most successful sense memory. All I had to do was close my eyes, clutching the imaginary china horse, and I'd see my father's pale naked form disappearing into the crackling flames; I'd hear his frantic calls of "The baby! The baby!" meaning my baby brother, who was in danger of being burned alive. I could watch the smoke billowing toward me, its acrid smell mingling with the pungent scent of the eucalyptus trees nearby.

Lee praised my work, saying it was a good example of using my concentration and imagination. Emboldened, I decided to test myself and perform in a scene where I had to undress.

But I just couldn't. I was too self-conscious—I couldn't go along with it—so instead I faked it, the worst thing you could do at the Studio, where behavior had to be authentic. After it was over, Lee said irritably, "The scene didn't work at all because you didn't do what you were supposed to do."

I nodded. He went on to order me sternly to "take off your clothes, darling."

The entire Studio membership seemed all eyes as I unbuttoned my blouse and flung it over a chair and then I stepped out of my skirt, shook off my ballet slippers, and stood barefoot in my bra and panties in front of Lee. I was trembling with embarrassment. *Had I shaved my legs recently?* I wondered dumbly.

Lee stared at me, and I stared back, thinking, *You are a voyeur, goddamn it!* But I kept quiet and then he commented, "You're not enjoying yourself, are you?"

"No," I mumbled, my cheeks flaming red. I was exposing my half-naked body to a bunch of virtual strangers. How could I enjoy myself? What I was doing went against everything Mama had taught me about being modest and private, and yet I could hop in the sack with nameless lovers. *Who was I?*

Lee was continuing to stare at me. Was I supposed to say something? Finally I exclaimed, "I've been married!"

Lee snorted. "Why are you telling me this?"

"I don't know. Now can I please put on my clothes?"

"Go ahead." As I dressed, he continued to lecture me. "You should remember this experience. How do you feel?"

"Awful. I want to crawl into a hole."

"Good, and it's okay to feel that way when you take off your clothes again. I asked you to undress for a reason. To make you aware of your responses. You were uncomfortable. Your skin probably prickled. Your heart was beating very fast . . ." (Good God, he was correct on all counts!)

He went on, "Everything you were feeling then and are feeling now, you can use for this scene. Do you realize that?"

"Do you think I'm a complete idiot?" I shot back. "I know it's about behavior!"

There was a murmuring from the members. Nobody talked back to Lee. And with that, Lee turned away from me and rose to his feet. The session was over; he was done with me.

I was surprised. I thought we'd finally connected. I tried to follow him and say something to that effect, but he turned coldly away from me, ignoring my stammered "Lee, thank you for . . ."

It was as if I didn't exist. Trailing behind him as he left the theatre were Shelley Winters, Jane Fonda, and Marilyn Monroe. Part of his inner circle, they would accompany him to his table at Sardi's and listen to him pontificate about theatre and show business. Part of me wanted to crash that hallowed circle, but I had this instinctual urge to protect myself. I'd heard about the actresses who were held hostage by Lee emotionally. Although I was still numbed by my brother's suicide, I wasn't sure I wanted Lee to be the person to release me.

"He controls some of the most neurotic and talented members of the Studio," Marty would tell me. "Kim Stanley won't make a move without him. He coached her when she played the tomboy in *Picnic*; he had her doing stuff that was dazzling but personally excruciating. Lee also coached her for *Bus Stop*. Kim thought he was a god because he could mobilize such deep painful feelings inside her through the sense-memory exercises he'd worked out so methodically. 'Do this and you will feel something.' And that's very powerful, especially for those who are not in touch with how they feel. Because of this, some actors make transferences to him the way they do to a therapist."

Marty took me to a couple of Lee's Sunday-night suppers, where Chinese food was served and the greats of Hollywood and Broadway showed up. I'd try to be helpful by picking up the dirty plates and carrying them to the kitchen, where Marilyn Monroe was stacking them in the sink. One time Lee came by to see how Marilyn was doing. He oohed and aahed about her talent for drying glasses. I stood there; he didn't give me the time of day.

Once I met Susan Strasberg, his bewitching, beautiful, complicated daughter, I stopped wanting to be a part of Lee's circle and just wanted to be Susie's friend. She was seventeen and was triumphing in *The Diary of Anne Frank*. She had never taken an acting lesson, and she had never studied with her father.

Nobody knew Susie was supporting her parents (Lee's salary at the Studio was small) or that she had bought a house for them on Fire Island with her movie money (she had done two films). She paid for the lavish spreads at the parties on Sundays—aside from Chinese food, there was champagne and caviar and rich cakes— and nobody knew that she endured her father's obsession with Marilyn. Susie often gave up her room in the apartment when Marilyn was having problems with Arthur Miller and had to spend the night. One time Marilyn was so bugged she cried in Lee's arms, and Susan heard him sing Marilyn a lullaby he'd sung to her when she was a little girl. "That really upset me," she said.

Susie and I spent many afternoons together. She was bright and funny and generous and tender. We'd go shopping at Jax and buy gingham blouses and slacks, and a couple of times we'd accompanied Jane Fonda to an exclusive spa on the East Side, where we'd had our faces slapped. It hurt, but the routine was supposed to give you hollow cheeks. I think we went there at least half a dozen times before we confided to each other it wasn't working. "All we have now are very red faces," Susie announced.

Marty picked Susie up every night from the Cort Theatre in his cab, and sometimes I'd hitch a ride and we'd go backstage. Before the curtain came down I'd stand in the wings listening to Susie give that famous speech of Anne Frank's: "In spite of everything, I still believe that people are really good at heart . . ." The spotlight would linger on her beautiful little face and then black out.

I WAS STILL living at home and not paying rent, but Daddy didn't give me extra money to live on, so I took odd jobs to make ends meet. For a while I worked as a waitress in a popular restaurant on the East Side called the Right Bank. I was fired for adding up checks incorrectly. Then I obtained temporary work as a demonstrator at Macy's, where I attempted to show customers how to work a combination nutcracker, coffee grinder, and juice-squeezing apparatus. It was an impossible feat and I was fired from that job too. I had better luck as a hat-check girl at the Stork Club. That job lasted three months; it was the graveyard shift. But I lost out on that one too when I refused to date the owner of the club, cigar-smoking Sherman Billingsley.

Chapter Fourteen

NEAR THE END of autumn that year I made a new friend, Lily Lodge, another new member of the Studio. The daughter of John Lodge, governor of Connecticut (and niece of Henry Cabot Lodge Jr., who would run for vice president with Nixon), Lily was to the manor born. A tall, statuesque woman with masses of brown hair and a gracious demeanor honed from years of living in embassies around the world, she had trained at the Royal Academy in London. Her mentor was Helen Hayes, the First Lady of the American theatre. She had been on State Department tours with Helen in *The Skin of Our Teeth* and in other plays too. Lily was virtually her surrogate daughter; Helen's real daughter, Mary MacArthur, had died tragically of polio in 1949.

Lils and I bonded immediately. Whenever she was between apartments Lils lived with my parents and me on East Fortieth Street. We became lifelong friends.

Sometime in November we decided to do a scene together at the Studio and chose Sophocles's *Antigone*—the intense dramatic scene between Antigone and her sister Ismene, when Antigone is fighting to get her brother a proper burial service. She must go to King Creon to get permission. I was playing Antigone. It didn't occur to me that it might be difficult to play this scene until we started to rehearse and I burst into tears, remembering Bart—remembering that I hadn't gone to his funeral and I still hadn't been to his gravesite in Sacramento. We stopped rehearsal. I calmed down and then we talked late into the night in the brick-walled theatre at the Studio. I poured out my heart to Lils and she was very compassionate. I had told no one about my brother's suicide. It was a relief to release some of my pain.

Not long after we met, Lils came to me with an idea. Helen Hayes was about to star as Amanda Wingfield in Tennessee Williams's *The Glass Menagerie* at the Palm Beach Playhouse. The part of Amanda's fragile crippled daughter Laura had not yet been cast. Would I like to be considered?

What a silly question. Of course I would.

The very next afternoon Lils drove me to Nyack, where Helen lived in a white-shuttered Victorian mansion high on a hill overlooking the Hudson River. She was waiting for us in the double living room when we arrived, a small round woman with amazingly bright eyes. She didn't stop talking as she showed us around: "Here's Duse's handkerchief, which I'm about to give to Julie Harris . . ." I noticed that her voice was bright and chirpy; it grated faintly in my ears. We walked through many rooms, the place decorated with chandeliers and Renoir paintings, not to mention numerous Tony Awards and the Oscar she'd won for her first major film, *The Sin of Madelon Claudet*.

I was most drawn to the pictures. The walls were covered with them, portraits of Helen at various points in her legendary career. She'd been on the stage since she was a toddler and had triumphed in a constellation of roles from flappers to matrons to Shakespearean heroines and Chekhovian old maids. There was a particularly fascinating series of photographs charting her remarkable performance as Victoria Regina; she had played the long-lived British monarch from girlhood to widowhood, aging visibly through the magic of makeup.

Soon we sat out in the garden near a swimming pool. A maid served us tea. Helen took a delicate sip. "Kate Hepburn once swandived into that pool," she announced. "Kate liked to show off."

We hadn't mentioned *The Glass Menagerie*. I longed to hear what she had to say about this great play, which had revolutionized the theatre with its lyricism and poetry, its insistence that memory could be a force of gravity. I assumed we were to read one of the mother/daughter scenes from the play. I'd even memorized a scene. I pulled a copy of the script from my bag and was about to say something when Lils put a finger to her lips. I kept quiet as Helen nattered on.

"I enjoy going to Palm Beach in winter. The weather will be wonderful. Paul Crabtree will be directing and playing the Gentleman Caller. Will Hare will be Tom. Lils tells me he's a member of the Actors Studio, so you will feel comfortable."

I nodded. Will was a kindly, burly journeyman actor who worked frequently on projects in session and was full of advice to all the younger Studio members.

Then Helen looked at me. "I phoned the Theatre Guild and spoke to Lawrence Langner. He saw you in *Blue Denim* and thought you were quite marvelous. And with my darling Lils's recommendation . . ." She reached out a small hand. "I am so glad we will be working together."

IT WAS SETTLED. Just like that. I couldn't believe my good fortune. But then everything in the last six months had been unreal—becoming a lifetime member of the Actors Studio, playing Janet in *Blue Denim*, and now I was about to inhabit Laura in *The Glass Menagerie*. For the next month I prepared, researching and taking notes.

The Glass Menagerie is Tennessee Williams at his most auto-biographical. In it, as the narrator Tom, he tells the story of his miserable life in a St. Louis tenement supporting a controlling mother, Amanda, and a delicate reclusive sister, Laura, by working in a shoe factory. Both Tom and Laura have unending battles with Amanda. All Tom wants to do is escape from his family so he can write.

Laura had been inspired by Williams's sister Rose, a pathologically shy girl whom he was close to. I related to the character of Laura and related to how she loved her brother. I imagined she hated fighting with her mother as much as I did. I understood her fantasies, her need to abandon reality and move into the make-believe world she'd created with her sparkling glass animals.

Every so often I'd go to the Studio to attend sessions. Once I bumped into a disheveled Tennessee Williams, hair awry, wearing clothes that looked as if he'd slept in them. He was on the way to watch Kazan improvise with Carroll Baker and Eli Wallach for *Baby Doll*, his latest movie project. How I longed to buttonhole him and ask him questions about his sister, but I didn't say a word.

Rose would be the model for at least fifteen characters in various Williams plays. But first he'd immortalized her as Laura, so I concentrated on thinking about her.

OVER CHRISTMAS, MAMA and Daddy gave their annual San Francisco "exiles" party; it had become something of a tradition and they looked forward to seeing their transplanted California friends who were now living and working in New York. Some of them were still homesick for the mild weather, the fog, the vista from the hills, the great blue bay.

The Roger Laphams came, and Paul Smith, editor of *Collier's*. There were others but all I remember was being introduced to an impressive young man named Mel Arrighi. He towered over me, very tall and very handsome in his cheap, ill-fitting suit, horn-rimmed glasses covering acute gray eyes, rumpled curly brown hair. His classic good looks reminded me of the poet Robert Lowell. I told him that and he shrugged, embarrassed.

"Yeah, so I've heard," he admitted, barely getting the words out. I tried to ask him other questions and he seemed unable to answer. His hesitant manner of speech, almost a stammer—although he could also speak with great force—suggested a discomfort in his own skin. Nick Lothar, a friend from San Francisco who'd brought Mel to the party, ultimately answered some of my questions for him, but as soon as we sat down to dinner—and we sat next to each other—I found out a great deal more.

We discovered we were exactly the same age, twenty-four. Mel was a playwright, a novelist, and an actor. He'd been about to teach at New York University when he auditioned for the Lunts and was soon to go on tour with them in *The Great Sebastians*.

He told me he'd been born and raised in California and had attended Reed College. Yes, he said quietly, he'd heard about my brother's death, but they had never met. He added he was sorry for my loss. He said it so compassionately my eyes filled with tears. Then he added that he had a brother to whom he was very close but this brother was now sick and living with their mother back in San Francisco. I changed the subject and asked where he lived in New York.

"In the Village." At the moment he was sharing an apartment with the painter Paul Resika. They were so poor they often existed on cornflakes, he joked. Sometimes not even that. To pay the rent, he was a play reader for the William Morris Agency. What excited him most was working with Joe Papp. Papp had recently founded a Shakespeare Workshop housed in a church basement on the Lower East Side. He'd gathered a band of ragtag actors, Mel among them, and they were doing readings of *Romeo and Juliet* and *Two*

Gentlemen of Verona. Papp's goal was to bring free Shakespeare to the masses, but so far there was no press about it. Mel added that he'd acted in Shakespeare a lot at UC-Berkeley, where he'd transferred in his junior year. He'd been taught by John Barton, one of England's foremost authorities in classical theatre.

After dinner he excused himself; he had an early rehearsal. He said he hoped I could see him in one of Joe Papp's productions when I returned from *The Glass Menagerie*.

I replied I would like to, very much.

Then he added, "I think you will be very good as Laura." He was no longer stammering.

As he walked out the door, I looked after him with interest. He was attempting to do everything just the way I was. He was trying to succeed as a writer and an actor. I wanted to see him again.

WILL HARE AND I both took the early flight to Palm Beach. We were playing brother and sister in *Glass Menagerie*, so we hoped to get to know each other a bit on the plane. But Will was hungover and I was so shaken by a fight I'd had with my mother that we barely spoke. At least we'd be on time for the first read-through; it had been scheduled for one p.m.

We were driven directly from the airport to the playhouse through a blinding hot sun. Along the way we passed palatial homes decorated with reindeer and Santa Claus figurines on emerald-green lawns. In the distance I saw a strip of ocean.

The director, Paul Crabtree, greeted us in the lobby. A polite gentleman in a seersucker jacket, he spoke in a thick Southern drawl. All around him people were pushing and shoving to get in the long line forming at the box office. As soon as Helen's name was announced, her fans had come in droves to buy tickets. *The Glass Menagerie* would be completely sold out for its weeklong run over Christmas and New Year's.

Paul guided us backstage. Helen was already in the wings, perched on a camp chair knitting. When she saw us, she called out a welcome. As introductions were made, her eyes twinkled behind steel-rimmed glasses. She radiated a buoyant supreme confidence. I noticed she was wearing navy blue tennis shoes.

The formalities over, Paul signaled the stage manager, and within minutes we were seated at a long table with pitchers of ice water at each end. There were no opening remarks. We began a read-through of the play. As it proceeded, Helen plunged into the role of Amanda Wingfield with an electric excitement that left everyone else at the table a bit stunned. She seemed to be giving the performance of her life that sultry morning—wheedling, badgering, ordering her son, Tom, to find a gentleman caller for Laura, her daughter, to save her from spinsterhood.

At our lunch break Will warned me that Helen's portrayal of the foolish but indomitable Amanda would probably remain the same at every rehearsal and throughout the run. "Some stars are like that," he explained. "They set their performances in stone early on. It may drive us crazy, but we will use it."

And use it we did, although I for one was so intimidated by Helen's assured external technique—in direct contrast to my more naturalistic internal one—that I didn't come into my own as Laura until after the dress rehearsal.

Helen had already starred in London as Amanda to great success. But she would tell me she could never come close to Laurette Taylor, who'd originated the role and had been unforgettable. Helen was a modest and down-to-earth soul. It was sometimes hard to believe that this diminutive woman was considered one of the greatest actresses of the twentieth century, with theatres named after her. She was pleased I was a Catholic and I would soon accompany her to Mass. She lit a candle for her departed daughter, Mary, every day.

*　　*　　*

AFTER PAUL BLOCKED the play and set our moves, we ran through it over and over for the next week. There was never any discussion about the scenes or notes given about our characters. When Paul wasn't being the Gentleman Caller, he'd sit out front in the house, letting us find our way into the remarkable story of a family whose lives form a triangle of quiet desperation. Somehow this *Glass Menagerie* directed itself; the language and poetry carried us along.

After rehearsals Will and I would work on our own. We'd have supper in the Barn Grill near us and then go back to our boardinghouse by the ocean and run lines. Sometimes we'd create subtexts, imagined thoughts and feelings that go underneath the dialogue. Sometimes we'd improvise. I was positive Tom and Laura felt like doubles. They finished each other's sentences; each knew what the other was thinking, as I used to long ago with Bart.

Before I left New York I'd found a snapshot of my brother and me taken when I was six and he was four. We are standing in front of our Berkeley house. I am in sunlight; Bart, pudgy and solemn, in shadow. Our nanny often took us for walks up into the hills behind the university. Williams and his sister also took walks when they were small and living in St. Louis, and they played together, told each other stories, shared secrets.

"You and I are the same person, only different," Will would say of us as Laura and Tom.

We would work until midnight, and were so keyed up that we couldn't sleep, so we'd wander down to the beach and watch the waves break onto the sand. We never talked about whether what we'd been doing was deepening our performances or making us come more alive onstage, because we didn't know. I was beginning to realize that the secret of acting is that it cannot be explained. I would never be able to say *how* I accomplished what I did. I knew only that Will was everything to me in that part. Relating to him, to that perspiring, kind, ruddy face of his, made all the difference. In connecting to others on stage you are halfway there.

THAT'S WHAT WAS so difficult about acting with Helen. During dress rehearsal we would be having a dialogue, and although she seemed to be looking at me, she wasn't *seeing* me, and that was unsettling. It was the main difference in the way we behaved onstage. I *made* myself look at Helen and see her, but after a while her commanding and theatrical voice threatened to imprison me. By the end of the dress rehearsal I felt as if I'd evaporated as Laura.

The morning after the dress rehearsal Helen and I took a walk on the beach. She tucked her arm in mine and we strolled across the dunes. We didn't speak; she seemed deep in thought. Then she murmured, "Don't be afraid to stand up to me as Laura in our scenes. Laura is timid and reclusive and she lives in a dream world with those glass animals, but she is also very stubborn. She won't ever give in; she is never going out in that terrible outside world again. Remember, she vomited when she went into the city that one time. Think about it. She stands her ground with her mother, don't you agree?"

I told Helen I did. Of course what she said had special resonance for me. I realized that every time I stood up to Helen as Amanda, it would be as if I were confronting my own mother. From then on, I did, and it worked.

The situation was that familiar. Amanda *did* remind me of Mama: edgy, wayward, domineering. Our battles ran on her energy as she insisted I stay with my peers. I should think about my future and security and finding a decent, responsible man. "You won't be young and beautiful forever, you know!" I never felt I was a match for her, but I kept on rebelling. Just recently she had been scathing after discovering that my latest companion was a jazz composer who'd been arrested for drug possession. I thought he was so sensitive and talented. I'd contributed to his bail. We'd argued about whether he was worth it until we were exhausted, and then, her voice cracking with emotion, she cried out, "You will hate me for saying you are a fool, but you are. You are careless and impulsive. You don't think about the consequences. Someday you'll regret that you didn't listen to me. You will miss me terribly . . . and you will realize how much I loved you."

I used these admonitions that my mother had been repeating to me over and over again since I was a teenager. They were imprinted on my brain and I absorbed them into my performance as Laura.

OPENING NIGHT HELEN and I both received bunches of yellow roses. I didn't look at the cards. I was too nervous—and I also couldn't read the telegram my parents had sent. I was overcome with stage fright, which took the form of dizziness, nausea, and heart palpitations. I prayed I would forget the terror by practicing my limp back and forth across my dressing room, but I remained petrified, so I tried Helen's remedy—wiggling my toes. That worked. Then I glanced at my face in the mirror; my gaze vibrated with intense confused feelings. Would I be able to inhabit Laura as I dreamed I could? I had no idea. I did know I had to overcome my fear. I began to shake; my mouth grew dry. I sipped some water and continued to wiggle my toes.

Miraculously, by the time the stage manager called "Places!" I'd pulled myself together and was able to walk straight and tall across the stage to cross over to my place on the set. In front of me was the Wingfields' shabby living room, which also served as Laura's sleeping room, and just beyond, separated by transparent curtains, the dining room. There an old-fashioned whatnot displayed the dozens of gleaming transparent glass animals Laura is so obsessed with.

Dusky lights washed over me as I sat down at the dining room table opposite Helen (who was already there, staring straight ahead).

The golden light warmed my shoulders; I felt stronger. (Williams had written, "The light upon Laura should be distinct from the others, having a peculiar pristine clarity such as light used in religious portraits of female saints or madonnas.")

I heard the audience murmuring and coughing as the curtain rose and Will sauntered onto the fire escape, lit a cigarette, and announced, "Yes, I have tricks in my pocket; I have things up my sleeve . . . But I am the opposite of a stage magician. He gives you illusion that has the appearance of truth. I give you truth in the pleasant guise of illusion."

Listening to that beautiful evocative language calmed me. I was no longer afraid, but I prayed I would inhabit the painfully shy, crippled Laura in a genuine way. Laura is frozen both by her mother's unrealistic expectations of her and by her own repressed sexual fantasies.

Will finished his monologue and pulled back the gauzy curtains to reveal Helen and me sitting at the dining room table. The audience went wild, and Helen would soon give them what they expected—flustered charm as a form of acting.

I hadn't expected this; she was doing a new variation on Amanda. I realized she could overwhelm me if I let her. I didn't. I held my ground. During our scenes we had actual staring contests. She often would not look back at me, but I never looked away. I responded to Helen as never before; I related to her as Amanda/Mama, finally connecting totally to this aging star.

The audience was adoring her; she had an awesome emotional hold on them. There was something endearing about her. She once told me, "I think I'm a plain Jane. If I'm popular, it's because people think I remind them of someone in their family." Maybe so. I'll never forget that fierce little face topped by a god-awful stringy wig. She would soon enter my dreams, her voice grating in my ear: "RISE AND SHINE! RISE AND SHINE!"

I had no idea how I did that night. I performed in a kind of trance, lights hot on my face. I felt utterly drained as the curtain came down and applause swelled. Helen received a standing ovation, the rest of us enthusiastic applause. Will hugged me tight in the wings. He was sweating profusely and breathing hard.

"I don't know whether I was any good or not," I whispered.

"Neither do I—we can't judge our performances. But I gave it my all," he whispered back hoarsely. "It's all you can do." He would give it his all every night after that and then go off and get roaring drunk.

I hurried to my dressing room to prepare for the opening night party. I was just zipping into the brocade satin cocktail dress I'd borrowed from Mama when there was a knock on my door and Tennessee Williams appeared, with arms outstretched.

"Baby, you look like my Laura and behave like my Laura," he crooned, and then he broke into a wild cackle and embraced me.

I couldn't speak. To me he was the epitome of the genius artist—one of the greatest playwrights of the twentieth century, along with Eugene O'Neill and Anton Chekhov. Then I noticed an elegant handsome man with a probing gaze standing next to him.

"Baby, this is Gore Vidal. He liked you too." Tennessee turned away. "We must congratulate Helen." The two of them disappeared.

I saw them briefly at the opening night party, sitting with Helen and her husband Charles MacArthur. I didn't go over to the table. I spent most of the time dancing with the theatre's press agent, a bespectacled boy who had a crush on me.

The following evening, Tennessee and Gore returned to see the show again, and afterward they took me to a seedy bar near the beach and we proceeded to drink the night away. Or rather they proceeded to drink. I could not keep up with them. I sat there in silence nursing a gin and tonic, thrilled to be in their presence as they bantered back and forth.

LEFT: Me, Daddy, and Bart at Lake Tahoe, 1937

BELOW: My brother and me in Carmel, California, 1938

BELOW: Me, Mama, Bart, and Daddy at Aptos, California, 1942

RIGHT: Mother and daughter in matching Lantz dresses at Aptos, 1943

ABOVE: Daddy (holding our cocker spaniel, Frisky), Mama, and Bart outside Aptos, 1944

RIGHT: Sitting in my hideout, 1945

BELOW, RIGHT: Daddy with President Harry Truman, 1948

BELOW: Me and Bart on our way to school in San Francisco, 1948

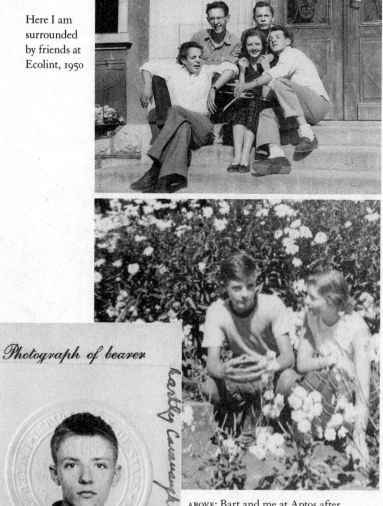

Here I am surrounded by friends at Ecolint, 1950

Photograph of bearer

ABOVE: Bart and me at Aptos after the Deerfield incident, 1950

LEFT: The last photograph of Bart, taken for his passport, September 1953

LEFT: My first modeling test shot, 1953

BELOW: High-fashion modeling shot, 1955

ABOVE: Testing for *Seventeen* magazine, 1955

RIGHT: Me and Lee Strasberg at the Actors Studio *(Getty Images)*

Burt Brinckerhoff, me, and Mark Rydell in *Blue Denim* at the Westport Playhouse, summer 1955

RIGHT: Playing Laura in *The Glass Menagerie* opposite Helen Hayes at the Palm Beach Playhouse, January 1956

LEFT: Joseph Schildkraut ("Pepi") and me outside the White Barn Theatre, August 1956

LEFT: *Small War on Murray Hill* curtain call at the Barrymore Theatre on opening night, January 3, 1957. Left to right: Stefan Schnabel, Nicholas Joy, me, Leo Genn, Jan Sterling, Daniel Massey, Francis Compton, Harry Sheppard

RIGHT: *The Sin of Pat Muldoon* curtain call at the Cort Theatre on opening night, March 13, 1957. Left to right: Elaine Stritch, James Olson, Gerry Sarracini, me

LEFT: My close-up as Sister Simone in *The Nun's Story* with Audrey Hepburn, directed by Fred Zinnemann, filmed in Rome, spring 1958

RIGHT: Me as Sister Simone and Audrey Hepburn as Sister Luke, about to say our penance in *The Nun's Story*

LEFT: On Broadway again as Sally Sims with Albert Salmi in Phoebe Ephron's *Howie* at the Forty-Sixth Street Theatre, September 1958

RIGHT: Before I went on as Mary in Jean Kerr's *Mary, Mary* at the Helen Hayes Theatre on Broadway, 1964

LEFT: Here I am in my dressing room before going on for Tiffany in *Mary, Mary* (and transitioning into journalism), 1964 *(Photograph by Jill Krementz. All rights reserved)*

BELOW: Mel and me on our wedding day, February 15, 1966

They both seemed infinitely worldly; they knew everybody. Between them they could hold forth on almost any subject—politics, the arts. For a while they discussed a new novel called *Lolita* by a Russian novelist, Vladimir Nabokov.

I noted that Williams was oddly good-looking. He wore a white linen suit and a white panama hat, and he appeared better groomed than when I'd last seen him at the Actors Studio. When I asked how the *Baby Doll* project was going, he answered mournfully, "I want Marilyn Monroe to play Baby."

"She's too old," Gore protested.

I wondered what Williams would be writing next. He'd been so prolific in the last decade: *Streetcar*, *The Rose Tattoo*, *Camino Real*, *Summer and Smoke*, *Cat on a Hot Tin Roof* . . . Plays poured out of him, works peopled with freaks, eccentrics, monster women, tormented souls—and on subjects seldom written about: aberrant sex, violence, and misfits. He wrote with religious fervor, and even with the sometimes shocking, repelling incidents there would be a kind of shining poetic epiphany that would stun you.

As the evening wore on, Williams became drunker and drunker, but he answered every question I put to him about the autobiographical aspects of *Glass Menagerie*. He admitted that his sister, Rose, was the inspiration; he confided he thought about Rose night and day and that he'd left the violence in Rose out of the play. She'd been subject to such uncontrollable fits that she'd been lobotomized at the age of twenty-six. Before her operation she'd been passionate and opinionated, with a terrible temper. Once she'd poked a knife at their father, a brutal indifferent man. Still, Williams felt guilty about not doing more to prevent the lobotomy. "Ah coulda, ah coulda," he murmured. He began crying when he told me a story about how, as kids, he would pull at Rose's curls and yell at her, "Dingdong, dingdong!"

"How could I have been so cruel?" He added that friends had

called them the Couple when they were growing up. "We were inseparable . . ." As he spoke of Rose, he would roll his eyes and burst into fits of hysterical laughter. I wanted to tell him their intense relationship reminded me of the one I'd experienced with my brother, but I didn't.

Opposite Williams, Gore—slender and quite beautiful, with such tawny hair—seemed to be cold sober. He listened to Williams's ramblings and then made a few caustic comments about Helen's performance as Amanda. "It was officious; it was 'cute.' She's too conventional and not spontaneous at all."

Williams disagreed. "Helen is virtuosic. No, she can't hold a candle to Laurette, who was incandescent, but an actress like Laurette comes along once in a century, like Duse."

Gore grew irritated. "The part must be played by a grand eccentric. Helen is mundane. The play is about the romantic individualism of the artist, and Tom emerges as a writer self-affirmed. Tom is Bird," he explained to me. "Bird" is how he addressed Williams.

("Why do you call him Bird?" I asked Gore once. He answered years later in a seminal essay on his dear friend: "The image of the bird is everywhere in his writing—the bird in flight, the bird in time, the bird in death.")

As the evening wound down, Gore drew me out, asking questions about where I'd gone to college and who my parents were. He knew of my father and his defense of the Hollywood Ten. When I said I'd worked with Arthur Penn in *Blue Denim*, he let loose with a tirade: "Untrustworthy prick!" Gore had just finished writing a screenplay of *Billy the Kid* for Paul Newman, with Arthur directing. "He cut some of the best scenes. He's an illiterate."

I would soon find out that Gore had a cruel streak in him, although he was never cruel to me. He had a real cynicism about human nature. I think he trusted few people. I made one mistake that night by praising a story I'd just read by Truman Capote. Capote was attracting a great deal of attention, and this bugged Gore, who didn't suffer rivals gladly.

"Truman stole from Eudora Welty and Carson McCullers," he told me. "The only thing he and I have in common is our mothers are both drunks." He ranted on for a while longer. By the end of the evening we were exchanging phone numbers, and before he and Williams escorted me back to my boardinghouse, Gore said he'd like to see me again.

BEFORE HE LEFT for New York, we took a walk on the beach. I felt shy. I was twenty-five and Gore was then thirty-one, but he seemed years older—his attitude about life was world-weary and his reputation daunting. He'd already written five novels, as well as numerous mysteries under pseudonyms; he'd produced scores of adaptations as well as shows for television. He would soon have his first play on Broadway, *Visit to a Small Planet*.

He confided that he wanted to make lots of money and be surrounded by a blaze of publicity. "Never lose an opportunity to have sex or be on television," he declared to me (and many others). I could tell he was restless, driven, on the move to fame and fortune in whatever form it might take.

I wanted to say that I'd read *The City and the Pillar* and it had changed the way I'd felt about homosexuality. I was starting to believe that maybe my brother and Clark had loved each other, but they'd been ashamed and kept it to themselves, and that after Clark killed himself, Bart had felt hideously guilty.

But I didn't say any of that. Instead I confided that I hoped to be a writer as well as an actress, and did Gore think that was possible? "Of course!" he exclaimed. "Acting and writing are both forms of showing off." Then he turned serious and wondered what, if anything, I had written. I was trying to finish a novel, I said, and I kept notes on the Actors Studio. Did I keep a journal? he asked. Yes, I nodded.

"Good, so just keep at it and at it. You never know what you think until you see it on paper." A long pause, and then he offered to read my work when and if I wanted to show it to him.

I couldn't believe what I was hearing. *Why* would he want to take the time to read my work? I couldn't believe my good fortune.

I DIDN'T SEND him anything right away, however. In the next few years we continued to see each other as I progressed in theatre and Gore in everything. Sometimes we'd have coffee at Downey's or a drink at his apartment on East Fifty-Fifth Street. We talked about books and writers and writing, and I finally did send him a rough draft of a story about Jason and the bird, which he pronounced "creepy." Gore never wrote his comments to me; instead he phoned and we'd discuss what I'd sent. Very often he'd ask, "*Why* are you writing this?" or say, "Too general."

Over twenty years passed and then in 1978, I sent him my biography of Montgomery Clift. He liked the book very much and gave me a wonderful quote for the jacket. After my Clift biography was published, Gore and I were having drinks at the Plaza and I finally asked him what I'd always wanted to ask him.

"Why did you suggest I send you my writing? You barely knew me at all."

"Oh, but I did know you," he answered. "I learned everything I needed to know about you after I watched you play Laura."

THE WEEK OF performances of *The Glass Menagerie* sped by. We played our last performance on January 2, 1956. I slipped into Helen's dressing room after the curtain came down. I wanted to thank her—it had been a privilege and pleasure working with such a legendary artist.

Helen was seated at her lighted dressing table, still in Amanda's wrinkled old robe. She was wiping the makeup off her face. Her wig was on its stand, her gray hair pulled back in a bun.

"Patti!" she exclaimed, looking at my reflection in the glass before she turned. "Oh my Lord, I am so relieved!" She gave a laugh that sounded like a sob and began to shake her head.

"What is it, Helen?" I asked, concerned, and she whirled around to face me.

"Great God, I hate this play!" she cried. "Hate it." And then the story came out. She'd seen the original with Laurette Taylor and Taylor was "magical. She managed to get a radiance and sympathy into a role that had been written with so much anger." Helen had gone backstage to tell Taylor how thrilled she'd been with her performance. Then she told a lie. She said she loved the play too, and she repeated the lie to Tennesee Williams when they'd joined him for dinner. Laurette planned to take the Broadway production to London, but she didn't live to do that. After her death, Helen was informed that it was Laurette's fond wish that if she couldn't do *Menagerie* in London, Helen should star as Amanda there. Helen was caught in a trap. "I couldn't back out without losing face"—so she agreed to do it. "I must say I gave the performance of my life because I still hated the play, but I was determined to rise above it."

HOW IRONIC. I loved *The Glass Menagerie*. The part of Laura would be the finest part I'd ever play. I would never forget the experience of being in a masterpiece that not only dramatized a mother's obsessive love and ambitions for her children but also explored the closeness of a brother-sister relationship. While I was in the show I had remembered Bart all over again, remembered our times in the hideout at Aptos when we escaped into fantasy and make-believe.

Sometimes we'd get silly and have belching contests, which would make us sick with laughter. Other times we'd run outdoors and play hide-and-seek in the woods on a hill covered with a thick bed of myrtle. It was so thick and green I could disappear into it very easily, but somehow Bart always found me. I could never find him; he could make himself invisible. Was it because he was smaller and quieter than I? I'd usually start giggling whenever he crept close.

I'd vow that somehow we'd always be together. But he would shake his head.

"Not possible," he'd say. "Nothing is forever, Attepe."

Chapter Fifteen

I RETURNED TO NEW YORK with a sheaf of good reviews, and for a couple of days I existed on a high. But then the bad winter weather arrived, and the snow, sleet, and freezing cold temperatures as I slogged to and from auditions left me depressed and feeling like a failure.

I hadn't yet developed the thick skin I needed to survive the onslaught of rejections as I went to cattle calls, lining up on a stage with dozens of other hopefuls, only to be eliminated time and time again because I was too short or too tall or too young or too blond (I'd been bleaching my hair). Once I was even informed I was the wrong astrological sign. Then there were the cold readings, where a script would be thrust in my hands and I was expected to give it my all immediately.

Marty advised me, "Learn to wing it," and then he'd add, "Go for an objective, like play you have asthma [I became an expert sneezer] or you are late for another appointment—that'll give the reading urgency, anything to make you seem alive and in the moment."

There was one agonizing series of auditions for the female lead in a Broadway comedy called *Fair Game*. I read the same scene over and over and over for weeks. Finally it was down to me and another actress, a very determined brunette with the professional name Ellen McRae. She got the part and changed her name to Ellen Burstyn. After my agent, Bret Adams, quietly informed me, "You lost out, honey," I slunk home and shut myself up in my narrow bedroom overlooking the back garden. I'd stay in my room until it was time to come down for cocktails. I hated living at home. I was worried about my career. Nothing was happening.

Marty said, "Feast or famine. You gotta adjust to it." But I couldn't. By March I thought I might be heading for some kind of nervous collapse.

UNBEKNOWNST TO ME, Daddy was very aware of what I was going through and he'd phoned his left-wing buddy, the Broadway director Herman Shumlin, and asked if he could help. It turned out Shumlin needed a new understudy for Bethel Leslie, who was playing the female lead in Shumlin's latest Broadway hit, *Inherit the Wind,* starring Paul Muni. The play was a fictionalized version of the 1925 Scopes "Monkey Trial," and Muni was playing Henry Drummond, a flamboyant crusading lawyer (a character based on Clarence Darrow) who represents a teacher on trial for teaching Darwin's theory of evolution in a Bible Belt school in Tennessee.

I auditioned for Shumlin, a bald husky man whose deep angry voice made me tremble even though he hired me straightaway. Not only would I understudy Bethel, he informed me curtly, I would appear in all the crowd scenes. I would be a spectator in the courtroom. I would be listed in the *Playbill* program as "the town hairdresser." He then ordered me to start memorizing my part immediately (Bethel was playing the teacher's sweetheart, and she had two big emotional scenes in the show).

The following week I had my first understudy rehearsal with the stage manager, who walked me through Bethel's part as I scribbled down the blocking in my script. Then I was fitted for my costume (a cotton print dress that hung on me unattractively). The next thing I knew I was hustled up the four flights of stairs to the attic of the Billy Rose Theatre to join seven other actresses giggling and smoking and slapping on makeup. When five minutes was called, we all trooped back down the four flights of stairs and were packed into the wings along with a wisecracking Tony Randall, who played E. K. Hornbeck, an H. L. Mencken–type journalist, and the bombastic Ed Begley, who played Matthew Harrison Brady, a three-time presidential candidate and noted Bible scholar (based on William Jennings Bryan).

Before I knew it, the curtain rose, lights blinded me, and I was pushed out onstage along with a crowd of fifty-five other actors. We were all there to greet Henry Drummond as he made his grand entrance. There was much banging of drums and tootling of horns from the small band that accompanied us.

It was my opening night on Broadway.

I felt myself being shoved center stage with the other actors. I found that I was leading the pack, dutifully waving my placard emblazoned with WELCOME HENRY DRUMMOND. Out front I could dimly see the audience—a thousand expectant faces—and then hear applause as Paul Muni made his entrance from the other side of the stage. The applause increased as he approached me in a rumpled brown suit and hat, carrying a bulging briefcase.

Suddenly, without warning—and just before he was about to launch into his opening speech—my shoe fell off. But instead of flopping off my foot, it flew up into the air and landed at Muni's feet just as he was about to say his first line. Muni glanced at the shoe, then at me, and went into his speech, giving it his usual brilliant rendition.

I stood stock-still. What had I done? What *could* I have done? I kept looking at the offending shoe. It was a big clodhopper of a shoe; it just lay there. The scene went on; the curtain came down.

Seconds later I heard a voice over the loudspeaker, requesting, "Patricia Bosworth go to Paul Muni's dressing room immediately."

I hurried to the star's quarters. When I got there, the door was closed, so I knocked.

"Come in." I found Muni at his dressing table, head in hands.

I approached him. "Oh, Mr. Muni, I am so sorry!"

He looked up at me sadly. "I just ordered you a pair of shoes that fit."

I gasped.

"Don't you know an actor should always wear shoes that fit?"

"Well, I'm a replacement. I knew they didn't fit too well [my costume was hanging on me]. But I didn't want to say anything."

"Well, now I have," he told me shortly. "You may go."

"Thank you, Mr. Muni. Thank you."

He waved his hand. "Go . . . go."

AFTER A COUPLE of weeks playing in *Inherit the Wind,* I had earned enough money to move into my own apartment. I found a one-room studio on East Sixty-Sixth Street off Second Avenue for $125 a month. It was a four-flight walk-up with a kitchen and bath, and it had a working fireplace. The building was next door to a convent. I felt that was a good omen.

When I informed my parents I was moving, all hell broke loose at cocktail hour.

"We just got you back after your divorce! We thought you'd want to live here for a while," Mama cried, gesturing to the double duplex with its two living rooms, three bedrooms, and deck overlooking the garden. "We rented it for you!" she went on dramatically. "You have all the privacy in the world."

"No I don't!" I shot back. "You monitor my comings and goings—"

Daddy sat hunched on the sofa with his drink and cigarette while Mama paced the floor and I continued to rant.

"I'm over twenty-one. I'm earning my own living and I am divorced."

"Don't remind me of that embarrassing humiliating period," Mama cried.

With that, I let loose: "It is my life, Mama, and I am leaving!" And I stormed out of the living room and started upstairs to pack.

"I have lost my own son and now I am losing my only daughter," she called after me.

I stopped. Mama always knew how to get to me. I walked slowly back into the living room and hugged her. "You have not lost me. I am going to be at the end of a phone and we are certainly going to see each other."

Mama was wiping her eyes. "I won't hold my breath."

For the next decade my battles with my mother went on and on and on. But at least I now had my own apartment.

MY LIFE SETTLED into a routine. I was now busy six nights a week with two matinees and understudy rehearsals as well. I was taught some rules: Always be on time and come prepared (of course I'd memorized the part of Rachel thoroughly). In the next months I learned how to project my character and throw my voice so it could be heard in the last row of the balcony. Until *Inherit the Wind* I'd played only in small houses. The Billy Rose was a big barn of a theatre that seated 1,500 people.

When Herman Shumlin took over from the stage manager and directed us, we had to be on our toes. I remember wanting to ingratiate myself with other cast members, until Shumlin ordered me to "stop yammering—you don't need to be liked, you need to do the work." In the few times I worked with him, he directed me with many specifics about my character. "You love this man," he said to me. "You'd fight to the death for him."

I never did go on for Frances Helm, who had replaced Bethel, but I lived in fear and trembling that I would have to, so I recited my entire part every day—later learning that Paul Muni recited his part every day too, even though he'd been playing the part of Drummond for months. It became a habit of mine whenever I did a show. It helped.

Appearing in *Inherit the Wind* was never boring because I was onstage with Muni and able to watch him. The audience was hushed whenever he delivered one of his soliloquies. It was a testimony to the transformative powers of this actor that he could be convincing not only onstage as the rumpled angry lawyer but also in films as the evil gangster in *Scarface*, as the gentle peasant farmer in *The Good Earth*, and as the dapper novelist Émile Zola. Muni's work was honed in the Yiddish theatre, where being versatile was much more important than being a star personality.

He always gave an impassioned performance, but then one night something quite unexpected happened and he handled it with aplomb. Although there were fifty-five actors in the cast, director Shumlin decided the stage should be littered with even more people, so two dozen extras had been hired to play spectators. Most of them weren't in the union; they were paid only twenty dollars a performance and were herded onstage to sit in the courtroom just before the scene commenced. They had been coached to react as we did—applaud at one point, murmur at another—but mostly we sat in silence as Muni cross-examined Ed Begley and tested him on his knowledge of the Bible.

Then one night a disheveled, wild-eyed extra pushed his way to the front row of courtroom spectators and confronted Muni center stage as he was about to give his summation to the jury.

"I can do that speech better than you!" the extra bawled.

Muni stepped back a few paces. "Oh? You think so?" he demanded

The extra was thrown; he hadn't expected such a confrontational response.

"Yes! Yes!" he bleated. "I can play your part better than you ever dreamed!"

Muni didn't answer. We realized he was trying to figure out what to do, and within seconds he had, putting his arm around the extra's shoulders and beginning to move him offstage.

"You should leave the courtroom for a while—relax—prepare yourself. Then come back."

Muni's voice was soothing as he guided him into the wings, where the two stage managers grabbed the unfortunate soul and took him away.

Then Muni returned to stage center and began his penultimate speech, letter-perfect, his voice rising to an emotional crescendo.

When the curtain came down, we all crowded around him; his face was ashen. "Never, never in all my years in theatre did I have such an experience," he told us excitedly. "But I don't think the audience caught on."

The stage managers started to apologize, but he cut them off. "Tell Herman he has to pay for genuine actors to fill up those seats in the courtroom or I quit."

With that he shuffled off to his dressing room, calling for a cup of tea.

THE SUMMER OF 1956 was sweltering. I bought a small air conditioner for my apartment. I wasn't going out much, except on Sundays, my day off. If the weather cooled off, I would take my folding bike and pedal around Central Park. Biking reminded me of my brother—biking into Santa Cruz, biking through the woods at Aptos. I would bike for hours and then stop and lie down on the grass and look up at the sky. That reminded me of Bart too—the sky, the clouds. I wondered if his spirit was happy and rested.

"Are you okay?" I would ask in our private language, and I would imagine him answering back, "What a silly question."

In the middle of the summer, Mel Arrighi sent me a postcard inviting me to the opening of Joe Papp's first production of free Shakespeare in the Park, *Taming of the Shrew*. I was surprised and pleased. The play was held in the East River Amphitheatre on the Lower East Side. I could hear the sound of tugboats and the rumble of cars going over a nearby bridge. Above me there was the crack of heat lightning, and all around me was an excited, volatile audience. Everyone was roaring with laughter at the antics of J. D. Cannon as Petruchio, Colleen Dewhurst as Kate, and Mel as Lucentio.

When the act ended, there were ominous cracks of thunder and bolts of lightning and then it started to pour. Joe Papp came out to announce that the show had to stop and there were cries of "No, no"—many of the disappointed shouts came from children.

I searched for Mel among the makeshift dressing rooms, a long row of tents behind the stage. Then I saw him poking his head out of one of the tents, a towel around his shoulders.

"Hello," I called out.

Mel squinted in the gloom and then adjusted his glasses; he hadn't recognized me right away.

"Oh, hey . . . You're getting so wet." He pulled me into his tent and tried to dry me off.

"I'm okay, I'm okay," I assured him, laughing.

"D-Did you like the show?"

"Very much."

"Come see it again when the weather is better." He was speaking very slowly so as to control his stutter.

We listened to the storm thundering outside.

"It's really coming down. I'd better go." I turned to leave, but he held my arm.

"I have an umbrella; you don't. I'll take you home."

"Okay." I watched as he zipped up his windbreaker. He looked so serious in his horn-rimmed glasses. I noticed he had long, sensitive fingers.

The next thing I knew we were splashing through the rain to the subway as lightning crackled above us. It was late and very dark; shadowy tenement buildings rose up on either side of us. I thought I saw a rat crawling into a garbage can. I guess my body tensed, because Mel immediately assured me, "I'm here, and I like the dark. It doesn't scare me."

He reminded me of my brother, who had often told me he felt more alive in the dark. Right now Mel was behaving in the same gentle courtly manner as Bart had whenever we'd walked in the rain together, holding the umbrella above my head with one hand, his other hand gently holding mine.

Our parents had never known how much Bart and I had explored the city at night during our first year in New York. They usually stayed out late at parties and dinners and our servants covered for us. "They are both sleeping like little angels," the butler would often respond when they returned home. Daddy was very tipsy and sometimes Mama was too; she was always more concerned about him than about us.

On weekends Bart and I would get bored and we'd sneak out of the Fifty-First Street brownstone and wander all over Beekman Place, ending up peering into the windows of Irving Berlin's townhouse hoping to catch a glimpse of him. When we grew bolder we'd sometimes hop a subway at night at Lexington and Fifty-First. The station was deep, empty, odoriferous—"like the pits of hell," Bart would say. The trains would pound in and out of the tunnels, headlights shining like gigantic eyes. We'd hop on and go down to Chinatown or the Battery. We'd count the "weirdos," as Bart called them, on the train. Once we saw a hunchback, another time a teenage boy who exposed himself to us. Then we'd take the subway home; we were gone only two hours, but it was exciting and risky and we loved it.

The station was almost empty. Mel and I didn't speak. We were in our own worlds, but I felt comfortable. He did not let go of my hand.

We both noticed a man in a tattered raincoat. He was mumbling to himself and pacing back and forth on the platform before he jumped onto the tracks. Everything happened very fast. A subway clerk tried to persuade the man to climb back onto the platform, but the man refused. We heard the recorded announcement that a train was on the way. The clerk managed to find a power shutoff in the tunnel and he threw the switch. Police and firefighters rushed to the scene and took the man to the hospital.

Mel pulled me out of the station and hailed a cab. It was still raining. We didn't say anything on the way uptown. He knew I was thinking about my brother, and I knew he knew.

I was grateful for Mel's silence. He simply dropped me off at my apartment and squeezed my hand in his; it was large and callused but warm.

"I'm glad you came to see the show. Thank you." And he disappeared into the night.

Later I sat on my bed in the dark. "I think I like Mel Arrighi. Am I fickle?" I was talking to Bart.

Is the Pope Catholic? my brother answered. *You barely know the guy. Although that hasn't stopped you before.*

"He didn't say anything about getting together again."

Give him time.

"That near accident on the subway . . ."

What about it?

"Made me think of you."

But I didn't fail in my attempt.

"Are you telling me you planned to kill yourself?"

For the longest time.

Part Three

Making Choices

Chapter Sixteen

I KEPT THINKING ABOUT Mel, but I didn't see him, although we were in touch periodically via the telephone and a few post-cards. He was on the road again with the Lunts.

I was still very much alone, but I'd begun to adjust to the loss of my brother, so I didn't feel quite as numb. When I wasn't at the theatre I'd hole up in my apartment and write. I was trying so hard to write, because as Gore said, it's only when you see the words on paper that you know what you're thinking. Sometimes I'd be scribbling away and I'd feel I had a passionate alter ego inside me that would be relieved only when it came alive on paper. Would it ever be possible then for me to find another self? A better self? A more fully formed, loving self?

When I couldn't write anymore, I'd visit Daddy at Silver Hill. He'd been in and out of that rehab center for the last year. It was an insidious cycle. He'd say he was making progress kicking the alcohol and pills, and then friends would sneak him some booze or a handful of Seconal and he'd be flying; then he'd say he was "definitely stopping" and I'd pretend to believe him, although I knew he was lying. But I didn't confront him. That was Mama's job. She was the "bad cop," exhorting him to stop or she would leave him. I was the "good cop," who entertained him and made him laugh.

Then one night he showed up backstage after a performance of *Inherit the Wind* to "see how my baby is" and I realized he was high. We wandered around Times Square and then we had coffee at Sardi's; I finally ordered a Carey Cadillac and took him back to the rehab myself.

We sped along the Hutchison River Parkway, close together in the backseat. Daddy smoked and coughed and coughed and smoked until I took the cigarettes away from him and he fell asleep. In repose his face appeared twisted and miserable.

I decided he had a powerful need to destroy himself. Was it over Bart? Did he ever feel remorse or shame or guilt about his son's suicide? I was sure he must be in agony, but we never spoke of it—the subject seemed off-limits—and there were no longer any pictures of Bart at home. Was this Mama's choice? I didn't ask. We remained a family full of terrible silences.

By the time we reached Silver Hill, Daddy woke up with a start. He seemed refreshed. "It was great seeing you, baby!" he exclaimed. "You are looking beautiful!" He patted my knee. "I'm getting some clients while I'm in here, y'know. Everybody needs a lawyer, especially when they're in a loony bin."

He hopped out of the limo, then poked his head back in. "I'm gonna quit, baby, I promise. You watch. I'm gonna be fine." And then he disappeared.

I knew he wasn't serious about quitting. He would never quit.

Returning to New York, I stared out the window and saw nothing. The black night enveloped me. I had never felt so wide-awake or despairing.

SO IT WAS a complicated autumn. Daddy would be at Silver Hill until mid-November, suffering from violent mood swings and two more escapes from rehab before he settled down. I would visit him as often as I could, commuting up to New Canaan in the morning; I'd keep him company, usually in the cafeteria, where he ate Jell-O and watched TV. It seemed enough that I was with him. He didn't talk much—he'd been given Valium. Around four-thirty I'd hop a train in order to make "half hour" (the actors' call time for the show) and go onstage in *Inherit the Wind*.

Then by chance I met the actor Joseph Schildkraut, otherwise known as Pepi, at a reading I was in at the White Barn Theatre. He was fifty-six, the exact age as my father—a fact I couldn't ignore.

In the movies Pepi usually played villains, like the sneering Don Francisco opposite Bob Hope's *Monsieur Beaucaire*. But he'd won two Oscars, the first for his sympathetic portrayal of the persecuted Alfred Dreyfus in *The Life of Émile Zola,* the second for his memorable performance as a tortured murderer in *The Tell-Tale Heart*. Now Pepi was starring on Broadway in *The Diary of Anne Frank*. I'd watched the show many times from the wings, and his portrayal of the stoic Otto Frank was as heart-wrenching as Susie's Anne.

Pepi came into my life at the perfect time. I was exhausted from babysitting my father. And although I was in a hit Broadway show, it didn't seem to be leading anywhere. I wasn't getting many auditions—and I had no hopes of ever falling in love—and then this imperious older man who walked into rooms like an emperor, this *celebrity*, was sweeping me off my feet with flowers and notes left backstage ordering, "Come see me at once!" It was flattering. He proved to be a diversion for a while.

At our first dinner Pepi announced, "Great actors are not necessarily great human beings." When he'd won his first Oscar, he'd played a decent sympathetic character. "But I am not a nice person." This was true. He was self-absorbed, petty, easily bored, often cruel. He threw tantrums, fired underlings, and was generally disagreeable, "unless I am with you, darling girl."

He could be very tender and loving. When we were together, he'd make me forget the loss of my brother and my father's torment. We'd attend midnight screenings of new movies; we'd eat supper at the Russian Tea Room with Garson Kanin, the natty little director of *Diary*. His tiny, supersmart wife Ruth Gordon was always with him.

However, I was nervous being with Pepi in public since he was a married man. I was afraid Lenny Lyons, who prowled the Tea Room for items, might write about me in his column, but Pepi thought I was silly. His wife, Marie, was back in Beverly Hills; they were rarely together. "She doesn't care what I do as long as I pay the bills," he insisted.

I felt more relaxed when we were by ourselves in his suite at the Hotel Meurice. We talked and talked, or rather I talked and he listened. Then I'd get tired of talking and put my head in his lap, and he'd stroke my hair or tickle my ears. We never had sex; I assumed he was impotent. But we'd lie together in the luxurious king-size bed he'd had shipped from California, and then we'd kiss and cuddle. He'd trace his finger slowly up and down my bare arm. His smooth hands were calming; his caresses made me sleepy, and somehow his touch made me feel as if he understood me.

PEPI AND I began seeing each other a couple of times a week. Otherwise, we led pretty separate lives. In those months I was mainly concentrating on getting Daddy well—keeping his spirits up, making him believe he still had a lot to live for. I reasoned that it was difficult for him to accept that until he got sober, so I was in and out of Silver Hill. I knew the Mass times at the local Catholic church Daddy liked to go to and I memorized the New Canaan train schedule. Grand Central Station became my second home.

Every so often I'd wonder what Pepi was doing when we weren't together. I didn't have a clue as to what he did away from me. Nor did he ask about my business, although he suspected I saw other men. I did see someone else, a folk singer called Paddie; he'd come over to my apartment and we'd pop corn in the fireplace and drink a bottle of wine, and then he'd make fierce love to me. Once I left Paddie and returned to Pepi's big bed, he scolded me for wasting time with a mediocrity.

I said, "How do you know he's a mediocrity?"

Pepi replied, "Because he is not me!"

Then he wondered if I'd ever been in love. "I don't believe another man has ever reached you to the core of your being," he remarked melodramatically. My father had said the same thing.

ALTHOUGH I RADIATED shyness and insecurity, inside, I was very ambitious—a trait I'd inherited from both my parents, who I knew were also ambitious for me. I was sick with fear I was disappointing them, so I admitted to Pepi that I needed a better agent. He got me one and I was immediately sent out on more auditions. Pepi coached me for a couple and I got called back. I was so overjoyed, I showered him with kisses. I was ashamed I'd been so calculating; I even told him as much and he scoffed, "Darling girl, we all use each other to get ahead. Join the club." I supposed that was true.

But I'd feel guilty anyway. Sometimes I'd wake up with him in bed and cling to him as if I were drowning. Yes, of course he was a father figure, a substitute parent while Daddy languished in rehab. Pepi gave me love, attention, and advice—I will never forget him for that.

Or for introducing me to Chekhov. He'd lecture me on *The Cherry Orchard* and *Three Sisters*, but we concentrated on *The Seagull*. Pepi had always wanted to play Trigorin, the overworked disappointed writer. I was Nina, the passionate innocent who thinks Trigorin is glamorous and falls in love with him. He leaves her; she loses his baby but becomes an actress. Pepi applauded the way I interpreted Nina—"like a survivor," he said. As time went on, we read the play more and more; we even memorized the lines and performed for each other in the hotel suite.

"We are finding ourselves in the play!" Pepi exclaimed at one point. He became so enthused about what we were doing that he approached Kermit Bloomgarden, the producer of *Diary*, and asked him to send us on tour in *The Seagull* after *Diary* closed.

Bloomgarden roared, "With an unknown? Never! But," he added, "it's an idea for you and Susie. First you play father and daughter, then lovers. Great box office."

Pepi was furious. He didn't get along with Susie, so he wanted me to play Nina. From then on, he buttonholed almost every producer he knew and tried to pique their interest. There were no takers. However, Pepi didn't give up and we'd keep reading the play to each other. By now he was calling me his "child mistress" and he'd given me a silver medallion engraved with "Pepi/Patti, Aug. 6, 1956," the date we'd met at the White Barn. He began talking about taking me to Paris on his vacation from the show. "You have given me a new lease on life," he'd say.

OCCASIONALLY THERE WOULD be unpleasantness. One Sunday, just before a Mahler concert at Carnegie Hall, we ran into Tobias, Bart's strange friend. He was on the sidewalk scalping tickets. I hadn't seen him in three years. He looked as if he'd crawled out of a sewer—ragged jacket, uncombed hair, grinning to reveal discolored teeth.

"Patti?" Sidling over, he stood so close I had to make introductions.

"Joseph Schildkraut," he murmured. "*The Diary of Anne Frank* . . ." Impressed, he leaned even closer, trying to shake hands, but Pepi moved away.

"Darling girl," he said sharply. "We must go." And he marched off to the concert hall, me trotting behind him as Tobias sing-songed, *"Darling girl . . ."*

As soon as we sat down, the image of Bart in Garrison came back to me in a flash—memories of my sweet, sad, pure little brother, so skinny in jeans and a T-shirt, shooting at tin cans while his sinister friend watched and applauded.

I gripped Pepi's arm and began repeating the painful conversation I'd had with Tobias after Bart's suicide. Pepi had heard the story innumerable times, so he hissed, "Be still!" His face took on a look of icy disapproval and he stared straight ahead.

As the music surged over us, I fought back tears and tried to excuse his behavior. He was, after all, being very helpful to me. He'd spoken to Garson Kanin, who was in preparation for a new Broadway play, *Small War on Murray Hill*, a period piece about the American Revolution. "There's a nice part in it for a rebel girl," Pepi said. "I told Gar you'd be perfect for it."

The next thing I knew, I was auditioning for the show; Pepi coached me. As a matter of fact, earlier that day I'd learned I was being called back for a second audition. I should have been excited, but I wasn't. Instead I felt anxious and forlorn; bumping into Tobias set me on edge.

THE CONCERT SEEMED interminable; when it was over, we walked in silence to the Meurice. It was only three blocks away on West Fifty-Eighth Street, but it took forever because Pepi was very tired. As soon as he got in the door he began disrobing, tossing his clothes this way and that. I dutifully hung up his jacket and trousers and placed his shirt in the laundry hamper. As I did, I again began to speak hesitantly about Tobias.

Pepi cut me off imperiously. He acted as if he were disgusted with me. "I will not listen to the story of your brother again. It is too terrible." With that he got into bed and turned his back to me.

I was so undone I ran into the bathroom and locked the door. Then I sat down on the toilet seat top and began communing, as I still did, with Bart.

"Pepi is so unfeeling. Why am I with him?"

Why are you with him? Bart repeated.

"I don't know."

Oh yes, you do. You are using him to get ahead in your career and it's not your finest moment. I had never heard him speak so sharply.

"Well, he is helping me audition . . ."

When are you going to develop some self-esteem?

"I'm so depressed."

Because you're not being true to yourself.

"What does that mean?"

You should at least be with a guy closer to your own age.

"I haven't met anyone yet."

Yes, you have.

"Who? Who?"

You'll know in a while. He seemed to be teasing me.

"I miss you," I blurted.

What else is new?

"Darling girl? What's going on? I have to use the loo." It was Pepi. I got up from the toilet and came back into the bedroom.

"Make us some tea," Pepi ordered. "Make us some tea and then I'll hold you in my arms."

AFTER BEING CALLED back three times to audition for *Small War on Murray Hill*, the new play Gar Kanin was directing, I won the role of the ingenue lead. I had stiff competition from dozens of actresses much better known than me. Pepi had bought me an expensive suit from Bergdorf's to audition in and he'd helped me develop an attitude for the part. "She's a patriot who has strong feelings about the American Revolution. Make your entrance like a soldier." And I did. I marched across the stage of the Barrymore Theatre with a purpose, an action.

The scene called for me to state my political beliefs. I could hear my voice ringing out across the aisles and up into the last row of the balcony. The experience of this particular audition was quite thrilling. I knew I'd been projecting and inhabiting the character. I knew I'd been good, maybe even inspired. When I told Pepi, he embraced me, and with more emotion than I'd ever heard him express, he told me this was a once-in-a-lifetime feeling. "Treasure it, darling girl—it rarely happens when you *know* you are good. It rarely happens."

I WAS BURSTING to tell Daddy the news. He was being released from Silver Hill the following day. I could hardly contain myself, but I decided to wait until we'd left the rehab.

I came up to help him pack. When I arrived, I found my father subdued, dressed in faded coveralls—the kind of outfit he'd worn at Aptos when he was working in the garden. He hadn't shaved and needed a haircut, but his eyes were clear, his expression focused. We were in his sparsely furnished room. There were books and newspapers by the bed, yellow legal pads on his desk filled with writing. He was starting a memoir, *My Life as a Liberal,* for Simon & Schuster.

"How far along are you?" I asked.

"Not very far." He turned and went to the closet, pulling out a small, polished wooden bench. Picking it up in his arms, he handed it to me. "Made this for you in woodwork shop." He grinned. "Good therapy." I felt like crying. "I may have a talent for this. If I can't practice law anymore, I could become a carpenter."

"What makes you think you won't practice law?"

"The law is very different now. It's all about money and connections. When I started, I was excited about a cause I could defend or a person who was in desperate need of help."

I knew he missed his radical past. I'd seen some of the clients he'd helped pro bono; a few of them even trekked up to Silver Hill to visit—a former Chinese alien, an old lefty professor down on his luck.

We headed outside. A couple of the nurses ran after Daddy; one of them hugged him. He was very well liked. Then the doctor who'd treated him came over to shake his hand.

We put the bags and the wooden bench into the trunk of the Carey Cadillac and then we were off. As soon as we were speeding over to the highway, Daddy let out a groan. "Christ, I hated being penned in like that."

"But you're not drinking anymore or taking pills."

He nodded.

"Will it last, Daddy? Are you cured?"

He rolled his eyes and shrugged.

"Daddy!"

"Baby, stop asking so many questions. I'm in the world again and I'm grateful." He stared out the window. It was a beautiful crisp November day.

We rode in silence for a while and then he took my hand. "What's been happening in your life?" he demanded. "I want to know."

So I told him about Pepi and the audition all in a rush. He interrupted with, "Isn't he that old geezer Lenny saw you holding hands with at the Tea Room?"

"He's not an old geezer—he's the most wonderful man. He found me a better agent and I just got this amazing part in a big new Broadway show."

Daddy didn't seem impressed.

"Pepi introduced me to Garson Kanin, who's directing *Small War*."

"Pepi? Funny name for a guy."

"He is different from any man I've ever known."

"How so?"

"He appreciates me. He believes in my talent. He cares for me and he's an artist."

"Isn't he around my age?"

"Well, yes, but—"

"Is this serious, baby?"

"We do spend quite a bit of time together. He's trying to get a production of *The Seagull* for us to do."

"Isn't he married?"

"I think he's going to ask his wife for a divorce; he wants to take me to Paris."

"I see."

"He doesn't love his wife," I hurried on. "They hardly ever see each other."

"Hmm." My father lit a cigarette. He seemed deep in thought.

The intense emotional ties that bound me to Daddy felt like they were going to break. *He's trying to wake me up to the reality of Pepi. He won't say that, but* The Seagull *is a fantasy. The Paris trip won't happen. My life with Pepi is a dream.*

We didn't speak to each other for the rest of the ride back to Manhattan. Anxiety overwhelmed me.

When we reached my parents' home, Daddy said briskly that he was going to Hollywood for about ten days—"to make a few speeches and earn a few bucks." He added that when he got back, I should come over to dinner. He didn't kiss me good-bye.

TEN DAYS LATER I came to dinner expecting I knew not what. Mama had said some friends were over to celebrate "Daddy's return to civilization." When I entered the living room I saw a few familiar faces—playwright Marc Connelly, cartoonist Abner Dean, the designer Pauline Trigère and her Argentine lover—and then I saw Pepi sitting rather uncomfortably on a couch next to a chic middle-aged woman, her reddish hair in a chignon.

Daddy called out his usual greeting. "Hey, baby, give your old man a kiss!" I remained in the doorway until he pulled me over to Pepi. "Darling, this is Marie Schildkraut and her husband, Joseph. I ran into Marie after I made a speech in Beverly Hills—she said she was thinking of coming to New York to surprise—is it Peepee?" He laughed. "Excuse me, I meant Pepi . . . I said, 'Why don't you come over to dinner?' and she agreed."

I shook hands with both Schildkrauts.

"What a lovely-looking girl," Marie murmured, smiling.

Somehow I got through that dinner. Daddy sat at one end of the table, Pepi at the other. I watched the two most important men in my life at the time plying each other with questions and telling anecdotes. Were they showing off for me? The other guests seemed entranced, but I'd heard the stories before—Pepi's description of how he'd shaved his head for *Diary* and "suddenly I was Otto Frank," and Daddy waxing sentimental about growing up in Sacramento with Earl Warren as a high school classmate . . . but then he stopped. "Enough about me." And he directed his attention at Marie Schildkraut.

"What do you plan on doing after *Diary* closes?" he asked, and she immediately answered, "Pepi is going to take me to Paris. It's my favorite city."

I made excuses as coffee was being served. I had a terrible headache, I said. Mama looked puzzled. I guessed Daddy hadn't told her of my involvement with Pepi.

WHEN I GOT home, the phone was ringing. I let it ring for a while. I knew it was Pepi.

I finally picked it up. He was calling from a pay phone. "Marie is at the hotel. I said I had to go to the drugstore. Oh, darling girl, I am so sorry!" I couldn't speak, so he rambled on, "Marie surprised me. I had no idea she was coming. She appeared at the Meurice; she'd met your father at this benefit. She's always admired him . . . She introduced herself, they got to talking . . . It was your father's idea to invite us to dinner."

"Daddy knows we've been seeing each other."

"Oh."

"You were never going to tell your wife about me, were you?"

"Oh, yes. Yes, I was."

"God, you're a lousy actor, Pepi."

"That hurts."

"And our trip to Paris?"

"I still want to take you to Paris," he murmured faintly.

"I better hang up."

"Wait, darling girl . . . Marie is going back to Beverly Hills in a few days. Then we can be together again. We can read *The Seagull* . . . We can hold each other close."

I felt slightly ill. He was trying to reach out, but he didn't know how. He didn't understand me and I didn't understand him either. It almost felt like a Chekhov play, except it wasn't. I hung up and we never saw each other again.

IT TOOK ME a while to recover. I put away the chic little suit from Bergdorf's and returned to my uniform of blue jeans and old sweaters. I rushed back to my friends who were my own age that I'd been neglecting. Nobody asked any questions, but I realized that everybody had been aware of Pepi and me as a couple.

The first people I saw were Marcia and Gene, now ensconced in their ramshackle farm in New Jersey. I began spending time with my Studio buddies, Geoffrey Horne and Marty and Susie and Lils. I'd missed hearing their stories; I wanted to share in their lives again.

I wrote some of my sprawling novel. I saw Rib on and off. But I missed Pepi terribly. I even had the urge to call him because for close to four months we'd been enmeshed in each other's lives even if we hadn't seen each other every day. For better or worse he'd propelled me to a different level in my career. But what troubled me most, and continued to for decades to come, was my father's behavior. He had cruelly interfered with my life. By giving that silly dinner party he'd destroyed my relationship with Pepi. Granted, it was probably doomed anyway, but Daddy had been out of line. I was sure he'd done it deliberately, but I never challenged him. Between us it was as if Pepi hadn't existed.

I never quite trusted my father again, although I still adored him. We behaved the same toward each other. He'd say, "Hey, baby, give your old man a kiss," and we'd embrace. He'd ask me, "What's happening, baby?" and I'd tell him, hearing my voice go childish and light. I was still acting like Daddy's girl whenever I was with him, but I was starting not to feel like one anymore.

Chapter Seventeen

I THREW MYSELF INTO my work on *Small War on Murray Hill*. I memorized my lines and posed for pictures with the rest of the cast. *Small War* was a classy stylish fantasy that would never be done on Broadway today, and even back then it couldn't last, but it was quite an amazing experience.

I kept detailed notes in my journal: "Show is rehearsing at the New Amsterdam Roof," I wrote. "It's a murky old theatre perched on the top of an office building overlooking Times Square. During the 1920s it was the home of the Ziegfeld Follies. Since then many hit shows have rehearsed here, like *Streetcar*. Starting out at the New Amsterdam is supposed to bring luck to a production.

"Because *Small War* is set during the American Revolution, our director, Gar Kanin, lectures constantly about George Washington and the Declaration of Independence in between blocking the show. The producers are spending a fortune to make sure everything is authentic, right down to elaborate Boris Aronson sets and lavish costumes by Irene Sharaff.

"I privately think we're going to need a lot of luck; the material is slight, even though the play was written by Robert Sherwood, who won four Pulitzers and is the author of one of Daddy's favorite books, *Roosevelt and Hopkins*. Gar continues to be in high spirits, even after the deaths of two older actors in the cast and Sherwood himself in November. 'Three guys croak in a show, it's a bad omen,' the stage manager told me.

"But being in the show takes my mind off my troubles. I love going to Irene Sharaff's atelier to be fitted for my costumes, which are absolutely sumptuous, all silks and satins and linens; I love learning how to walk around in a petticoat and funny buckled shoes. Every day I lunch with different members of the cast. One day I had Caesar salad at Sardi's with Jan Sterling, the bosomy star of the show. We play sisters. After we were photographed by the *New York Times*, I found out she's a member of the Actors Studio too.

"Next day hamburgers at Downey's with Michael Lewis, the gloomy son of novelist Sinclair Lewis; Warner LeRoy, very funny and manic (his father Mervyn produced *The Wizard of Oz*); and last but not least, the infinitely charming Danny Massey (son of Raymond, who's best known for his portrayal of Lincoln). Gar has loaded the production down with as many names as possible to draw attention to the play, but I'm not sure anything will help. Gar remains enthusiastic, even when the show got royally panned in Boston. He invited everybody for drinks at the Ritz, and Thornton Wilder, the author of *Our Town*, joined us and proceeded to speak about theatre and art and the wonder and necessity of it all, as well as the importance of failure. Walking back to the Colonial Theatre with Danny Massey that night, we agreed we'd been inspired."

I WAS ESPECIALLY taken with Danny; I loved acting with him on-stage. We had several spirited scenes together (which began when he climbed in a window and started flirting with me). He had a kind of grasshopper lightness when he moved. He'd inherited a dry buoyant charm from his godfather, Noël Coward, who'd raised him. Later during the Boston run I was lucky enough to spend an evening with Coward in Danny's dressing room, where he regaled us with tales of being injected with sheep's urine in Switzerland "to keep me young."

The legendary English playwright-composer-director-actor did everything with wit and flamboyance. To be with him was invigorating and exhausting. Danny said later, "When you're with Uncle Noël, you *know* he has star quality. It's the lodestone of his life."

"And what is that exactly?" I asked.

"Star quality is the ability to project, without effort, the outlines of a unique personality."

Looking back on it, I lived in a kind of dream the entire time I played in this show—even after Marty came backstage on opening night, bearing flowers and telling me, "You looked beautiful in your costumes, honey, but the play is a bomb."

The reviews were respectful, but not very good. The producers, out of respect for Sherwood, kept the play open for a while. We continued to act our hearts out and Gar would visit us every night to cheer us on. So he was standing at the back of the house one matinee when Warner LeRoy didn't show up in the middle of the second act to deliver a letter. Jan and I had to ad-lib for several minutes. I froze; Jan took over and improvised some dialogue while Gar raced up to the fourth floor of the Barrymore Theatre and found Warner deep asleep on a cot in his dressing room. He was so ashamed of what he'd done that he insisted on taking the entire cast to Frank Sinatra's midnight show at the Copa.

I'll never forget walking in through the nightclub's kitchen (à la *Goodfellas*) and out to ringside tables, where Sinatra greeted Warner and all of us personally and then began belting out his songs in true Sinatra fashion. As he sang, he lounged at the piano holding a smoking cigarette and a glass of Scotch. His voice was so supple he could take banal Tin Pan Alley songs and transform them into something very personal and poignant. I felt as if he were singing directly to me.

DESPITE OUR BEST efforts, *Small War on Murray Hill* closed after twelve performances. I felt depressed; when a show ends it's as if you've lost part of your family. I'd become especially close to Danny, who remained a lifelong friend. It pleased me to see him in London triumphing in shows as diverse as *Betrayal* and *Follies*. I kept in touch with Warner too; he would soon turn his restaurants, Maxwell's Plum and Tavern on the Green, into sparkling fantasy palaces.

But I had little time to miss anybody, because a few weeks after the demise of *Small War* I was cast in another Broadway show called *The Sin of Pat Muldoon* by John McLiam. It was about an Irish Catholic family and James Barton, an old character actor best known for creating the role of Hickey in the original *Iceman Cometh*, was playing the irascible Muldoon. He spends most of the play slowly dying in bed, but is alive enough to argue endlessly with his children about heaven and hell.

I'd won the role of Muldoon's long-suffering daughter Theresa, who cares for her father even as she is falling in love with someone he disapproves of. The part was even bigger than the one I'd had in *Small War* and it was more challenging, since I was going to sing two Irish ballads in the show a cappella. I took singing lessons every day and thought I sounded pretty good until I learned that the role of my older sister had been taken by Elaine Stritch. Elaine was a brassy, tart-tongued actress/singer who'd done only a couple of shows—among them *Bus Stop* and *Pal Joey*—and already everyone was talking about her "I've seen it all" manner and her whiskey voice. She could stop a show with her wild inventiveness and manic energy.

I thought I'd be intimidated by her, but Elaine was subdued and quiet when we were introduced. She was beanpole tall and skinny and she had acne scars on her cheeks. We discovered we had a lot in common, not the least of which was that we were both practicing Catholics and had gone to Sacred Heart.

A COUPLE OF days before rehearsal started (and just before I signed my contract), the associate producer of *Muldoon*, sleek, debonair Richard Adler, invited me for a drink. Adler was the composer and lyricist (along with Jerry Ross) for two smash hits then running simultaneously on Broadway, *The Pajama Game* and *Damn Yankees*. He'd won a couple of Tonys, so he was pretty pleased with himself.

Richard took me to Dinty Moore's and ordered champagne. We toasted each other. He said I was going to be "lovely as Theresa," and then he got down to business. He'd decided I should be "his girl" on the road. He'd have a suite at the Taft Hotel in New Haven and another suite at the Ritz when we played Boston. We'd enjoy each other. Then when the show opened on Broadway "we will be finito," he explained very calmly, and then he clasped my hand.

His proposition sounded like a variation on the casting couch, a phrase used to describe lecherous casting directors and actresses willing to trade sexual favors in return for roles. I knew this kind of thing went on all the time in show business, and it was disgusting.

I withdrew my hand from Richard's, told him that I would never agree to such an arrangement, and left him sitting by himself at Dinty Moore's. I was sure I would lose my job.

But the following morning my agent called; he informed me that although he'd put up a battle, "Dick Adler will only pay you minimum. Even though you have the second lead, you are getting the last billing." (Later when I saw the program, my name was in the tiniest print.)

So that's how he's getting back at me, I thought. *So what? I'm still going to do my damnedest.*

I came into the first rehearsal defiant, but worried that Richard might be there. He wasn't, and as far as I could tell, nobody in the production knew that he'd propositioned me. I saw him periodically throughout the run, but we never spoke of the matter again. It was as if it hadn't happened.

IT WAS SNOWING outside when the cast gathered in a rundown office on West Forty-Sixth Street. Everybody was a Studio member (James Olson, John Heldebrand, Cliff James, and Katherine Squire, once again playing my mother). The director, Jack Garfein, was Lee's special protégé. A Holocaust survivor, he'd been responsible for the Studio's first big theatrical success, *End as a Man*.

Coffee was served. That's when I noticed there was one non-Studio actor, Gerry Sarracini (who would be playing my lover). He stood apart by the window watching the snow blanket Times Square. A powerfully built man, he had a wary jug face. I went over to say hello, but he turned away. He seemed to be favoring a bandaged hand.

Just before the start of our first rehearsal, Jack cautioned, "You mustn't look at James Barton, okay? He was in a terrible fire and he lost his nose. He always wears a fake one when he's doing a performance, but in rehearsal he likes to work without it. So act natural around him."

"You mean don't ask, 'Pops—where'd your nose go?'" Elaine demanded. Everyone laughed nervously, except for Gerry.

"That's exactly what I meant," Jack told her.

At that moment Barton appeared in the doorway, a bent, white-haired old man. He shuffled toward us and then took his cap off with a flourish. "Hello there, everybody. I am so glad to be here." We murmured our hellos back, trying not to stare too hard at the two gaping black holes in his face. Jack made quick motions for us to gather around the big table in the center of the room for the first read-through.

*   *   *

WE WORKED LONG hours, but the play didn't come together. After the second week Elaine and I slipped into St. Malachy's Church to light candles and pray for the production.

Gerry Sarracini's antics didn't help our uneasy mood. He'd shamble into rehearsal sporting a black eye and he'd fly into rages with Jack over his direction. The rest of the cast started keeping their distance from him, but I couldn't—we were playing lovers. I wanted us to be able to connect to each other onstage.

"Be careful," Katherine Squire warned.

I didn't listen. I'd often bring Gerry coffee if he appeared hungover. "Thanks," he'd say. He knew I felt self-conscious whenever I sang for Pat in the play, because Elaine was onstage listening. He'd whisper, "Forget Stritch—you're not entertaining her, you're entertaining your father." That suggestion helped; it reminded me of the times I'd sung at parties for Daddy and my voice would wobble horribly until I saw my brother in a corner smiling his encouragement. Gerry did that too, nodding and smiling as I sang "Molly Malone" clear and true. "Thanks," I'd tell him afterward, and he'd shrug. "*De nada.*"

We were having problems with our own scenes; they were so underwritten. There wasn't enough dialogue to suggest our so-called illicit passion. Gerry suggested, "Let's improvise" during one of the stop-and-go run-throughs. We figured out a nice little moment. No words. We're sitting in the kitchen in the middle of the second act; Gerry's playing the guitar. He notices I'm chilly, so he puts down his guitar and wraps a sweater around my shoulders. He caresses the sweater; his hands clasp my arms just for a second and our eyes lock and then he goes back to playing the guitar. It was make-believe rapture and it seemed to work. Jack told us to keep it in the show.

Gerry and I began going to the Theatre Bar after rehearsal. I'd sit there watching him drink and then strum on his guitar. He'd be frowning, his thick, powerful fingers plucking away at the strings. I had no idea what he was thinking. He was inscrutable. Whenever he spoke to me, it was slowly, almost lazily, through half-closed eyes. I decided after a while that the world seemed too bright for him to handle. He shied away from talking about himself. Sometimes I was afraid that if I asked too personal a question he might slap my face. But I did discover he hated phonies (as did my brother), and that before he became an actor in Canada, he'd been a professional boxer.

The happiest times for us before we left for New Haven were the nights at Birdland or the Five Spot. Gerry loved jazz. We'd sit in the smoky darkness listening to turbulent, lyrical, raucous music, and between sets he'd introduce me to his friends—the drug addicts; the black trumpet player, his face shiny with sweat; the fighters from Stillman's Gym. Oh, I'll never forget those nights. They seemed to gratify my hunger for experience devoid of thinking. Gerry never once touched me or kissed me, and whenever he left the room, I was afraid I'd never see him again. He was so busy burning himself up in front of my eyes. Nobody could live at his pace and stay the course, and every so often in bursts of intimacy he said as much. He seemed to want me to know this.

WE PREMIERED *The Sin of Pat Muldoon* in New Haven to mediocre reviews. Playwright John McLiam attempted some rewrites; we tried them when we opened ten days later at the Colonial Theatre in Boston, where we received even more mediocre reviews. By that time Jack had decided to "freeze the show"—no more repairs. We all thought the show was worse; cast morale sank.

Only Elaine seemed jubilant; she was stealing everybody's scenes with her brassy hard-boiled performance, plus she'd fallen madly in love with Ben Gazzara and he seemed equally crazy about her. Sexy, magnetic, hard-drinking Ben with his deep, rich, taunting voice and Italian good looks—he'd just finished a successful run in *Cat on a Hot Tin Roof* playing the enigmatic Brick. Now he was either in Elaine's dressing room or watching her from the wings whenever she was on. After the curtain came down, they'd often get roaring drunk and loudly proclaim their boozy passion for each other.

One night Elaine insisted I join them in her suite at the Ritz, and she also asked Gerry. The evening started off by Elaine ordering sandwiches from room service, and then she passed out martinis. I'd never had one. When I took the first swallow, the gin burned my gullet and I choked.

"You don't know how to drink, do you, kid?" Ben asked. He was sprawled on a couch smoking a cigar and already three sheets to the wind.

"Of course I know how to drink," I insisted. Daddy had given me my first taste of liquor when I was fourteen, an Old Fashioned. And he would frequently give me sips of his late-night drink, Jack Daniel's on ice.

"So take a man-sized swallow, twerp," Ben teased.

Gerry was observing me from a far corner of the suite. "Leave the girl alone," he ordered Ben quietly. Gerry had a strong gravelly voice, a commanding voice even though he was speaking softly.

"Why don't you fuck off?" Ben retorted. His words slurred.

Elaine was busy mixing up another batch of martinis. "Boys, boys!" she trilled tipsily. "Patti is gonna learn how to hold her liquor!"

With that, Elaine began dancing around the room shaking the martini shaker up and down like a castanet. "It gets better and better, don't it, Benny! What did Tennessee say? You wait till you hear that click in your brain . . . and then you start feeling relaxed and you feel almost tired, but you aren't scared or anxious anymore and nothing can harm you!" Elaine bent and twirled, still holding the martini shaker—her long slender legs flying, her blond curls bobbing. She went around the room refilling our glasses. When she finished, she cried out, "Oh, Gawd, do I love to drink! Do I love to drink!"

(Elaine didn't stop drinking for many years until she suffered a severe hypoglycemic attack and almost died. When she recovered, she joined AA and fought to stay sober for the next decade. I once asked her what she wanted most when she got to heaven. "A big fucking bar, sis, with every kinda liquor imaginable! Oh, do I miss drinking—I miss it every goddamn day of my life!" The year before she died, she confided fiercely that she'd started drinking again, but furtively—secretly. "Had to! Had to! Had to have that one little drink every night." Then she rolled her eyes. "That's how I survive. Do you hear me?")

The evening progressed. Ben and Elaine grew impatient with Gerry's dourness. He sat in his corner, drinking steadily right along with them but not saying a word.

"You are a boring drunk, you know that, Gerry Sarracini?" Elaine declared. "I wish I hadn't asked ya."

Gerry looked at her balefully. "I only came to make sure you weren't gonna fuck with Patti."

"You don't think Patti can take care of herself?" Elaine demanded. "She's stronger than you realize, asshole."

I sat there barely able to focus. Did I really come across as strong?

"Patti!" Elaine bellowed. "Aren't you stronger than we realize?"

When I didn't answer, she singsonged, "You remind me of myself when I was your age—pure innocent as the driven snow, but with demons underneath. You had to go to Confession all the time . . . Back in Michigan my parents taught me how to drink. I learned from them."

"My father is an alcoholic." I stopped. Why was I saying this? So they might feel closer to me or that I might feel closer to them?

I sank back in my chair wondering why drunks were such gifted, lovable bright people. Men and women with brains and talent, yet totally focused on destroying themselves . . . I'd watched Daddy progress as an alcoholic for years—the endless cocktail parties he and Mama gave in New York and California. Daddy would get loaded, but he never seemed drunk until very late, and then after Bart's suicide, he'd had blackouts and couldn't function.

In front of me Ben stumbled around, trying without success to re-light his cigar as Elaine primped in front of a mirror. I noticed Gerry sat morosely staring into his drink. They were all lost in their own little worlds . . . and I was too. Tonight I crazily, irrationally, wanted to see if I could drink and maybe it would make me feel better, melt my reserve, my numbness—maybe I could also understand *why* my father drank, why Elaine drank, why *anyone* drank. "Cuz we're all scared shitless of life, of going to hell," Elaine had confided once.

BY THREE A.M., Elaine was staggering around the room holding forth on her love for Ben. "I was a virgin until I hopped in the sack with Benny," she announced. When nobody reacted, she cried out, "Ya hear me, babies?"

I stared at her. "I don't believe that. How old are you?"

"I am thirty fucking years old, sis! I was raised by nuns at the Convent of the Sacred Heart and my uncle is Cardinal Stritch, for fuck's sake! I was taught to believe that sex was bad, sex was dirty, sex was a sin until you got married."

After hearing that, I downed another martini and confessed I'd married my first husband because I felt I had to. "I'd gone to bed with him and I knew I'd committed a mortal sin. That's why we eloped."

Elaine screamed with laughter. "And didn't you regret it? Didn't you realize you'd made a mistake?"

I nodded. She poured me yet another martini and I drank it.

"How you feelin'—feelin' no pain?"

"I'm feeling a little nauseous."

"It'll pass—drink up!"

So I tried to keep up with her and to keep up with everybody else in the room. Elaine exhorted, "Keep goin', Patti baby, it'll put hair on your chest!"

AROUND FOUR A.M., Ben seemed to turn cold sober. He recited the "To Be or Not to Be" soliloquy from *Hamlet* and then he passed out. Soon Elaine passed out as well and began to snore.

Gerry remained in his corner drinking steadily. Every so often he'd stare hard at me. I'd stare back. A kind of electricity flowed between us. I was drunk, but I felt aroused; my skin prickled; my heart pounded so loudly it seemed to vibrate in my eardrums.

By now the room was littered with plates of half-eaten turkey sandwiches; a gin bottle rolled around on the floor. Then I realized I was very nauseous and staggered into the bathroom, where I heaved and retched and then collapsed, hugging the toilet bowl like a life preserver. Moments later Gerry stumbled in and held my head while I vomited some more. Then he washed my face very gently with a wet towel and half carried me back into the living room, where he deposited me on a couch. I watched as he poured himself another drink.

"I haven't touched you all these weeks because I knew if we ever got together there would be trouble," he said.

"Trouble?" My voice sounded so weak. "What kind of trouble?"

He sat down and put his arms around me. "I am the worst kind of drunk. Worse than Ben or Elaine. They enjoy drinking. I don't. But I have to drink," he told me. He was very drunk, but he was an amazingly controlled drunk, like my father.

We left Elaine's suite and walked out into the street. It was snowing heavily. We were both staying at the Touraine, a cheaper hotel not far from the Ritz. We went back to my room and fell asleep. From then on we were inseparable; we even decided to share a dressing room.

After the show we'd go back to the hotel and crawl into bed. Gerry would play the guitar and then we'd pass a bottle of whiskey back and forth until we got a wonderful buzz and then we'd make love. I'd count the number of times we made love during those nights because each time was different and we experienced deeper pleasure, sometimes so hot it seemed to burn our skins. We were brimming over with desire. Afterward we'd just hold each other; we didn't talk, two lost animals cuddling in a hotel cave.

Once while I was lying naked in Gerry's arms, my father called me from New York. I usually phoned him when I was out of town, but this time I hadn't. Daddy wanted to know if everything was all right. I said it was. I had the impulse to cry out, "I'm in love for the first time!" But I swallowed my words.

In retrospect Gerry filled a more powerful need than Pepi ever did, because Gerry was an alcoholic. I could take care of him as I tried to do with my father. I could take a drink away from Gerry when he got too soused; I could take his cigarette away before it burned his finger. Being drunk and miserable was a familiar condition to me. I knew how to handle such men. But of course at the time I wasn't aware of any of this.

WHEN I RETURNED to New York I made the mistake of bringing Gerry home. The meeting was a disaster. He came over to the duplex very hungover. He didn't say much and he bolted right after the meal, saying he had an important appointment to get to.

As soon as he was gone Mama lit into me. Daddy did nothing to stop her.

"Another long-suffering artist!" she cried out, her eyes filling with tears. "You seem to invest every one of your losers with noble qualities. When will you settle down with a decent, responsible man who will take care of you and give you children? Right now you are living to be possessed and consumed."

With that I jumped to my feet, trembling with anger and frustration because I didn't know how to answer her. I put on my coat and left the duplex, with Daddy calling out to me, "Don't do anything rash!"

I knew where Gerry would be, at the Bolivar, his fleabag hotel. It catered to drug addicts and prostitutes, and it was on Broadway and Sixty-Fourth Street, where Lincoln Center is now. In those days the area was dense with tenements and delis, some Chinese takeout places, and numerous falling-down bars.

Gerry was lolling on his bed and playing his guitar. But he wasn't drunk; he was cold sober.

"Your mom is a piece of work." He chuckled.

"How come you're not drinking tonight?"

"Want to be able to see you, feel you, touch you . . . Love you with a clear head."

"Oh my God."

"Yeah, oh my God. I surprise myself sometimes. We better take advantage of this. I don't know when I'm gonna be like this again."

We spent a beautiful night together.

THE OPENING OF *Pat Muldoon* was a disaster. I'd been playing assuredly in front of audiences for four weeks, but opening night I froze when it came to singing my song at the end of the first act. I sat next to James Barton on his bed and stared blindly out at the sea of faces. I could not for the life of me remember the opening lyric of "Molly Malone." Barton waited for a couple of minutes and then sat bolt upright on his pillows and, in true musical comedy fashion, belted out, "In Dublin's fair city, where the girls are so pretty . . ."

The curtain came down. Jack Garfein and John McLiam rushed backstage to confront me as Barton raged, "If you ever do that again, girlie, I will knock yer block off!"

Moments later Jack and the playwright descended on me angrily. "You changed the meaning of the first act! Pat is supposed to be dying. Pat isn't well enough to sing a song."

I slunk back to my dressing room, sure that nothing worse could happen now—but I hadn't bargained on Elaine. She'd always hated the monologue she had at the end of the third act, which was directed at Barton. She'd been threatening to do something about it, and in the last five minutes of the show, she did. Sashaying center stage, she swooped over and held Barton down on the bed, adlibbing a funny, scathing torrent of words designed to total her father and tell him off for all the stupid things he'd done in his life.

The entire cast gathered in the wings to watch, goggle-eyed, as Barton thrashed on the pillows. Elaine kept at him, flaunting her long, slender legs and tossing her blonde curls; she brayed, she yelled, she even sang a few bars of a song. The controlling daughter let her old bastard daddy have it. It was completely improvised and it brought down the house.

Afterward we all crowded outside her dressing room to hear her explanation. "What were you trying to do, Elaine?" the playwright wailed. "You have ruined my play!"

"I don't know what you are talking about," Elaine replied demurely. She was seated in front of her dressing table staring impassively at her reflection in the glass.

Jack Garfein was irate. "You gotta apologize, Elaine. What you did is not acceptable. You changed the play . . . you . . ."

Elaine whirled on him, eyes blazing. "I don't know what you are talking about! Now please get out of my dressing room!"

The reviews were terrible, except for Elaine's. She received raves. *Pat Muldoon* closed four nights later. After the last performance Gerry and I wandered over to the Theatre Bar and sat at "our" table surrounded by shopping bags full of our stuff from the show—makeup, dying flowers, and telegrams.

Gerry seemed quiet and depressed.

"What's the matter?"

He told me swiftly that we were finished. "I don't want to fuck up your life."

"You're not fucking up my life! I love you."

"I *would* fuck up your life. I fuck up everybody's life if they stay with me. Trust me." He got up. "I mean it. This is good-bye. Don't follow me, don't call me. This is it." With that, he left the bar, calling over his shoulder, "You can keep the guitar."

AFTER GERRY LEFT me, I felt bereft; my life seemed so painful that the only thing I could think of to do was to escape back into the Actors Studio and be enveloped by the manic energy of the place. There was always so much going on—such an abundance and variety of talent—it continued to amaze me. Norman Mailer was writing plays there for the newly formed Playwright/Directors Unit, headed by Kazan and Arthur Penn. I immediately got involved with Mike Gazzo's *All That Jazz*, improvising scenes with George Peppard. And of course the Studio remained in the news, mainly because Marilyn was still attending classes. Reporters had sneaked in to hear Lee talk. There had been accounts in the press that he was encouraging eccentric, uncontrollable behavior—that actors were working out "personal problems" onstage.

A portrait of the Studio actor was emerging in the public's mind as a rebel against refinement, decorum, and gentility. Kazan defended the Method as a revolt against romantic rhetorical theatre, and Harold Clurman had added that this rejection of gentility and decorum was another step on the road to a greater "reality," truthfulness, directness of expression. That said, to many outsiders Studio actors were crazy mixed-up kids.

But I didn't think so. There was the astonishing morning when Lee directed Anne Bancroft and Viveca Lindfors in *The Stronger* by August Strindberg, a tour de force in which Annie's character remained mute as Viveca's unleashed a boiling torrent of words about their rivalry. All the while, Lee softly advised "not to give anything away." Annie chafed under that restriction, growling as Viveca continued to goad her. Finally Annie could stand it no longer and struck Viveca; the two women struggled, then started punching and slapping each other. It was so violent that Shelley Winters screamed, "Stop it! They are hurting each other!" Lee thundered back, "Let them continue. This is really a fight. Two washerwomen couldn't do it better." (In subsequent sessions Viveca and Annie continued to work on the scene, confiding that their fight had pushed them to a new level of acting.)

I was inspired to try something new in session too. I'd adapted the last chapter of a long-forgotten pulpy novel for myself be-cause the heroine was so vibrant and alluring, and she had an angry monologue directed at her stepfather, who was trying to seduce her.

None of my friends were available to work with me, so I chose a middle-aged actor I barely knew to be my partner. His name was Ernie. We didn't have much time; everybody had projects, so the downstairs rehearsal room was almost fully booked. We ended up rehearsing for only two hours.

Ernie had difficulty memorizing lines, and he was annoyed by the fact that I had most of the dialogue. "I'm basically the straight man," he complained.

I suggested we improvise. I'd been doing a lot of improvs with George Peppard in Mike Gazzo's play earlier that month and I felt a new confidence in myself, but Ernie didn't. He balked even when I told him there was no right way to do this kind of playacting. "You're simply in the moment," I said. "Let's experiment with the situation. It invariably intensifies the reality onstage." I didn't know he would take me so literally.

As usual, the Studio was packed. The scene began: Ernie as my stepfather attempts to embrace me; I struggle with him, telling him off. But I'd said only a couple of lines when Ernie, in response, began hitting me. He'd never done that in rehearsal. His blows immediately triggered memories of Jason when he'd catch me off-balance with slaps. Then I'd cower to protect myself, to ward off more blows.

But this morning I found myself fighting back, kicking and crying and pulling Ernie's hair until he yelped. He hit me again. I grabbed his hand and bit his wrist, and after that I managed to speak a few more lines of the actual monologue.

Ernie was so surprised by my vehemence that he lost his balance and toppled to the floor. Luckily he was really out of shape, so I took advantage of this, hopping on top of him and straddling him as one would a bicycle. I began pinching his forearms hard. He huffed and puffed. "For Christ's sake, stop," he bleated, writhing under me. I kept on squeezing his flesh.

God, this felt good! I was finally in control. In the past I'd always been pushed to the breaking point before I protected myself. I hadn't left Jason until he almost strangled me to death.

For a few minutes Ernie made a tremendous effort to move out from under me, but I wouldn't let him. We rocked back and forth until Ernie grew so exhausted that he stopped fighting me and his body went limp. I gazed down at his red, perspiring face and a triumphant groan filled my throat. I opened my mouth for the be-reaved creature inside me; the groan turned into an exultant scream and I began to cry, tears rolling down my cheeks.

A patter of applause rippled through the membership (applause was something that wasn't encouraged at the Studio, but it meant people had liked what they'd seen). There was no point in continuing any further, so I hopped off Ernie's inert body and struggled to my feet. Ernie followed. We tottered over to Lee to hear what he had to say.

Lee was smiling at me. "Darling," he said, "you were alive and in the moment. This was the best acting I've ever seen you do."

"I wasn't acting, Lee," I heard myself saying in a trembling but clear voice. "Ernie was *hurting* me. What I did had nothing to do with acting."

With that Lee held up his hand imperiously. "No, you weren't 'acting,' darling. *You were being. Being* in character, experiencing genuine emotion before you act. Before you inhabit a part." He glared at me.

I glared back, shaking, quivering with so much emotion I felt incapable of continuing our discussion, so I ran out of the theatre. Nobody stopped me. I could hear Lee calmly questioning Ernie as I ran down the stairs and out into the street. My body ached from Ernie's blows. I got as far as Forty-Fourth Street and Ninth Avenue before I realized somebody was calling, "Hey, Patti, wait up! I wanna talk to you!"

I stopped, and there was Marty Fried jogging up to me, rumpled, swarthy, handsome, his expression concerned. For years, unless he was working, Marty attended sessions. If anyone knew what Lee was talking about, Marty did.

Now we were vaulting through traffic to the other side of West Forty-Fourth and into the local greasy spoon where we often gathered, heading to our regular table by the window. Marty ordered coffee and doughnuts for two.

After we settled ourselves, Marty proclaimed, "You had an emotional breakthrough—you know that, don't you?"

Yes, I thought, but I was bothered by the distance between actor and character. The inevitable gap between *simply being* (as Lee said) and *giving a performance*. This hadn't been clarified for me. It was as if to be "yourself" in a real and believable situation was enough.

"Lee can be confusing," I told Marty. "I'm not sure I know what he's saying half the time."

"It's like learning Chinese. You gotta be patient."

"I've been working professionally for almost two years," I blurted. "I still don't know what I'm doing onstage!"

That thought silenced both of us. For a while we didn't say anything. I realized I had come close to cracking through my frozen emotions, but it didn't mean that I knew how to act.

"Maybe I'll study with Sandy Meisner for a while," I confided to Marty.

Marty shrugged. "Most people end up doing that. But you'll be back."

SANDY MEISNER WAS Lee's archrival; they'd both been members of the Group Theatre. They disagreed so violently about how to teach Stanislavski's Method that they no longer spoke. Sandy believed Lee overemphasized personal emotions at the expense of other key elements in acting. Sandy's approach: *The Reality of Doing*—creating truthful behavior within the imaginary circumstances of a play.

I made an appointment to see Sandy almost immediately and found myself in the presence of a tall regal man who chain-smoked Pall Malls. When he discovered I was a member of the Actors Studio, he didn't want me in his classes. I pleaded that I had to study with him, that I had no training. I was working a lot, but I needed to be taught the basics—"Lee doesn't teach the basics," I said.

"That's right," Sandy snapped. "You will learn to *act* with me. At the Studio you work on yourself."

I confided I might have been accepted as a member of the Studio because of my "quality," not because of my talent.

"Very possibly," Sandy nodded. "You are a lovely-looking girl. Hides a multitude of sins."

He finally agreed to let me join his professional classes, but he tried to persuade me not to return to the Studio "ever! Lee supports the cult of personality. The place is a hotbed of celebrity fuckers and Lee is the worst. And you know it."

I didn't answer, but I knew I couldn't promise I'd never go back to the Studio. Many Studio members—Julie Harris, Eli Wallach, Lee Grant, Sydney Pollack—had trained with Sandy at the Neighborhood Playhouse before they studied with Lee.

I studied with Sandy very diligently and I learned a lot. His teaching was simple, direct, and not pretentious. He stressed good diction and bodily grace; he made me aware of character motivation and breaking down a script.

I WAS ABLE to test what I was learning with Sandy quite soon. I got a great job on a TV soap opera, a running part on a CBS show called *The Secret Storm*. For a couple of months I played the ubiquitous girl next door. Except she was a rather neurotic girl next door, so I could occasionally chew up the scenery.

The Secret Storm was directed by the chain-smoking Gloria Monty, who went on to be part of that show for forty years. I'd never been directed by a woman before, and Gloria brought all sorts of feminine insights into my character, including, "She's very tightly wound; she has one goal in life—to lose her virginity." I tried to "play" that whenever I could, and it worked.

It was the so-called golden age of live television, and you never knew what would happen next. Christopher Plummer (who also worked in soaps) said it was like doing summer stock with cameras. I remember one sequence when the character I was playing became suicidal and jumped out a window screaming bloody murder (the camera didn't catch me landing on six thick mattresses). I was paid $500 extra for that jump. I received hundreds of letters from worried fans concerned I'd hurt myself. Meanwhile my character recovered and went on to suffer more emotional turmoil.

It was a fourteen-hour day, up at dawn to rehearse and block the show, have a dress rehearsal, then do it live at three p.m. I had to memorize up to forty pages of dialogue a night; sometimes my memory would fail me (as it did most of the actors in the cast), so we invented frantically, often improvising entire scenes. During one show I was moving into camera range carrying a breakfast tray to bring to my ailing mother when I tripped and the tray crashed to the floor. Zero in on close-up of my face ad-libbing, "I'll be back in a flash with some coffee." Blackout while Gloria bellowed from the control room, "After the commercial, tell her you're sorry and you will clean the mess later."

I learned a lot doing *The Secret Storm*. I couldn't take hours preparing as I did at the Studio. I learned to think on my feet and forgot about being nervous. The accident-prone quality of live TV made me feel as if I was living on the edge as an actress.

"Nothing better than a job, even if the part doesn't always make sense, huh, baby?" Elaine Stritch commented. She was working nonstop too. We had continued to see each other. We'd go to a late Sunday Mass, have breakfast at Schrafft's, and then hike through Central Park. Elaine loved to walk, usually in slacks and a windbreaker with a cap perched on her blond curls, no makeup, and huge dark glasses. She kept up a stream of conversation about the heady highs and lows of show business. Elaine was timeless, fearless, on a roll, climbing steadily up the ladder of stardom and celebrity, rarely referring to the darker aspects of her life battling alcoholism.

She was having an affair with Gig Young; Noël Coward was

writing a show for her. I talked to her about Gerry: "I need to see him—I miss him terribly." "So call him, baby."

Elaine and I remained friends until she died in 2014 at the age of eighty-nine.

THEN IN THE winter of 1957, Christmas Eve to be exact, Gerry phoned me. I hadn't heard from him in months. He'd just opened on Broadway in *Romanoff and Juliet*. I started to congratulate him on great reviews, but he interrupted to ask if we could meet for a drink that night after the show at his favorite bar on West Sixty-Fourth Street. Of course I said yes, even though I'd never liked the place; it was gloomy and chaotic and seemed to be peopled with only drug addicts, prostitutes, and drunks. But Gerry felt comfortable there and knew many of the regulars. He'd often spend hours listening to their tales of woe.

I found him waiting for me at the back; he looked tired and hungover, but when he saw me he jumped to his feet, drawing me down into the booth. We embraced but didn't speak. I was thinking, *Oh God, maybe we'll have another chance for something special to happen to us . . . Maybe we'll have the opportunity for both of us to fully realize ourselves together.*

I was about to tell Gerry what I was thinking, but he murmured, "Shush"; then he kissed me very gently on the forehead. "I'll get us some drinks."

I watched him cross the long smoke-filled room, a big hulking giant of a man with muscular shoulders and curly hair. There were so many couples packing the bar that he was soon engulfed by the crowd and I could no longer see him.

As I waited, I watched a heavyset, swarthy man with tattoos stagger out of the john and begin threatening a beat-up woman with a scarred face. Some black and Puerto Rican boys frugged near the jukebox. One of them had a knife sticking out of his back pocket.

A half-hour went by and Gerry never reappeared with our drinks. I grew increasingly nervous. Then I heard a commotion at the far end of the room. I couldn't see clearly—it was so dark—but heard a thump and a scream and someone called, "Hey, guys!" I knew I had to get out of there. I ran through the bar and out onto the street. It was snowing and then I saw a man pummeling another man lying on the sidewalk. It was Gerry. Aside from feeling sick, I had this fantasy urge to leap over and save him, but of course I couldn't. People crowded around, a cop car pulled up, then an ambulance, and Gerry was carried away.

HE WASN'T AT Roosevelt Hospital, where I'd been told he'd been taken. After another couple of hours of fruitless searching I returned to the East Side. It was around eight in the morning and bitterly cold. It was also Christmas Day, so church bells were ringing in the Church of St. Vincent Ferrer. When we'd lived on Sixty-Eighth Street, it had been our family's parrish; I often went to Mass there with Daddy. It was also down the block from my own apartment, so I still prayed there pretty regularly.

Now I climbed the steep stone stairs and into the nave. There were nuns in the chapel at the side of the nave; they were lighting candles for the first Mass. I knelt down in one of the ornate carved pews at the back of the church and had the overwhelming realization of how important my faith was. I'd always believed I could talk to God, that I had a personal relationship with Him. My non-Catholic friends kidded me about that. I would tell them, "Look, I know you can't reach God directly all the time—you have to go through patron saints and all sorts of religious experiences—and every so often I can catch *glimpses of God*."

Memories flooded back. Of my teenage self rushing into the same ornate pew at the back of the church after I eloped with Jason; I'd knelt there pleading with God to help me explain my reckless act to my parents. And then I'd prayed for my brother after his violent death, and lit candles and kept on asking, "Why? Why?" And now I asked God to please save Gerry, and then I burst into tears. Because Daddy always said, "Don't ask God for favors. You get what God thinks is best for you."

Did He want Gerry to die? I couldn't believe that. Gerry was a good person. Didn't that count for something? I stayed in the church praying until Mass started, and then I left and returned to my apartment.

I didn't even take off my coat; I lay down on my unmade bed, my heart pounding so loudly that I experienced reverberations in my ears. My parents called. I was expected for holiday lunch. I played sick. "Terrible flu. I have been throwing up all night." Then an actor friend of Gerry's phoned and told me Gerry had died of a brain concussion and the man who'd hit him had been arrested.

I SUBSEQUENTLY LEARNED more details about Gerry's death from a *Daily News* feature. Apparently a two-hundred-pound laborer named Monroe Gibson admitted to the police that he'd knocked Gerry out with one punch right outside the Broadway bar. Gerry and a friend of his, ex-boxer Tommy Bell, were on the street talking. Gibson wanted to get into the bar, but couldn't; Gerry told him it was past closing time and he couldn't go in. That's when the fight began. Gibson was ultimately charged with homicide.

FOR THE NEXT couple of days I stayed in my apartment. Friends kept calling and leaving messages. I didn't answer most calls, but I did listen to Elaine's. "Where are ya, babe? Don't fall too far down into a hole. The hurt may always be there, but you will get used to it." I did.

Then Mama appeared bearing hot soup in a thermos. I was so glad to see her I felt like hugging her, but I didn't. She was all bundled up in her mink, blond hair swept off her proud little face, bright red lipstick on her mouth. She looked amazing.

After bustling around and pouring the soup into a mug, she insisted on washing my face and hands with a warm towel. Then she plumped up the pillows on my bed and made me lie back and drink the soup.

"Feel better now, lamb-pie?"

I remembered the times she'd nursed my brother and me through colds and flu and chicken pox. I had flashes of our nursery in Berkeley with its view of the San Francisco Bay and Bart and me being served lovely suppers on trays.

"So." Mama shrugged off her mink. "You really did love him, didn't you?" Her voice was surprisingly compassionate.

I couldn't speak.

She shook her head. "Terrible ending. I'm sorry. I'm truly sorry."

"But you didn't even like him."

"That has nothing to do with it."

"What's going to happen to me, Mama? Why do I always choose the wrong man?"

She didn't answer; she just took me in her arms and held me so I could cry and cry and cry.

"I wish I could cry," she said after I had cried all I could and blown my nose. She wiped my cheeks with the towel.

"I have rarely cried," she announced. "My father said it was weak to cry and I wanted to be strong for him, so I have always held back. So I didn't cry when he died, although I loved him more than anyone in the world, and I didn't cry when Bart . . ." Her mouth tightened. "Saul said it was good to cry. I cried when we said goodbye, but that was long ago."

"You still think about Saul, don't you?" I'd almost forgotten about Dr. Saul, Mama's longtime lover in California.

"Oh, yes." Although they hadn't seen each other in five years,

Mama and Saul communicated by phone and letter, and she thought about him every day. She said she loved him passionately, but it was a different kind of love from that which she felt for Daddy. She smiled very sadly when she said that and added that I wouldn't understand what she meant now, "but someday you will." (She was right. I did.) "Saul made it possible for me to go on and continue as your father's wife," Mama continued. "You won't understand that now either, but someday you will." (As I do decades later, remembering my own infidelities and secrets, the longings I had for men other than my three husbands.)

"Oh Mama, I care so, I feel so, about the men I love."

"You should care. You are a beautiful, sensitive spirit. But," she added, "you have to face reality in these romances. This Gerry fellow was a big drinker and a brawler. There were bound to be problems. That other man, Pepi, was *married*. That was the reality of *that* situation." She laughed. "I like to think I am both realistic and romantic. Otherwise I couldn't survive. You have got to start assessing the situations you're in with a man—figuring out what the hell you are doing. When I was a crime reporter, I got involved with some real bastards. They were very seductive. I knew they were; I was very aware of what I was doing, so they could not take advantage of me."

She paused again. "In the end—you have to pay a price for being in love. It never comes easy."

We continued to talk late into the evening. When she left I thanked her for coming. She told me I shouldn't be such a stranger and that she was here for me whenever I needed her. I loved her very much in that moment and ever after, although we continued to have brutal arguments and never-ending disagreements, mostly about men.

Chapter Eighteen

I T TOOK ME a while to get over Gerry. For months after he died, I moped around; I was very lonely. Then I started dating a French photographer named Michel. We both agreed we weren't going to be serious, we were just friends. We were also seeing other people. But then we went to bed and I got pregnant.

I'd rarely taken precautions when I had sex. Stupid, but there you are. I was twenty-four and had been sleeping around pretty indiscriminately ever since my divorce. I'd gone to a gynecologist once to find out about contraceptives and I'd used a diaphragm for a while, but the diaphragm kept slipping. It wasn't comfortable and I stopped using it. I'd been very lucky. Now I wasn't so lucky anymore.

The day I found out I was pregnant, my agent phoned excitedly to say I'd been cast in a movie called *The Nun's Story* starring Audrey Hepburn. I would be playing Audrey's best friend at the convent. It was difficult under the circumstances to share my agent's giddiness, but I forced myself to listen to what else she was saying: "It's a Warner Brothers movie—very big—Fred Zinnemann is directing. The movie will start shooting in Rome next month."

That's when I knew I was going to have to make one of the most important decisions of my life. Only if I terminated my pregnancy would I be able to play Audrey Hepburn's best friend. I couldn't ignore what was going on in my body. Already my belly seemed a bit distended.

I didn't tell my mother—that was out of the question. Of course I told Michel; he was properly sympathetic. We discussed the situation at length. We both knew we weren't in love—we couldn't commit to each other and neither one of us wanted to take responsibility for raising a child. I never considered being a single mom (that was almost unheard of in those days). The only other alternative was abortion.

I'd never thought about abortion until I had to have one. I'd never thought about going to hell either. The Church considered abortion a sin, so if I had an abortion, I would have a mortal sin on my soul and I wouldn't be forgiven unless I went to Confession.

It's hard to describe what the atmosphere was like back in 1958 vis-à-vis abortion. Nobody, but *nobody*, talked about it. There was so much stigma attached to the subject that women who had abortions believed they were "bad," as did I. After I got pregnant, I'd stare at my reflection in the mirror and a terrified, confused young woman stared back at me. I couldn't sleep and started biting my nails to the quick, something I hadn't done since I was married to Jason.

I was scared. In 1958 abortion was illegal; you took a big medical risk if you had one. There was so much misinformation and there were so many dangerous "abortion mills." I heard a ghastly story from a former high school classmate who'd gotten a punctured uterus from some amateur in Chinatown. He had poked at her insides with a catheter. Luckily she survived.

I HONESTLY CAN'T remember all that I did in the next weeks as Michel and I sought out abortionists. But somehow I tried to go on living my life, having dinner with my parents and attending sessions at the Actors Studio.

My agent kept filling me in with more details about *The Nun's Story*. Peter Finch would be costarring with Audrey, and almost every major character actress I could think of was playing a nun: Dame Edith Evans, Peggy Ashcroft, Mildred Dunnock, Beatrice Straight, Patricia Collinge, Margaret Phillips. These women were all remarkable artists; I was thrilled to be joining their ranks.

Then I received my script and I read and reread it. It took my mind off my troubles for a while. The screenplay by Robert Anderson was based on the bestselling novel *The Nun's Story* by Kathryn C. Hulme. It told the story of Sister Luke (Audrey), a strong-willed young woman who joins a celebrated nursing order of nuns. As World War II approaches, she is sent to a hospital in the Belgian Congo, where she passes many trials—spiritual, medical, political—especially when she assists a charismatic doctor (Peter Finch) who shakes her faith, a faith that is enmeshed in the vows of poverty, chastity, and obedience.

I would be playing Sister Simone, who befriends Sister Luke while they are both young postulants. Their devotion to God keeps warring with their rebellious natures. Sister Simone leaves the convent years before Sister Luke finally does. It is virtually impossible for either of them to hold to the vows of obedience.

I thought Bob had done a compelling job dramatizing the ordeals of self-sacrifice that nuns must endure, and I was personally grateful to him. After seeing me in *Pat Muldoon,* he'd told Fred Zinnemann I should audition for the part of Simone.

But I wasn't screen-tested. Instead I'd been photographed in a nun's flowing black habit and white wimple by Vandamm, then Broadway's greatest portraitist. Fred said he'd chosen me because I resembled a Burne-Jones painting. Apparently Burne-Jones painted young women who were "ethereal, wistful, angelic, and otherworldly." I may have appeared that way in the photograph, but I sure as hell didn't feel like it in real life as Michel and I continued going over lists of abortionists.

EVERYBODY RECOMMENDED A legendary abortionist in Pennsylvania because his operating room was clean and safe and he charged only $100, but for some reason he was unavailable. Some women we spoke to had traveled out of the country to places like San Juan, Havana, even Tokyo. I ended up choosing a doctor in Manhattan suggested by a college friend. He was "really good," she said, and he was trustworthy. The cost: $500 in cash. Michel agreed to pay.

I spoke to the doctor on the phone. When he learned I was in the first trimester, he said it would be no problem. I was to fast the night before; the operation was called a D&C. I would be in the office for about four hours and the operation would require heavy sedation. He assured me it wouldn't hurt too much, "maybe a little cramping." He did not tell me that the operation would include an electric suction machine and some very sharp instruments. When I explained I had to fly to Rome in less than two weeks for a job, he said I should come right away.

I went by myself; Michel had an assignment, but he said he'd check up on me later and wished me luck. It was all very impersonal.

The doctor's office was in a brownstone on East Seventy-Second Street between Lexington and Park. I rang the buzzer. A voice on the intercom asked, "Who's there?" I gave my name, and after much clicking of locks and the unbolting of a door, a nurse let me in and sat me down in the nondescript waiting room. I was surprised to see another woman waiting too. Middle-aged, with sad pouchy eyes. She felt it necessary to whisper that she wasn't going to have an abortion; she was picking up a friend.

As if on cue the friend appeared from an inner room. She was young and freckled and sobbing uncontrollably. The middle-aged woman ran to her.

I was hustled away by the nurse, who murmured, "Sorry about that," and then she asked for the money. I gave it to her in an envelope, five hundred-dollar bills. She counted them, thanked me, and then led me into another room, telling me to take off my clothes and put on a hospital gown.

I remember little after that, but I do remember Frank Sinatra records were playing the entire time as I lay on the white-sheeted operating table, legs splayed apart. Very bright lights. Before I went under, I noticed the doctor needed a shave. He was cheerful but businesslike. He assured me, as he washed his hands and put on rubber gloves, "Won't take too long, blondie."

I closed my eyes. Even though I was pretty much knocked out by the anesthesia, the scraping and sucking was excruciating. When I woke up, I initially felt relieved, but then sadness enveloped me, as well as a feeling of loss so powerful and painful I couldn't believe it. And then I thought, *I may never be able to have a baby. I have probably ruined my chances of ever becoming a mother.* I began to cry.

I was now lying in an alcove in what I supposed was the recovery room. I was surprised to see another girl next to me on a cot. She was being minded by a black man feeding her ice chips. I couldn't stop crying and the nurse came in to chide me. "Please stop. You are upsetting the patients in the waiting room."

"I'm hurting," I sobbed. My womb seemed to be on fire; it was throbbing and cramping. I kept on crying until the doctor came in and, in businesslike fashion, stuck his hand up me and began massaging my womb.

"It will stop cramping soon, I promise," he said. And thank God it did.

Before I left, he gave me pills to take to keep me from hemorrhaging. He warned me that the high altitudes on the transatlantic flight to Rome could be harmful. "The stitches in your vagina might burst. You must take the pills." I said I would.

I'd arranged to have Lily Lodge pick me up. She was the only one I'd told aside from Michel. Lily helped me into a waiting cab and then took me back to my apartment and stayed with me. I slept on and off; every so often I'd wake up feeling crampy and nauseous from the anesthesia. Lils nursed me with ginger ale and cracked ice. After twenty-four hours I felt much better, and Lils left. I made a pot of coffee for myself and then washed my hair and started packing for Rome.

Mama came over to help. As soon as we hugged I longed to tell her everything; then she would take care of me and put a hot water bottle on my stomach, as she had when I was a little girl. But I kept quiet and pretended I felt fine, even though I was still cramping and I looked very pale. Mama didn't seem to notice; she kept insisting that I pack unnecessary items like monogrammed hankies and white gloves.

She didn't want me to travel alone to Europe, so she phoned Mildred Dunnock (whom she had never met) and asked if I could sit next to her on the plane and would she watch out for me? Dear, elegant Millie, who'd created the role of Linda Loman in *Death of a Salesman* and was playing Sister Margarita, mistress of the postulants in *The Nun's Story*, was a truly unique lady. She said absolutely, of course.

THERE WAS A stopover in Paris on the long flight to Rome. I accompanied Millie to an airport coffee shop and somehow left the pills I was supposed to take to keep from hemorrhaging in the ladies' room. I realized this with a start just as the plane was taking off.

I didn't know what to do. I sat in my seat staring straight ahead as Millie dozed beside me. I could not tell her or anyone. All I could think of was "I may die."

By the time we landed, I'd started to bleed. I got a Kotex from the stewardess and checked my outfit, standing in the plane's toilet. Luckily I hadn't stained.

Millie and I were driven directly to the Cinecittà Studios an hour outside of Rome. We were needed there for preliminary costume fittings. As the car rolled in, we were confronted with a maze of low gray sound stages that stretched for miles, all of which were being used for movies from *Ben-Hur* to *La Dolce Vita*. Cinecittà was the largest international movie studio in the world.

We finally found the wardrobe department for *The Nun's Story*. I undressed with extreme care, terrified the blood might leak through the Kotex. I remained stiff and tense as the seamstress began measuring my long habit.

At the end of the afternoon our director, Fred Zinnemann, a wiry finely featured man with a slight Viennese accent, dropped by to say hello. I could barely concentrate as he told us that he'd arranged for us to visit several convents for research throughout the following week.

The entire cast had been booked at the Hotel De La Ville on Via Sistina, at the top of the Spanish steps. We were a block away from the gushing Trevi Fountain, and nearby I could see the green sweep of the Villa Borghese gardens. Except there was no way I could enjoy the scenery; the cramping was so extreme, I resisted having dinner. I just wanted to lie down.

But then Millie and I ran into Dame Edith Evans in the lobby, and she intoned grandly, "I refuse to eat alone. Let's all go out together." We accompanied her to a trattoria down the cobblestoned block.

Dame Edith was a formidable woman, tall, stately, considered by many to be the greatest actress in the English-speaking theatre. I thought she'd hold forth on Laurence Olivier and the Old Vic. Instead she wondered in a stage whisper, "What do you know about

Audrey?" In 1958 Audrey was the biggest star in the world, second only to Ingrid Bergman.

"She's something of a mystery," Millie answered. "Engimatic, detached, but irresistible."

Dame Edith murmured, "It's as if she's from another world. In *Sabrina* when she plays the chauffeur's daughter, she falls from a tree . . ." The two women went on extolling Audrey's virtues. I would soon learn that the entire cast of *The Nun's Story* was bedazzled by Audrey Hepburn. They'd accepted roles, however small, in *The Nun's Story* just so they could work with her.

Throughout the meal I remained silent; Millie commented that I must be very, very tired. I said I was.

All I wanted to do was remain in bed, but the next morning I was scheduled to do research at the Salvator Mundi International Hospital, which was run by the Congregation of the Divine Savior. It made sense for me to do my research there, since *The Nun's Story* revolved around an order of nursing nuns.

My appointment was with a sensible-looking woman with a round, kind face who spoke English very well. "My name is Sister Rose," she said. As we shook hands, I tried to hide the pain I was feeling.

"Are you all right, Miss Bosworth?" she asked. "You look very ill. Can I help you?"

I protested that I was fine and attempted to ask her questions about her life as a religious.

She kept looking at me. "You are not well. I know it. Please let me help you."

I heard myself lying, "No, no, Sister, I'm okay." Inside myself I was pleading, *Tell her, "I need help."* But I couldn't.

We talked only a few more minutes and then she cut the interview short. "You should go back to your hotel and rest, and you must promise you will call me if you don't feel better. Will you promise?" She scrawled her name and phone number on a slip of paper.

She gazed at me with such compassion and concern I had to stifle a sob. "Yes, Sister, I promise."

By the time I returned to my room at the De Ville, blood was streaming down my thighs; it stained the carpet and trickled onto the polished floor. I grabbed the phone and called Sister Rose. I told her I'd had an abortion and that I thought I might be dying.

She sent an ambulance immediately. The next thing I knew I was on an operating table at the Salvator Mundi and a doctor was looking down at me angrily. (I found out later he was Ingrid Bergman's doctor and had delivered her twins.)

"You little fool!" He glared at me. "Do you know how many actresses I've had on this table? Why didn't you at least take precautions?" Then he gave me a shot that knocked me out. He sewed my stitches up and I was rolled, unconscious, into a private room.

I SPENT THE next few days recovering. Various doctors looked in on me and made notes. So did a number of medical students. Was I an oddity, I wondered, an example of a "bad woman"? When I asked Sister Rose, she assured me that my "real condition" had been kept secret. Indeed, Warner Brothers had been told I was suffering from a stomach ailment, so they paid all the bills, no questions asked. And my absence from the set didn't cause problems, since the picture was a week behind schedule. No time would be lost.

I lay there, thinking, *I almost died*. After my brother killed himself, I didn't care whether I lived or died, and yet somehow I was here; I'd survived. I wondered how many hours I'd lost screwing strangers, wasting time daydreaming, eating candy, smoking cigarettes, staring at myself in the mirror. I hated myself for my weaknesses and my self-indulgence and my lack of purpose.

My breasts were sore; my uterus throbbed, but I felt I deserved the pain. Nurse-nuns hovered, bringing me hot cocoa and cups of steaming tea. When I complained of cramping, I was given a heating pad. It was then explained to me, very quietly, that cramping was normal and necessary for my uterus in order for it to return to its normal size.

I had such an abysmal lack of knowledge about my body. I didn't even know whether I'd ever menstruate again. Then, as if by magic, an intern dropped by to inform me that I could expect my menstrual cycle to begin again within four to six weeks and that I could become pregnant during that time if I went "unprotected." I had no intention of letting that happen. For the first time in my life I thought about my body and what I'd done to it. I touched my breasts, I caressed my vagina. I even tugged at the soft hair between my buttocks. I'd never been aware of my body before. It was something that was just *there*.

Then I began to miss my mother. I yearned for her comfort and support, but of course I would never tell her what I had done. She'd kept me in the dark about sex and never encouraged me to take responsibility for my body, and she'd instilled in me a fear of doctors when I was growing up. I'd never asked my male gynecologist any questions. I didn't question him about fees or procedures either, nor had I discussed the possibly adverse effects of my abortion with the doctor who had performed the operation the week before. He had given me those pills so casually ("Just take 'em on the plane so you won't hemorrhage . . ."), but I'd been only half listening. I still hadn't learned to concentrate when it came to taking care of myself.

I knew that I was at a turning point. I couldn't go on living in the same careless, reckless manner, never giving a thought to what I was doing. I had to take stock. I had to change. Easier said than done. My growing up would take a long, long time.

*　　*　　*

JUST BEFORE I left the hospital, Sister Rose came to visit me. She sat near my bed and we talked. I noticed how tall and straight she seemed, and how serene. Even though I'd grown up with nuns, I could never fathom their singular way of being. Sister Rose's calm warmth reminded me of my beloved Mother M back in San Francisco. We were quiet for a while, and then I said, "Thank you for saving me, Sister. I am so ashamed."

"A waste of time."

"I feel guilty, so guilty."

A long pause, and then she suggested gently, "Go to Confession."

"I hope God forgives me."

Sister Rose didn't answer. Instead she murmured in conspiratorial tones, "I shouldn't be here." She continued to stare at me very hard. "You could've died, you know."

"I know."

"God has saved you for something," Sister Rose noted. "There is a reason you are still alive. What do you want to do with yourself?"

"Well, I started out wanting to be an actress," I explained, speaking very slowly and carefully because I realized this could be an important conversation. "After I became an actress and started to work, I had to face the fact that I didn't enjoy performing all that much. I didn't like to be that focused on myself. Sometimes I think I am not as committed as I should be to acting, that it is not my vocation. That I should be—well, I really want to be a writer."

"Writers are dreamers," Sister Rose murmured.

"I have been writing," I assured her. "I haven't gotten very far. I'm not published. But I'm writing a novel and some short stories. It's very hard."

"How old are you?"

"I'm twenty-four."

"You have time. Pray for guidance. You should offer up your struggles."

I sat bolt upright in bed. "I pray every day," I cried. "I say the prayer I learned at the Convent of the Sacred Heart. 'Oh Jesus, through the immaculate heart of Mary I offer up all my prayers, works, and sufferings of this day.'"

"That's a good start," Sister Rose said. She rose and moved toward the door, rosaries clinking by her side. I didn't want her to go.

"I was supposed to ask you questions about what it's like to be a nun," I called after her.

"It's not for everybody," she said. "But I wanted to be a nun from the time I was fourteen years old."

"What's it like?"

She thought for a moment. "It's a life primarily of silence, although you wouldn't know it from the way I'm talking. I'll have to do a penance. It's about love and living the Gospel. I make it sound simple, but it's hard."

"What's the hardest part?"

"The vows of poverty, chastity, and obedience. The most difficult is obedience. The religious life has to begin every day as if it was a first."

"Have you read the screenplay of *The Nun's Story*?"

"Oh, yes. We were all asked to read it when we agreed to advise Warner Brothers and Mr. Zinnemann."

"What do you think?"

"It's quite accurate." She moved closer to the door. "I have to go." Her skirts rustled; her rosaries clinked.

"Please pray for me, Sister."

"I will. I promise." And then she was gone.

As soon as I was alone, I scrambled to my knees and clasped my hands fervently together. "Oh my God!" I cried. "Thank you, thank you, thank you!"

I looked out the window and I could see Rome and its jumble

of churches and crumbling palazzi. On my bedside table was a vase of flowers from Fred Zinnemann and Warner Brothers and a note: "Get well soon."

Was it fate or destiny or just plain luck that had put me together with Sister Rose at the Salvator Mundi International Hospital? At that moment, my survival seemed an incredible wonder.

I was alive. I was healing. Due to a series of totally unplanned circumstances.

Chapter Nineteen

AFTER A FEW more days the doctors said I was well enough to leave the hospital, so I went back to the Hotel De La Ville, feeling very disoriented. I would continue to feel this way for the next few weeks. I remember standing in front of my desk leafing through call sheets and schedules from Warner Brothers and finding it hard to believe that I was about to be featured in a big Hollywood film. Then I glanced down at the carpet, relieved that the maid had washed all my blood away.

I couldn't tell anybody what had happened to me. I had to act healthy, so when the PR department called to set up a photo shoot with the *Rome Daily American*, I immediately agreed.

That same afternoon I established a routine that I maintained until my job was over. I had supper almost every night with various members of the cast. I loved hearing Dame Edith talk about Shakespeare; Pat Collinge would tell me about writing for *The New Yorker*; Millie Dunnock might discuss the differences between Arthur Miller and Tennessee Williams as playwrights. These distinguished women were a comfort to me in my vulnerable state. I listened hungrily for anything they might tell me. They had discovered themselves and the world in ways I hadn't yet.

Millie was my favorite, although we would occasionally eat our meals without talking. I was uncomfortable with that; I thought we should fill our silences with chatter. But when I did, Millie would often not answer. She remained deep in thought, her enormous eyes filled with melancholy.

"Is something the matter?" I would ask.

She would shake her head. "It's inexplicable. It's emotional. Words would destroy what I am trying to figure out inside myself."

So I let her go on pondering. Keeping quiet, keeping one's conscience. It was a lesson that took me decades to master.

THE INTERIORS FOR *The Nun's Story* were all being filmed at Cinecittà. I began going out there a lot for more costume fittings and makeup tests. The sheer size of the place overwhelmed me: offices, piazzas (Fellini had an apartment there), so many sound stages I couldn't keep count.

I lost my way the morning I had an "emergency meeting" with Fred Zinnemann. I hadn't expected him to be waiting for me in my dressing room.

"You're late," he said.

It was 7:05 (I had been called for 7:00 a.m.). Millie had warned me, "Fred is *always* on time." To me, he was the artist who'd discovered Montgomery Clift for *The Search* and directed Brando as the tormented paraplegic war vet in *The Men*. I loved all of Fred's movies, especially the suspenseful Western *High Noon* and *From Here to Eternity* (which had won eight Academy Awards). I knew he was a meticulous craftsman; every detail had to be perfect. Which may have explained his next comment to me: "We must do something about your teeth."

"What do you mean?"

"Your teeth—your two front teeth," he replied briskly. "In your color test they photograph yellow. We can't have that. So I've arranged for a dentist to make you some porcelain caps." Fred's assistant appeared as if on cue to hand me a slip of paper. "You will be driven directly to the dentist's office. He's waiting for you. This has to be done right away because we are shooting your first scene with Audrey tomorrow morning."

"Oh." My head was spinning. I followed the assistant outside to the long driveway between the many sound stages where limos and cars were forever idling.

"Hopefully this won't take too long," the assistant murmured as he helped me into my car.

It didn't take long. *The Nun's Story* was a multimillion-dollar Hollywood movie, so the dentist (who could speak only a little English) worked feverishly, bringing out tray after tray of caps for me to try on. None of them seemed to work. Some hung over my lower lip like fangs. Others were too short. After about an hour he slipped on a pair he thought would be "bella!" They did at least feel secure, but when I smiled in the mirror I was horrified to see a cartoon character gazing back at me. The teeth were so bucked I resembled none other than Bugs Bunny.

The dentist assured me it was the best he could do. I decided I should go back to Cinecittà.

I had to wait for about an hour for Fred to reappear in my dressing room. Finally he hurried in. "I've been in conference with the Vatican," he explained, rolling his eyes. Then he clapped his hands together. "Let me see your beautiful smile."

I flashed him my Bugs Bunny grin.

"Good Lord!" Fred exclaimed. "You look like a—"

"A cartoon character. I know. The dentist said this was the best he could do."

Fred crossed his arms together in what I would soon remember as a characteristic gesture. "I guess you won't be able to smile in the movie. But," he added, "you aren't expected to smile much anyway, so I don't think it'll be too big a loss."

Now I was worried about speaking at all. "Will my teeth show when I'm saying my lines?"

"Not enough for there to be a problem."

From then on, before I came to the set I would always run my lines in front of the mirror, making sure my teeth could barely be seen.

WHEN I RETURNED to my hotel I ordered dinner in my room and thought about my role as Sister Simone, the devout, clumsy farm girl who befriends Sister Luke when they are both young postulants. I had only three scenes with Audrey, but "they were plot points, so they couldn't be cut." Bob Anderson had explained this to me when he'd given me the rough draft of the screenplay back in New York. At the start of the movie, we see Simone and Luke constantly breaking the rules. Before they take their final vows, Simone tells Sister Luke that she can't take the rigorous life of a nun, so she's leaving. Sister Luke remains in her order for seventeen years, struggling with her conscience, before she leaves the convent too.

THE FOLLOWING MORNING, bright and early, I filmed my first scene. It took place in the parlor of the convent where the novices were all saying good-bye to their families. Although I had no lines, I was told I'd be in close-up and I was understandably nervous—and excited too, because I was finally going to meet Audrey.

Everybody was milling around, talking and giggling as the lights were being adjusted. Then all talking stopped on the set as Audrey herself appeared. I watched spellbound as she glided across the floor toward me, her feet barely touching the ground. Then I felt her slender delicate hand in mine and heard her say in that in-imitable accented voice of hers, "I'm so glad you're going to be my little friend for a while."

Nobody has ever made quite the impact on me that Audrey did at that first encounter. She greeted me as if she'd been waiting to meet me all her life, which I suspect is how she greeted everyone. I'll never forget gazing into that remarkable face of hers; it radiated such beauty and sadness.

When we shot the scene proper we had no dialogue. Our fathers do the introducing, but our eyes meet; we are both in tremulous close-up for a second, connecting. I have a cap on my head and am smiling shyly (lips together, teeth hidden); then we break and join the line of novices trooping into the convent chapel.

Just before the cameras rolled, Fred took me aside and whispered, "Do something that will make us notice you."

I decided to fake a sneeze. After the shot was completed, Fred came over to me. "Nice touch," he said, "but you should have told me beforehand what you were going to do." Nevertheless he kept that take—it's a nanosecond-long part of my debut on the big screen.

I SPENT THE next week filming transitional scenes: Audrey and I walking down a corridor, sitting in a class, working in the convent hospital. While reciting our culpas to the Reverend Mother, I had one line—"I accuse myself of daydreaming"—and I wondered as I said it whether Bob Anderson had written it especially for me.

I was finding movies difficult to act in. I preferred the theatre, where you can build your performance in unbroken arcs. Movies were made up of bits and pieces that are assembled *after* the fact into an illusion of wholeness. I couldn't get used to that.

And then for ten days we were drilled for the long, complicated processional scene inside Cinecittà's biggest sound studio. There were two hundred of us, counting the extras, all moving slowly through an enormous replica of a Belgian convent chapel. It seemed as big as Grand Central Station—big vaulted ceilings, stained-glass windows, and a copy of Michelangelo's *Pietà*, which I confused with the original.

It took hours. There was much adjusting of lights and cameras, but everybody was very patient. The atmosphere remained hushed; we spoke in whispers to the real nuns, who hovered near us making sure we kept our eyes cast down. We knelt and then prostrated ourselves over and over again in front of Reverend Mother Emmanuel (aka Dame Edith, looking properly magisterial).

Just before we began filming, Audrey joined us, gliding up to Fred and Franz Planer, who were huddled in front of the cameras. She seemed almost transfixed. We'd been told she'd been building her character from the inside out. She was on a regime of convent-type meals; she refused to look at herself in the mirror and turned off the radio in her dressing room so she could be totally quiet while she prepared.

I'd heard that the character of Sister Luke challenged her; she'd grown bored with the fashionable gamine creatures she'd perfected on the screen. Sister Luke's fierce dedication to her conscience and her attraction to an interior life and doing for others appealed to Audrey. She would later say that she never felt comfortable being a celebrity. She'd never enjoyed the constant narcissistic focus on self.

OUR LUNCH BREAKS were always a relief and we'd go together, Millie and I—still in our flowing habits—to Cinecittà's noisy commissary where pasta and wine flowed from eleven onward. As soon as we entered the room we could always count on the same greeting from the lone man in our movie, the diabolical, often-drunk Peter Finch. "*Get out of my sight, you fucking nuns!*" he'd growl, and then he'd collapse laughing.

The place teemed with familiar faces: the beauteous Sophia Loren and Gina Lollobrigida bursting ripely out of their dresses, Marcello Mastroianni chain-smoking in a corner, Fellini in his big black hat. There were movie stars from Hollywood too, like Rock Hudson and Jennifer Jones. Charlton Heston strutted around in a toga; he was about to start shooting *Ben-Hur*. It was rumored that one thousand horses would be used in the chariot race. I could watch them from the commissary windows being exercised, cantering around two enormous dirt fields far below me.

One morning I ran into Gore Vidal; he was rewriting the *Ben-Hur* script with Christopher Fry. Gore took me back to his office. I'd never been to a writer's office before. I was impressed. It was so organized—much research on ancient Rome, books and papers and a storyboard of the entire movie up on a bulletin board. We made plans to get together when we could.

BECAUSE I HAD such a small speaking part in the movie I was often free for days at a time, so I spent them sightseeing around Rome with Millie. We went to Hadrian's Villa; we trudged all over the Seven Hills. When I was alone, I'd wander into a church and kneel down, praying I'd have the guts to go to Confession. I never did.

I still felt ashamed and unhappy. One morning I took a day-trip to Florence with a lawyer from Warner Brothers, a trim slender man named Tonino who'd been my escort at several big parties.

We parked near the Piazza della Signoria, the L-shaped square opposite Palazzo Vecchio. Then we went on a whirlwind tour of the Uffizi Gallery, where crowds of tourists were craning their necks to study Sandro Botticelli's mythological *The Birth of Venus*. When I saw that painting, my eyes welled with tears. It brought back memories of my childhood in Berkeley with my brother, when Mama was trying to teach us about art.

When we were very small she festooned the walls of our nursery with copies of masterpieces—Velázquez's *Las Meninas*, Van Gogh's *Wheatfield with Crows*. She'd keep changing the images, so sometimes we'd wake up to a portrait of *Bacchus* by Caravaggio or a Monet landscape. Mama's favorite was Botticelli's *Birth of Venus*. She had a postcard of it framed on her desk, and there was a larger copy of it in the nursery. She said she'd seen the original many times at the Uffizi. Botticelli had used a special alabaster paint, she told us, so the colors of the sea were shifting shades of green around Venus. Venus herself glowed pink in her nakedness, standing on her shell, hair flowing down—one hand over her breast, the other covering her vulva.

Daddy compared Mama to the Venus, and she didn't contradict him. Once we were allowed to watch as he sponged Mama in her bath. Her hair was flowing down her back and she had one hand covering her breast as in the painting. Daddy called out to us, "Mama is Venus on the half shell, kiddies," and he laughed and we could see his shirt getting soaked as he kissed her.

Then Mama decided that Bart and I should participate in a costume contest; it had something to do with Spanish culture at the university. She dressed me as the Infanta Margarita from Velázquez's *Las Meninas*. Bart was around six; he was one of the Infanta's entourage.

At the contest we were trotted around in our finery, but we didn't even get honorable mention. A skinny, funny-looking girl dressed as Carmen Miranda wearing a hat made of bananas and berries won the grand prize.

Mama burst into angry tears; art books in hand, she marched up to the judges and cried out, "How dare you! My babies were the genuine article."

Subdued, we returned home. I remember standing next to her patting her hand after she collapsed in a chair still sobbing. Bart climbed into her lap and asked her very sadly, "Mama, why are you crying?" She wrapped her arms around him and said, "Because I wanted you both to win!"

Bart shook his head. Later in the nursery he asked me, "Why do you have to win in life?" He seemed too small and young to be asking that question.

We pondered this for a long time, and when Daddy came upstairs to kiss us good night, I told him what had happened and asked, "Why is it so important to win?" He told us it was more important to make an effort, "to do the best you can. Nobody can win everything in life—it wouldn't make sense if you could. It is far more interesting to struggle, to strive. All you can do is your best."

I remembered Bart then; I could see him listening so attentively to Daddy. His big eyes got rounder and rounder. I'm not sure if it was before or after that he tried to make those wings to fly into the clouds.

THAT AFTERNOON IN Florence I attempted to tell Tonino about my brother and me and the costumes based on the Velázquez painting, but he wasn't interested. I missed my brother so much. As soon as I reached my hotel room and shut the door I began talking to him in our private language. I hadn't spoken to him for a long time.

"Oh God, I wish I'd never told that story."

It's not a particularly compelling one. Interesting only to us.

"Do you remember what Daddy told us?"

Sure. Something about winning and losing and it's supposedly better to try, to make the effort. I say bullshit; now I say it's better to win.

"Why haven't I spoken to you for so long?"

You've had a lot to do.

"You knew I'd had an abortion."

Silence.

"I'm sorry."

You are not sorry. You are glad. You made the movie. You didn't die on the operating table.

"I could have."

Don't be so dramatic. They were just sewing up busted stitches, for God's sake.

"I'm worried about Daddy; I'm worried about Mama."

Worry about yourself. Think about yourself.

"I feel differently now. I'm going to be more sensible."

I should hope.

"MORE SHORT TAKES," I wrote in caps in my journal, dated April 21, 1958: "I am starting to feel better . . . This experience in Rome is emotionally intense on so many levels—just being in this ancient city! . . . In the morning I'll be shooting a scene and then I'm off to tour the catacombs, and in the evening I find myself at a party dancing with Anthony Quinn. When I get back to my hotel it's Daddy on the phone telling me he misses me and he's gotten a weird new client, a comic named Ernie Kovacs—whose children have been kidnapped and Daddy has to hunt them down before he can get paid.

"I'm acting in a movie that may be iconic . . . Fred Z is amazing—he admits to improvising—he was both a documentary filmmaker and an assistant director, so two attitudes exist as he works in film! And then there is Audrey, who I have not gotten to know at all . . . A big disappointment . . . But she is a star and as Lenny Lyons says, 'Stars want to be with stars . . .' She remains a total mystery to all of us; she is regal, she is childlike—obviously tamping down her high spirits (which I am sure she has) to inhabit Sister Luke in *The Nun's Story* . . . We have barely exchanged a sentence, but she did scold me for smoking too much on set. I get nervous. 'I smoke too, you know,' she told me quietly. 'It doesn't do any good.'

"I wanted to ask her if it's true about her mother, who is apparently very cold and very difficult and once told Audrey, 'You have absolutely no talent, so it's amazing you've come so far!' And Audrey is loving to her and supports her financially."

April 24, 1958: "Mama sent me a birthday cake! It's my birthday, April 24—I am twenty-six. She arranged to have Millie order my favorite white cake with caramel frosting. Millie invited Pat Collinge and Dame Edith, and we sat in the hotel garden. They toasted me with champagne. The birthday celebration—blowing out the candles and making a wish—brings back memories of the other birthday parties Mama gave me and my brother when we were small. She hired a magician and he took live white rabbits out of hats . . . and then the rabbits shit on the dining room table. Mama was furious! . . . Another time she asked the opera singer Lily Pons to sing "Happy Birthday" to Bart when he was seven and he started to cry. He told me, 'Her singing hurt my eardrums!' It's all so long ago."

I REMINDED GORE VIDAL that I was trying to write a novel the first time we'd met and I was still trying.

"But why?" Gore wondered.

We were in his office in Cinecittà. The lights were on; the room had no windows; it was stuffy. But I didn't care because we were talking about writing, though I couldn't explain why I was writing the novel.

"*Four Flights Up*, it's called, maybe because the heroine is a young girl living in a four-flight walk-up in New York, as I do."

Gore's eyes glazed over in boredom and he switched the subject to families. "Much more interesting to write about a family, to write about somebody you *know*," he said.

I told him my parents, especially my father, had always encouraged me in everything I'd wanted to do and they'd encouraged me to read—I'd read prodigiously as a little girl.

Gore said, "My mother worried that I spent too much time reading—escaped into the magical *Oz* books and Edgar Rice Burroughs, *Tarzan*..." We both agreed that we'd preferred to live in a world of fantasy by the time we were teenagers, "to get away from our reality," Gore said.

I began telling him about Bart—his suicide and the circumstances surrounding it, the hanging death of his friend at Deerfield and the school's fearful, dismissive attitude about the friendship.

Gore would later write an incisive piece on the complicated matter of sexual identity. "The American passion for categorization has managed to create two new non-existent categories—gay and straight. Either you are one or the other. But since everyone is a mixture of inclinations, the categories keep breaking down; and when they break down, the irrational takes over."

Was my brother homosexual? I wondered.

"*This* is what you should be writing about, Patti, not a novel," Gore said. "Write about your brother. Write about what *you* know. His torment, your torment."

"Oh God, it would be too painful."

"Of course it would." His voice grew irritated. "It won't be easy. *If* you can do it, it will take years."

"But how—how could I even approach it?"

Gore thought for a minute. "You will have to go to a place inside yourself you cannot bear to go. You have to ruminate on everything about your brother. You have to swim in the pain, absorb it, understand it, and then when you do, you detach, because you must be detached to write something like this. You can't be mawkish or sentimental."

He gazed at me. "You are still so young. You won't be able to do it for a while, maybe not for a long time, since you have absolutely no technique whatsoever."

"I know that."

"Maybe in thirty or forty years. By that time you'll have some distance, some perspective." We both laughed, but I knew he was telling me the truth.

I hurried back to my dressing room and scribbled down what Gore had told me. That I should write everything I could remember; it's only in writing it down that you know what you think. Pull from the raw material of your life—how is it possible to tell the story a personal narrative needs to tell? Important events: the fire in the nursery where my brother was almost burned alive . . . Bart struggling to make those paper wings and fly far, far away . . . The rose gardens at Aptos . . . The view of the Hudson River from our house on the hill in Garrison . . . And above and beyond everything, my brother's spirit hovering. My brother, who was always my co-conspirator, my savior, when we were growing up. He would never forget me or leave me stranded. He was the silent one, but he was the one who helped me cope. I was the clown who entertained our parents' guests and then often fell apart.

Chapter Twenty

THE MORNING I filmed my good-bye scene with Audrey, I felt like crying because I would be leaving Rome soon, but I realized I had to concentrate. I watched Franz Planer, the great cinematographer, wheeling the cameras into view before he conferred with Fred. I'd already been told I'd be in close-up through most of the scene; that scared me, since a close-up in a movie is the high-wire test of an actor's skill.

As the lights were being adjusted, Audrey drifted over to me and took my hands in hers. "Patti," she said softly and intensely, "don't *do* anything. Above all, don't *act*. The camera picks up everything. But do mean what you say."

Then she whirled around and began her own preparation, withdrawing into the character of Sister Luke. In another moment the cameras would begin rolling. I had to enter from a hallway and then step into position opposite Audrey.

It's an illusion to think that the ability to project in front of a camera is easy. It's hard to act natural and hold the camera's eye—to fill the space. That eye catches *everything*. In the space between my face and the camera, I would be undefended; my eyes and the set of my features would be my only means of expression.

But when I gazed into Audrey's mobile, translucent face, that's all I seemed to need. Focusing on that face, I believed it when I told her, "I'm leaving the convent because I know I'm not like you—as strong as you . . ."

Our eyes met as the camera recorded me in close-up. I kept on looking at Audrey. Nothing moved as she listened to me. Eyes unblinking, she conveyed without words sympathy and affection.

Fred shot a couple of versions. He was making a big Hollywood movie, and while these scenes were essential, they were but tiny ones to be stitched together into the intricate mosaic of a picture. So when he called, "Print! Take! And now on to the next," he was very brisk with me. "Good job," he said.

I watched Audrey disappear; there was a sinking feeling in my stomach.

I was on my way back to my dressing room when Audrey's assistant ran after me. "Miss Hepburn would like you to join her for tea tomorrow [it was Saturday]. Givenchy is flying in from Paris to show her his new collection and she thought you'd enjoy seeing it with her."

AUDREY'S SUITE AT the Hassler was filled with her favorite things. It was said she traveled with forty pieces of luggage crammed with possessions, everything from china to linens. She traveled so much she needed to have objects around that she cared about, such as silver candelabra, white silk pillows, crystal dishes, a white cashmere blanket for the cream satin chaise. There were piles of books and scripts and photographs of family in silver frames. Her mother, Baroness Ella van Heemstra, with Mel Ferrer and Audrey on their wedding day in Switzerland. Snapshots of her beloved tiny dog, Famous, who was barking and scampering around when I came in.

The minute I entered the suite I was enveloped in the sweet fragrance of L'Interdit, the perfume Hubert Givenchy had personally created for Audrey. She was the only one who wore it for two years; then he started selling it commercially. Audrey came into the living room almost at once dressed in a favorite outfit—toreador pants, flats, and a man's shirt tied at the waist. After kissing me lightly on the cheek, she drew me down on the sofa. "Tell me a little about yourself—we don't know each other at all."

"I was born in San Francisco."

"I love San Francisco! My mother loves San Francisco."

I noticed she wore no makeup and she looked tired, but she was animated. She'd been working nonstop since January and had even fallen deathly ill not long before I had my two scenes with her. She'd suffered from a painful bout with kidney stones, but she hadn't wanted to be operated on. Instead she opted for rest and relaxation, "and now I'm fine," she insisted. She was bone thin, but she maintained she had "a healthy appetite. Yes, I am skinny, but it's metabolism."

She confided, "Hubert is in the next room preparing the models. He's one of my best friends in the entire world." They'd met in 1952 when she was about to start filming *Sabrina* and decided she wanted Givenchy to do the costumes. "I had the chance to wear high fashion for the first time. It was a dream come true."

"Clothes are positively a passion with me," she had said to a journalist at the time. "I love them to the point where it is practically a vice."

Givenchy was twenty-six when they'd met; he'd only recently left Schiaparelli to open his own atelier. He heard a Miss Hepburn was coming to see him. He expected Katharine Hepburn, and then this very thin girl with beautiful eyes and very short hair and thick eyebrows, tiny trousers and ballet slippers and a T-shirt waltzed in. She was anxious about her acting because she'd had no training, no experience, when she was pushed into the spotlight. After she won the Oscar, she made a decision—she would concentrate on her image and make it as perfect as possible. It would become her shield. "I always knew what looked good on me. Simple dresses, beautifully cut. Flats. Then I found Hubert. We started talking and we have never stopped. He is like family. He is my dear friend."

In public she had often referred to him as a "personality maker." "I've never stopped worrying about my acting ability." She had even gone so far as to say that Givenchy's clothes made up for what she lacked in dramatic technique. "It is a help to know I can always *look* the part. Then the rest isn't so difficult. I don't need a psychiatrist; I have Hubert." She laughed.

At that point I interrupted to tell her that my favorite dress of all time was the ball gown she'd worn in *Sabrina*. "Yes, it was heaven," she agreed. "Angelic bouffant layered gown . . ." She appeared magical in it, the chauffeur's tomboy daughter turned into a swan. (A strapless organdy sheath with a buoyant overskirt, it so captured Audrey's essence—the slim boyish figure with the airborne femininity. When Audrey walked in it, it was as if she were walking on air.)

Then Givenchy entered the room, a very tall man in a white suit. *"Tu est prête?"* he asked in French. ("Are you ready?")

"Oh, absolutely, darling."

He clapped his hands. Models glided in wearing various dreamy outfits. There were tailored suits and flowing gossamer gowns; there were blouses (I learned that the blouses were $3,000 each); there were ravishing black cocktail dresses; there were boxy coats and turbans. Everything was delectable.

When it was over, Audrey turned to me. "Would you like to order anything, Patti?" she asked.

I demurred, "But thanks anyway."

Then tea was served and Givenchy began to reminisce about Audrey's talent for fashion. "She always puts the finishing touch on my work." He gave as an example the black cocktail dress and hat that she wore in *Sabrina*. She chose the hat—it suited her face. It was like a bathing cap and it covered her eyes, showed off her good profile . . . "She knows her good profile from her bad. She is very professional—so disciplined, so organized."

Soon Givenchy departed for Paris. I lingered in Audrey's suite. I didn't want to leave. I was in another world.

Audrey lit a cigarette. "Did you enjoy the experience of working in *The Nun's Story*?" she asked in that lilting distinctive voice.

"Oh yes," I breathed. "I'll never forget it."

Audrey smiled. "Neither will I." And then she added, "I love fashion, you know. Really love it. But fashion has nothing to do with *me*. The *me* in here"—and she touched her heart—"the private me, the interior me—inside I'm not fashionable at all."

AUDREY AND I kept in touch until she died in 1993. We wrote notes to each other, and whenever I went to Rome, we'd have coffee or a meal.

Bit by bit she shared some confidences. She made more movies like *Breakfast at Tiffany's* and *My Fair Lady*; she divorced Ferrer (by whom she had a son) and married Andrea Dotti, a Roman psychiatrist, with whom she had another son. She had always wanted children. "They are my biggest blessing," she said. She confided she'd never been happy as an actress. She suffered constantly from melancholy and depression; she still had nightmares remembering her experiences in the war—seeing some of her family put up against a wall and shot. She hid people in her house during the Resistance, Jews who were trying to escape the Nazis.

Audrey spent the last years of her life working tirelessly for UNICEF with refugees, mostly in Africa, seeing that children and their parents were fed and clothed, generating hope and goodwill. The last time I saw her was at the gala tribute Lincoln Center gave her in 1991. She was wearing a white satin Givenchy gown and she looked painfully thin. She invited me to the greenroom before the tribute began. When I entered, I saw her flanked by her partner Robert Wolders and by her good friend Ralph Lauren. The minute she saw me she stretched out her arms and cried, "My little nun!"

I ran to her and we hugged. She then explained who I was and said we were friends.

The tribute concluded with many vivid excerpts from her films. There were several beautiful sequences from *The Nun's Story*. Audrey is truly luminous as Sister Luke. In the movie she achieves everything through her remarkable face—the spiritual struggle, the emotional anguish. It is all internal, all deeply felt. It is her finest performance.

BUT BACK IN June 1959, Warner Brothers didn't have high hopes for *The Nun's Story*. They were surprised when it broke all records on opening day at Radio City Music Hall. My father and I attended that first performance sitting in the balcony; he gripped my hand when I appeared on the screen and did my scenes with Audrey. There I was in a tremulous close-up. We were stunned when a line I uttered, "So I can talk without saying a culpa or doing a penance," got a laugh. The packed house, roughly six thousand strong, howled, and Daddy whispered, "You have the audience in the palm of your hand." A bit of an exaggeration, but he was my doting father.

The movie went on to be nominated for many Oscars, including another nomination for Audrey.

The film remains popular today around the world, shown constantly on Turner Classic Movies and at film festivals. I always get a kick out of it when a friend will call me late at night and say, "I think I'm watching you playing a nun on the tube. Am I crazy?"

MY PLANE TOOK off from Rome in the early afternoon. It was clear, balmy weather. As we rose into the heavens, I peered out the window to gaze at the terrain far below. There were the Vatican and the dome at St. Peter's, then the rolling Tuscan hills and vineyards, the manicured tapestries of green. I was reminded of California; as my parents drove my brother and me over the Santa Cruz Mountains, we would see vineyards and rows of cypresses and, in the far distance, the blue of the Pacific Ocean.

Midflight I realized I'd started to menstruate. I had to ask the stewardess for a Kotex. I put it on in the ladies' room. It had been six weeks to the day.

I DID NOT admit to having an abortion until 1972, when I signed a petition in *Ms.* magazine entitled "We Have Had Abortions" along with fifty-two other women active in politics and the arts, including Susan Sontag, Gloria Steinem, Grace Paley, and Billie Jean King. I wanted to join them in a campaign for honesty and freedom.

It was the height of the women's movement. Consciousness-raising groups abounded. Wives, mothers, college girls were all baring their souls.

I remember at one consciousness-raising session several of us were asked, if we had to do it all over again, given the change in the laws, would we still have had abortions?

I was not so sure.

Part Four

Changing

Chapter Twenty-One

What next? IT's my brother's voice asking me a question.

"I can't answer yet," I say.

Try!

I'd been back in New York a couple of weeks and I'd had surprisingly few calls for jobs. I was getting anxious; I'd assumed that my career would take an upward swing now that I'd been featured in a multimillion-dollar film. Then I saw my agent at MCA and he punctured any fantasies I might have had.

"Look," he said, "once you play a nun in a movie, Hollywood typecasts you as a nun."

I asked about *Splendor in the Grass*, because Kazan was directing. It was a William Inge screenplay, an intense adolescent love story. I'd heard several Studio actresses were up for parts. I assumed I could be too.

"Nope." My agent shook his head. "Casting's done. Natalie Wood and Warren Beatty have already been signed as the leads."

I left his office so frustrated that I phoned Ruth Gordon, Gar Kanin's tiny, indomitable wife. We'd become acquainted when I was with Pepi and she was triumphing on Broadway in *The Matchmaker*. Ruth was a woman rare among theatre performers in those days—an actress/writer. She and Gar had collaborated on several screenplays, including one for the extraordinary pre-feminist film *Adam's Rib*. Ruth told me that whenever she couldn't get work as an actress, she'd write something "either for myself or Kate Hepburn."

When we got together at her Carnegie Hall office, Ruth chewed me out for whining. She said I had to "hang on." I argued that I was so despairing, I wanted to give up acting entirely and concentrate on writing.

"Don't stop acting until you know whether you *can* write, or whether you have anything worth writing, for that matter." She paused. "I've seen my life as one long improvisation. I've never focused my energies on just one ambition. I've failed a lot. But in the meantime, keep on moving and stop kvetching!"

It was good advice. I continued auditioning—and I kept on trying to write. Then at the end of the day I often biked in Central Park.

I HADN'T EXPECTED to run into Mel Arrighi, but there he was one afternoon, walking around the reservoir mouthing lines. I almost biked past him, but he called after me and then I braked. He held my bike handles while we spoke, towering over me at six-foot-four. His words came at me in a stuttering stammer because he was so excited. A play of his had been optioned for Broadway, affirming his dream of himself as an artist.

He added that he was on a break from a rehearsal for a bus-and-truck tour of *Julius Caesar* that Joe Papp was bringing to the five boroughs. Would I be his guest at a dress rehearsal the following night? I said I would.

We began to see each other pretty regularly. We discovered that we lived only a few blocks from each other in Yorkville. Mel had a cold-water flat—two narrow rooms (bathtub in the kitchen, toilet in the hall) on East Seventy-First Street. "Not bad for $33.50 a month." He grinned.

The first time I visited him there, he insisted I read his play "before we do anything else," and he sat opposite me smoking until I finished. It was the story of his Italian immigrant family in San Francisco and of a brother lost to him. I was moved because my brother was also lost and I reminded Mel of that. Only then did he take me into his arms, his big strong body pulsing with energy as he covered me with passionate kisses. I felt very protected.

The following morning Mel brought me coffee in bed and he began to talk. Words poured out of him, anecdotes about his life on the road and reminiscences of growing up near Golden Gate Park with a mother who refused to speak English and left the house only to go to the opera. His older brother (now infirm) taught him to read and write, took him to the movies and concerts, told him the most important thing is to get an education. Mel had master's degrees in philosophy and history; there were stacks of books everywhere in his apartment. I would soon be awed by his erudition.

After listening to him, I admitted that I felt wildly ignorant. He replied, "A fool can be educated. It's more important to learn how to think."

MEL DIDN'T TEACH me how to think—he *caused* me to think. With him, I seemed to have found an articulate tongue. Everything unsaid throughout a lifetime of holding back—there were layers and layers of unpeeling for both of us. From then on, no night was ever long enough. We were both crazy to know and to do and to see. We had found in each other the perfect audience.

During the first months of our affair, we talked constantly about ourselves and asked each other a lot of questions. Ordinarily Mel treated me in a courtly fashion; he was polite, devoted, thoughtful.

304 • Patricia Bosworth

He seemed to respect my privacy. Except when it came to sex—he insisted on knowing about all the men in my life.

So I described, but not in too much detail, my strange marriage to Jason. But I refused to tell him anything else. It was none of his business. And a voice inside me was murmuring, *I might be penalized. I might lose his respect if he knew how many men I've gone to bed with. He might stop loving me.* So I hedged.

"Anybody better in the sack than me?" he'd ask after a passionate night of lovemaking. I'd tell him no.

"Sweetheart, ever go to bed with a black guy?"

"Ever go to bed with a black girl?" I countered.

Mel nodded. Then he launched into a long story (which he later incorporated into a novel) about this particular girl. She was lovely, a schoolteacher in Harlem. "We had a long relationship. But I broke up with her when she got pregnant."

"You broke it up?"

He nodded. "I didn't want her to have my baby. I tried to get her to have an abortion. We had a great many arguments; then she disappeared. After she left, I had a change of heart. I thought, *My God, I'm so stupid. I'm being racist.* I wanted her to have the baby—black, white, yellow, what did it matter? I wanted a child. But by that time she'd quit her job. I couldn't find her. I think she may have gone back to L.A. where some of her family is."

"Oh, dear."

"I wonder if there is a little half-black, half-white Arrighi baby toddling around somewhere." He tried to smile. "I do want kids." He said it so intensely and then he stared at me hard. "Have you ever been pregnant?"

"No," I lied.

BUT MEL'S QUESTIONING continued off and on for weeks, in between his obsessive hours of work. One night after he'd finished part of a novel, we met for supper and he demanded once again that I tell him about all the men in my life.

"Did you ever make a list?" he wondered.

"No," I lied (although I had). "Please stop," I pleaded.

"Look," he said, "I have nothing to hide. I had one girlfriend through college and we made love every night. Period. And then the girl in Harlem."

"It goes beyond hiding," I told him angrily. "It's a choice on my part. It's a choice whether or not I tell you my 'secrets.'" I was sure there were things that he didn't want to share. I was positive he had *something* he was trying to conceal. Wasn't that true? Mel avoided the question.

WE WERE BOTH busy; we didn't see each other that much, but we hated to be separated. When we weren't together, we'd call each other on the phone constantly. The intensity and possessiveness between the two of us was almost suffocating.

We were in love and quite dumbfounded by the experience. *Nobody* had been in love the way we were. We'd observe friends who said they were in love and we'd whisper to each other, "They don't know what love is." Love for us was warm, golden bliss under wrinkled patterned sheets . . . hours talking nonstop, holding hands on the street. We literally didn't want to let each other go.

When I was with Mel, I felt I was in another world where values, ideas, and even language moved away from what I'd known. He was so honest and forthright, so up-front in ways that were foreign to me. I was used to playing games with Daddy, with other men like Pepi—double-talk or no talk at all. Growing up with my parents had been disorienting, and now a virtual stranger had moved into my world and I felt more comfortable with him than I did with my own family (except for my dead brother).

We took care of each other. If Mel had a cold, I'd bring him hot tea and honey. If I lost out on an audition, Mel would be there for me with a fistful of daisies and words of encouragement. We shopped at the A&P together. We did our laundry at the Laundromat side by side. I felt comforted by the whishing sound of the water, the steamy soapy smell of the place, and Mel near me, our thighs touching.

I depended on him. I remember one dark night I was alone in my apartment and around two I was sure I saw an intruder lurking on my fire escape. I phoned Mel hysterically. He assured me he'd be right over and he came bounding up the four flights of stairs and burst into my studio with a hammer in his hand.

He was panting and heaving and coughing (he smoked four packs of Pall Malls a day and would eventually develop emphysema), but that night he lunged at the window, opening it wide. "Nobody there, hon . . . All clear." Then he dropped the hammer and enveloped me in his arms.

IN JULY I brought Mel over to dinner with my parents. It was the first time he'd seen them since their San Francisco exiles party. Mel had been eager to be reintroduced to my father; he admired his politics and he'd read about his defense of the Hollywood Ten and his writings on Israel. I hadn't mentioned Daddy's dark side, the alcoholism and the pill-taking. But then Daddy was in surprisingly good shape that night. Mama whispered, "He's sober."

Apparently he'd been sober for over a month ever since he'd started working for Robert Kennedy. Kennedy was chair of the Senate Rackets Committee, and his brother Jack was right alongside him. The brothers, along with forty other lawyers (my father among them), were investigating the corruption within the Teamsters union.

"Jack and Bobby will stop at nothing until they destroy Jimmy Hoffa," Daddy told us that evening. "I've never met such driven, ambitous men." He and Mel sat in a corner smoking and discussing what a volatile age we were living in. The Eisenhower era was winding down and these men, these Kennedys, my father declared, were rising up as powers in the Democratic Party. They represented something unpredictable.

In the next year, Daddy would be helping the Committee challenge the validity of Hoffa's 1958 election as Teamster president, since the unions were riddled with corruption. After thousands of anti-Hoffa ballots were discovered, dumped into a laundry chute, nineteen dissident Teamsters got an injunction against Hoffa to keep him from taking office. Then their lawyer Godfrey Schmidt and Hoffa's lawyer Edward Bennett Williams met in secret. As part of an attempt to remove all gangsters and mobsters from the union, Schmidt was appointed as one of three monitors to keep Hoffa honest. Hoffa knew Schmidt was out to destroy him, so he kept him from being paid. That's where my father came in—he was Schmidt's lawyer. He'd been hired specifically to collect Schmidt's fees, which by spring of 1959 amounted to more than $100,000. My father's fee was contingent on whether he collected.

What followed was a bizarre series of clandestine meetings with my father, the Kennedys, and the FBI. Teamster goons would appear at the duplex. Once Mel and I were in Garrison visiting my parents. Eddie Cheyfitz, Hoffa's loyal PR man, appeared in the garden and ordered my father to "stop nosing around." Another time the phone rang and a guttural raspy voice demanded, "Is Bart Crum there? Jimmy Hoffa wants to speak to him."

Daddy told Mel and me that he enjoyed being back in the corridors of power, on a first-name basis with the Kennedy brothers. Whenever he was in Washington, Bobby would grab my father for a quick lunch in the Senate cafeteria, and often Jack would join them. Daddy would report off-the-record stuff he'd been collecting from the pro-Hoffa Teamsters. He was discovering the same pattern in all his secret talks, that Jimmy Hoffa had total disregard for the welfare of the rank-and-file Teamsters.

FOR A WHILE I lost track of what was happening with my father because I was working so much. I appeared in an Off-Broadway revival of *The Moon Is Blue*; I went on tour with *Inherit the Wind,* starring Luther Adler. I played the part I'd understudied on Broadway.

Then I flew to Chicago, where I was featured opposite the pop singer Tommy Sands in the mystery *Remains to Be Seen*. It was a memorable experience for me. Something was happening now when I tackled a part—I enjoyed the process of discovery. Sandy's classes were paying off and so were the years I'd spent soaking up Lee's ramblings. I was starting to know what I was doing. During the run of *Remains to Be Seen* I reveled in being able to create genuine behavior for a character—in this case Tommy's mistress, who was a call girl. A character who was nothing like me. I talked out of the side of my mouth, I paraded around the stage in an iridescent bathrobe, and I had a great time.

The same was true in the show I did right after that, a comedy that toured all over the eastern seaboard in which I played Henry Morgan's long-suffering secretary. Henry was a celebrity panelist on the popular TV game show *I've Got a Secret*, so he had a devoted following. In person, Henry was a nasty, horny man and I couldn't stand him, but we loved to improvise.

I remember one night we threw pillows as we ad-libbed and taunted each other. I could feel the audience bouncing back and forth between us, an "I'm on his side," "No, I'm on her side" kind of thing. I'd never connected so viscerally to an audience before. It was exhilarating.

I had started to find things inside myself that connected to the roles I was trying to inhabit. I would look for a particular energy and let it grow inside me. I finally started to enjoy acting. I was still not sure I wanted to continue in theatre forever, because my desire to write was so strong, but this was a turning point for me. I was no longer dissatisfied; I felt I was making some kind of progress in my career.

BUT WHEN I returned from the road, my mother phoned me about Daddy. He'd fallen off the wagon. In July 1959 Robert Kennedy had asked my father to testify in front of the committee and describe what was going on behind the scenes vis-à-vis the monitors. Daddy agreed immediately.

But he was in no shape to testify, Mama said; the drinking and the pills made him jittery and forgetful. His law partners cautioned him not to testify as well: "It won't help your career." However, my father didn't listen to anybody and went down to Washington by himself on the train.

Mel and I watched the proceedings on TV. When Daddy appeared on the screen, he was pale and bespectacled as he recounted in detail the pressure he'd been getting for the past year from pro-Hoffa Teamsters. He ended his testimony by charging that just the day before he'd had lunch at Duke Zeibert's in Washington with Edward Bennett Williams, Hoffa's lawyer, who had said he'd pay part of Schmidt's fee of $5,000 immediately if my father agreed not to testify in front of the committee.

At that point Williams jumped to his feet and denied it was true, saying that he had a witness to prove it.

Daddy's testimony was a front-page story across the country.

The following day Hoffa got on the stand to deny being party to a bribe.

THERE WERE HUMILIATING repercussions. My father's law partners told him that if he didn't recant, he would be asked to leave the firm immediately.

"Perjure myself?" my father cried out in anguish.

The following week he returned to Washington. He agreed to accept Williams's statement that he did not intend to offer a bribe.

When he returned to New York he had dinner with Mel and me at 21. "I told the truth," he insisted. "I did tell the truth."

I discovered years later that Daddy *had* been telling the truth. I would learn that Edward Bennett Williams did indeed offer my father a bribe, but he'd done so at lunch in New York at the St. Regis on a Tuesday rather than at Duke Ziebert's in Washington on a Thursday. Tragically my father's consumption of pills and liquor had made him suffer memory loss. He often made mistakes about dates and places.

I discovered the truth myself on an old calendar decades after the event, when I read Williams's FBI files as I was writing my first memoir about my father. The file confirms that Williams "offered a lawyer a bribe in July 1959—the lawyer was to be bought off," the informer states. But Williams was too shrewd and smart to be caught in a lie.

I NEEDED A break from what was happening with my father, so I escaped into theatre. In the fall of 1959, the Great White Way was electric with activity. Sometimes on a matinee day Mel and I would buy standing-room-only tickets for $2.50 and see a play like *Chéri* with the tremulous Kim Stanley or *Gypsy* for the third time or *A Raisin in the Sun* with Sidney Poitier, which had won every award. The play was by twenty-eight-year-old Lorraine Hansberry, and it told the highly charged story of how a black family survives in white supremacist America.

Then one morning I brought Mel to the Actors Studio. I'd returned there because I was still absorbing, still listening and learning from Lee and other artists. The Playwrights Unit had agreed to give Edward Albee's *The Zoo Story* a first reading directed by John

Stix. He'd been my original contact at the Studio and he'd phoned, urging me to see it. "It's like nothing I've ever read—it's poetic, it's shocking."

Mel and I joined the crowd of the curious, including Molly Kazan (who ran the Unit), Norman Mailer, Israel Horovitz, and María Irene Fornés. Romulus Linney, then an aspiring playwright, was stage-managing.

The setting was a bench in Central Park. With scripts in hand, the two actors began reading: Lou Antonio as Jerry, a scruffy outcast who's fearing and longing for human contact, and Shepperd Strudwick as Peter, a complacent, uptight middle-class fellow. What followed was a searing, blistering confrontation between two opposites; the dominant emotional note was anger, but there was pitch-black humor in it too. The playwright's distinctive voice was eloquent in documenting the base animal in our natures.

The play ended in bloody violence and left the Studio audience visibly rattled. Everybody began quarreling, saying things like "It doesn't go anywhere," until Norman Mailer jumped to his feet. "I'm surprised nobody's said what a marvelous play this is. This is the best fucking one-act play I've ever seen."

Mel and I were shaken by Albee's words, and from then on we saw everything he wrote. To us *The Zoo Story* seemed to suggest that there could be a kind of poetry in a character's conflicted impulses, and that a diffident soul like Peter could be brutally surprised by what lurks inside himself. We heard later on that Albee had based both characters on himself, "the two Edwards—the one who lived in Larchmont when he was a lonely rich kid and the ambitious, dissolute drinker who lived in New York City." Everything, he insisted, was an amalgamation of what he observed and experienced and then subsequently invented. "The thing that happened in *The Zoo Story* was I suddenly discovered myself writing in my own voice. It's that simple."

Discovering your own voice in your writing isn't easy. It took a long time for me to find my voice.

After *The Zoo Story* opened at the Provincetown Playhouse Off-Broadway on a double bill with Samuel Beckett, it became an international hit and Albee became the most important new voice in theatre since Arthur Miller and Tennessee Williams. Off-Broadway became a cultural force and Mel and I got caught up in seeing everything, like Jack Gelber's *The Connection* (about a drug addict in need of a fix) and all the Phoenix Theatre productions too. We'd haunt La MaMa and Caffe Cino, and we weren't alone. Young playwrights and actors and directors all over the Village and Lower East Side were seeing everything, talking, arguing, and experimenting.

Mel would get a play of his, *An Ordinary Man*, produced at the Cherry Lane Theatre (about the rise of black power and its inevitable backlash). It proved controversial enough to have FBI agents visit backstage to investigate. But the Broadway option on his most personal play about his Italian immigrant family back in San Francisco had been dropped. We soldiered on; I organized readings of Mel's other plays at the Actors Studio, and we started writing a musical together.

THEN I GOT cast in another Broadway show called *Howie*. It was a slight comedy by Phoebe Ephron, a slender, quick-witted woman who'd written some very successful screenplays with her husband Henry, among them *Desk Set* starring Katharine Hepburn. The biggest plus as far as I was concerned was casting fellow Studio member Albert Salmi as Howie; he would play the title character with such sweet lumbering modesty that audiences sympathized with his problem. Howie has a genius IQ but can't get a job, so he stays at home and drives his family crazy. I played his exasperated teenage sister-in-law, Sally Sims; I spent much of the show either on the telephone or trying to get him out of the house so that everybody could have some peace.

We had a terrific supporting cast: Leon Ames, Peggy Conklin, and the hilarious Gene Saks. The first read-through was fine, but then in rehearsals the atmosphere turned tense because Henry Ephron would barge in and start interrupting. He'd criticize Phoebe's rewrites. Once or twice he leaned close to me and I smelled liquor on his breath. We knew the Ephrons usually partnered on scripts, but this one Phoebe had chosen to do alone. Henry had no business interfering, but our director John Gerstad, an urbane, mild-mannered fellow, didn't know how to deal with the situation. So tempers kept flaring.

In New Haven the reviews were so lukewarm that Phoebe began more rewrites. We were told we'd be trying out some new scenes once we reached Boston. I'll never forget what happened next. The entire cast had gathered on the stage of the Colonial Theatre when we saw Phoebe running down the aisle with Henry following her. They were both shouting at the top of their lungs, something about a couple of lines of dialogue. When they reached the footlights, Henry socked Phoebe so hard he broke her jaw and knocked her out cold.

Confusion reigned; Phoebe was rushed to the hospital. Somehow amid all the chaos we managed to rehearse. Phoebe had her jaw wired and she gave us more rewrites. She and Henry calmed down. They behaved as if nothing had ever happened. *Howie* opened on Broadway to tepid reviews on September 6, 1959.

It was nice to meet Phoebe's daughter Nora backstage. She came into my dressing room to say congratulations, a small, dainty young woman with high cheekbones and a toothy smile. I immediately wanted to ask her how she coped with her alcoholic parents. Was she an enabler? I'd never known someone close to my age who was going through what I was going through. But of course I said nothing. Instead we made small talk.

"Did my mother tell you Sally was inspired by me?" Nora asked.

"No, she didn't," I told her. I knew Phoebe had four daughters; she'd bragged about them and said they would all be writers. "Do you see any resemblance?" I asked.

Nora shook her head. "Maybe a line or two, and I do talk on the phone a lot." She paused. "Why are you wearing such big falsies in your striped top outfit?"

"Your mother specifically bought me falsies to wear. I didn't want to, but she insisted."

Nora smiled thinly. "How weird is this, considering that my mother hates bras. She never wore a bra until after she gave birth to her fourth child." (Two decades later Nora would write one of her most notorious essays about being flat-chested.)

I changed the subject to colleges. Nora was about to attend Wellesley. I spoke about graduating from Sarah Lawrence.

"I want to be a newspaper reporter," Nora said. I told her I hoped to be a writer too.

We went on to the opening night party at Sardi's. My parents had a ringside table. I brought Nora over to meet them. Daddy tried to stand up, but he couldn't; he was too loaded. Nora pretended not to notice. She moved on and joined the Ephron party. *Howie* closed after four performances.

As my father's alcoholism worsened, I longed to confide in Nora, but I never did. Nora was private; she was stoic. She'd stopped talking to a mutual friend when he mourned too much over his dead wife. Nora's motto was always "Get on with it!"

I did see her more frequently after we both became journalists. We were together at demonstrations during the women's movement; we'd picnic in East Hampton. We'd have long evenings at

Elaine's. At that point Nora always spoke of her mother in glowing terms—how she'd raised four daughters, was a wonderful cook, had a terrific career. She did it all, she'd brag. Later she would write the following: "Alcoholic parents are so confusing. They're your parents, so you love them; but they're drunks, so you hate them . . . They have moments when they're still the people you grew up idolizing; they have moments when you can't imagine they were ever anything but monsters. And then, after a while, they're monsters full-time. The people they used to be have an enormous power over you . . . but the people they've turned into have no power over you at all."

Chapter Twenty-Two

BY NOW MY father had completely fallen apart after the debacle at the Senate Rackets Committee. Alcohol had poisoned his system. I felt sad about him all the time. At night I'd lie in bed with Mel describing what he'd been like when I was a little girl and he'd been my hero, so smart and brave and funny. Now it was very difficult to be with him, but in those final months Mama and I kept cleaning up his messes, stashing his liquor away, hiding his pills. Every so often he would cry out, "My son, my son . . . I think about you every day."

At a party to celebrate his birthday on December 9, 1959, he seemed briefly his old self. With ravaged intensity he conjured up his glory days as a young radical lawyer yakking with President Roosevelt on the phone, sharing a Chinese dinner with Harry Truman. His friends laughed and applauded before they left the duplex; they did not see him stagger off to bed.

The following morning, Mama found him slumped over his pillows, dead from an overdose of Seconal.

I rushed to the duplex in time to see my father carried out in a body bag. Mama was sitting in the living room, looking shell-shocked.

"Did he leave a note?"

She shook her head.

"Are you sure?"

No answer.

I raced upstairs and into his room. The bed was unmade; there were pillows on the floor, his glasses by the lamp, which was still burning. I went over to his desk and took his crucifix—the one his grandmother had had blessed by the Pope—and the yellow lined pad he made notes on, put them both into my tote, and ran downstairs.

SIX YEARS EARLIER, almost to the day, my brother had shot himself in the head. Now my father was gone, and nothing would be the same. His death unleashed a terrible blackness in my soul and spirit. The grief hit me, and along with it, memories so painful I couldn't bear to relive them. At the opening of *Howie,* he'd appeared so sick and drugged that one of my friends had commented, "Your father shouldn't be seen in public."

I had so many unanswered questions. Was his suicide a rational choice deliberately made? Did he mean to do it, like my brother? At his birthday dinner he'd seemed almost jubilant. By then, I surmised, he'd decided to do away with himself and he felt good about it.

Within hours I discovered that he'd left no will and Mama had only $11,000 in the bank. Also, most of his papers had disappeared. How could a lawyer who'd defended the Hollywood Ten and worked for Truman, Roosevelt, and Willkie leave only a small paper trail?

"I'm counting on you to take care of Mama when I'm no longer around." He'd been saying that to me since I was a teenager. So I sprang into action like a mechanical doll, even though I felt hollowed out from so much loss.

But underneath I was seething too. A huge anger rose up in me, but I couldn't access my fury—my rage at all that was happening to me—so much responsibility along with the pain.

I managed to borrow $10,000 from a wealthy friend to keep Mama afloat. Then I organized the funeral in record time, inviting the guests, choosing the casket, even wiping the excess rouge from my father's waxen face just before the viewing at Campbell's.

The ceremony, held in the Church of St. Ignatius Loyola, was brief and melancholy. Daddy's oldest friend, Peter Cusick, gave the eulogy. He spoke of Daddy's brave political stands, his kindness and generosity. "He always had a talent for hope."

In the middle of the Mass I was surprised to feel an explosion of happiness course through my body as well as a surge of relief. I would always love my father and I would always admire him. But the hideous struggle to save him was over, and I didn't have to relive any of it again. I confided this to Mel when we were by ourselves. He applauded me. "Yes, you will still grieve, but you can go on with your life."

After the funeral I phoned my grandmother Mo and told her that the body would be shipped out to California. We agreed that Daddy should be buried in the family plot next to Bart. She expressed disappointment that I wouldn't be accompanying the coffin. I told her that it was honestly too much for me. I'm not sure she understood.

After I hung up the phone, I felt guilty all over again. I still had not visited the cemetery where Bart, and now Daddy, would be interred. At that moment I vowed that someday I would pray over their graves.

FORTUNATELY I WAS diverted by a visit from my beloved cousin, Elena Bosworth (we'd spent so much time together at Aptos that we were as close as sisters). Now she'd arrived in New York on the eve of her marriage to Howard Eaton. Blonder and more irrepressible than ever, she was staying at the duplex with Mama. Mama, in fact, was organizing the wedding reception and I was to be maid of honor. We were both very happy for Elena because Howard was a Yale graduate and head of the TV department at the advertising agency Ogilvy & Mather. More important, he was turning out to be one of the kindest, most decent men I'd ever known.

At the reception champagne flowed. The guests were in a mellow mood. Then, as the cake was being cut, I heard Mama whispering to someone that she wished I could find a man "worthy" of me.

I felt awful. Mama would not accept Mel; she'd even refused to allow him to come to the reception, although Howard and Elena had wanted him to be there. When I could, I slipped away and called Mel on a pay phone. I made no mention of Mama's cruel remark. I told him I hadn't had a good time because he wasn't with me.

"So come over to my place and we'll celebrate by ourselves." Mel laughed.

"Celebrate what?" I asked.

"That we found each other, sweetheart."

THE FIRST THING Mama did after we paid off some of her creditors was to move to a less expensive studio apartment. The next thing she did was almost empty her bank account to pay a plastic surgeon to wipe all the experience from her face and transform her once-strong nose into a button. I visited her in the hospital and cried when I left; she was so sure she looked young and desirable again. She had just turned sixty.

As the weeks went by, I noticed she no longer displayed Daddy's photographs. She started going out on dates and for a while she had a younger lover.

I, meanwhile, continued to mourn for my father. I sought out his friends: left-wing speechwriters, California politicos, Holocaust survivors he'd met when he was working for the Anglo-American Committee of Inquiry in Palestine. I discovered nobody knew Daddy very well. Some didn't realize he was married or had a daughter, although they knew he had a boy who'd died. He'd received a lot of attention for the speeches he gave around the country for Israel, but he'd seemed very lonely, a rabbi said, "and somewhat of a stranger to himself."

Sometimes I felt that way about myself too. My reaction to Daddy's suicide was even more physically extreme than when I'd grieved over my brother's violent death. I dragged myself around the city. My body ached; my legs cramped; I couldn't sleep. I finally went to Rado in an attempt to understand the intensity of my suffering. Would I end up diminished? I asked him. "I feel immobilized, stuck in my tracks."

He explained that my emotions were, in essence, frozen. "It's a survival mechanism. Be glad you are protecting yourself from feeling."

"You compared my emotions to an iceberg when my brother killed himself."

Rado smiled thinly. "Think *two* icebergs. Your emotions may take even longer to melt now."

"What else can I look forward to?" My tone sounded so sarcastic that we both laughed.

"You will continue to be driven. You will go on being a workaholic, but you will still feel worthless; you will get little pleasure from your successes, but you will still endure."

"Great."

"But this is a good thing. You are a suicide *survivor*. Don't you realize that? You are very strong."

RADO MAY HAVE been right. My actions had proven I could be strong. I hid my true feelings of confusion and fear behind a shit-eating grin. I kept quiet about the suicides for a long time. When I did mention them to people, conversation would stop; there would be sympathetic clucking, followed usually by some embarrassment.

I noticed that the term "suicide survivor" was alluring—scary, even. I wondered whether there was a kind of honor in being a survivor. If there was, I believed I'd won my so-called strength under false pretenses.

I'd try to explain my bewilderment and sadness to Mel and he'd listen, somber, gentle, devoted. He'd hold me tight. We were both enveloped by clouds of smoke because, after comforting me, he'd have to light up again—inhaling, exhaling, coughing, inhaling, stubbing out cigarette after cigarette and lighting up again, just like Daddy.

Chapter Twenty-Three

THE SINGLE HIGH point for me in 1960 was campaigning for John F. Kennedy in his run for the presidency. For two weeks I sat in an office above Madison Avenue and made and answered calls from the ever-ringing banks of phones, talking with voters, convincing them to cast their ballot for this amazing man with the movie-star smile. By early fall, most of America was enthralled by Kennedy's boundless enthusiasm and mesmerizing media presence. He had charm and fire and eloquence, and most intriguing of all to me, he was married to Jacqueline Bouvier, a young woman of notable beauty and style.

After the phone campaign I immediately went into rehearsal for Anouilh's *Romeo and Jeannette*, directed by Harold Clurman and starring Harold's then-wife Juleen Compton. It had a brief run on Forty-Second Street. At breaks, Harold impressed us with his knowledge of French theatre and his reminiscences of his time at the Group Theatre, immortalized in his book *The Fervent Years*. Right after that I appeared in Molly Kazan's *Rosemary and the Alligators*, with Jo Van Fleet and Piper Laurie; I learned how to tapdance for that show.

But Off-Broadway didn't pay much, and I wasn't being sent out on enough auditions. I needed money, so *Esquire* editor Clay Felker, who'd worked with my father on the *Star*, found me a temporary job assisting his friend, the blustery hotshot journalist Peter Maas. Peter would ultimately make a fortune writing about the gangster informer Joe Valachi and renegade cop Frank Serpico. While I was working for him, he was finishing up an exposé of Igor Cassini, aka Cholly Knickerbocker, a gossip columnist for the Hearst press. Peter had evidence that Cassini was an unregistered agent for the Trujillo regime in the Dominican Republic and he'd been using his column to promote clients for his own PR firm.

Peter lived and worked in an apartment on West Eleventh Street. Whenever I arrived in the morning he'd greet me, often hungover and scowling, in his pajamas. He mellowed in later years, but at the time he was a thoroughly disagreeable man with a hair-trigger temper, his mouth twisted as the result of a barroom brawl. He was usually cold and businesslike in his dealings with me, but every so often he would throw me a hot look, as if to say, "I will come on with you if you come on with me." I didn't give him any encouragement.

For six weeks I knocked myself out making Peter coffee, going to the deli or to the post office to mail letters or send presents to people he was sucking up to—like Robert Kennedy, then attorney general of the United States. Mainly I typed draft after draft of the Cassini piece while Peter swaggered around his office puffing on a cigar, yelling into his phone, browbeating the last of his sources to "level" with him. As soon as he hung up, he'd spring over to my desk to look at how I was retyping his latest draft. I wasn't an expert typist, so I'd often make mistakes and he'd start shouting at me, "Do it over again, you idiot. You can't take this over to *The Saturday Evening Post* until it's clean copy!"

Then the phone would ring, interrupting his harangue. I would answer while Peter tensed up; he was always waiting for

important calls. Often it would be Mel, needy and depressed—
he'd received another rejection of his novel. I'd whisper, "I'll get
back to you, hon," while Peter glared. As soon as I hung up he'd
demand, "Who the fuck was that?" I'd say, "My boyfriend," and
Peter would shout, "Tell your friggin' boyfriend your boss needs
his phone to be free."

I would do as I was told and then would go back to work;
I'd stay late as he labored over rewrites. Whenever he got a new
quote—another detail—he'd dictate the material to me and I'd
type the insert into the copy. I enjoyed the process; it was fun gath-
ering information about a person. Being with Peter gave me the
idea that I might be able to write nonfiction; it seemed less lonely
than writing fiction, where you are always alone in a room with just
your imagination.

EVERY SO OFTEN Peter would invite me to tag along with him and
Clay Felker when they went to one of George Plimpton's parties.
Plimpton was the legendary editor of *The Paris Review,* and he entertained frequently in his apartment overlooking the East River.
The minute I walked into the long, low room I was reminded of
the sexually charged atmosphere that rippled through the Actors
Studio—spirited, horny macho males joyfully throwing their
weight around as women waited, lovely but docile; most of the writers at Plimpton's were horny too, but they seemed either too bored
or too drunk to act on their impulses.

I wandered around, recognizing William Styron lounging truly
soused on a sofa. Nearby Philip Roth, Norman Mailer, and Bruce
Jay Friedman were exchanging caustic remarks. I said hello to Lillian Hellman, the only well-known woman writer there. In those
days literary female role models were rare. She was holding court
with a bantering Truman Capote.

But the center of attention was Plimpton, very tall, very skinny, and quite noble-looking. He was invariably surrounded by at least four ravishingly beautiful young women. Whom would he end up with? It was always a matter of who could outlast the others. Meanwhile, George seemed blithely above it all as he drank himself into oblivion.

I would soon revere him as the creator of the masterful Writers at Work series, to which I would eventually contribute. He would become known for his participatory journalism—playing the piano at the Apollo, competing with tennis champ Bobby Riggs, conducting a symphony at the Philharmonic—and then he would write about how these experiences *felt*. ("It took tremendous self-confidence and talent to do that," Cal Trillin once told me.)

By midnight, the party was dying down. I left and trudged back to Mel's cold-water flat, which was only two blocks away. I was keyed up from hearing about Mailer's latest book, *Advertisements for Myself*, an inventive collection of short stories, essays, and polemics—and from meeting Jules Feiffer, the cartoonist who drew the bitterly hilarious *Sick, Sick, Sick* for the *Village Voice*, which I read religiously. Jules's cartoons and Mailer's writing were part of the general cultural revolt of the 1960s against 1950s conformity and restraint.

The prospect of sharing pizza with Mel in his grim tenement apartment began to depress me. We had many arguments about the way he was spending his time.

"I need to be alone," he explained quietly. "It's the only way I can accomplish what I want to accomplish." He wasn't impressed that I'd been introduced to Jules Feiffer. "So what? You should take life more seriously."

I said I *did* take life seriously, but I wanted to enjoy myself too. I needed a break now and then; I enjoyed being with artists who were doing things—"the movers and shakers."

"They won't help you. You've got a novel to finish. You should quit working for Peter Maas. He's putting the wrong ideas into your head."

But I was learning about journalism, I said. In fact, I might even *become* a journalist.

Mel took off his glasses and rubbed his eyes.

I decided we should stop seeing each other for a while. We separated for a week and I felt better for it. Then we made up in bed.

MEL MET PETER only once when he came to pick me up after our reconciliation. We were planning to celebrate it by going to our favorite Italian restaurant, the Grand Ticino in the Village.

Peter was already pouring himself his first drink of the evening, but he didn't offer one to Mel. Instead they had a kind of staring contest, sizing each other up. Mel was taller and bigger than Peter. A deathly silence. I stepped between them. "Peter, I'd like you to meet Mel Arrighi."

"Arrreeegee—what kinda name is that?"

"Northern Italian."

"Oh yeah—what do ya do?"

"I'm a novelist and a playwright."

"Well, good for you." Peter's tone was sarcastic. "I gotta meeting uptown. See you tomorrow, Patti! Be on time!" He ushered us out the door. When we reached the street, Mel was shaking his head.

"What an unpleasant guy. Wish you didn't have to work for him."

"I need the money."

He nodded. "Let's hope it won't last much longer."

IT DIDN'T. A couple of nights later I finished typing the final draft of the Cassini piece. It was word perfect. After reading it Peter gave me a big wet kiss.

"Hey," I murmured.

"Hey yourself," he answered back. "I liked that. Did you?"

He didn't wait for an answer; he put his arms around me and moved me in the direction of his bedroom. I balked. I assumed he wanted to have sex with me simply because I was *there* and I was not about to comply; I was no longer the willing, eager-to-please chickie who hopped in the sack with whoever.

Peter watched me as I gathered up my purse and coat; he was breathing hard, a sure sign he was miffed. "What's-His-Name Arreegee—he's a nobody," he taunted. "Does he have any dough?"

"Enough."

"Oh, for fuck's sake! He's the proverbial artist starving in the garret for his art, and you are his handmaiden."

I didn't answer. I was getting angry, but I couldn't let it out.

"I'm a man who has money and I am going places," he bragged.

"What a cliché," I murmured.

"You sure as hell enjoyed the places I took you to."

"Yes, I enjoyed them and thank you very much and I'm going home now." I slipped out the door. Reaching the subway, I breathed a sigh of relief.

I wasn't surprised when I arrived at work the next morning to find a check on my desk and Peter lounging in his pajamas, saying genially, "You're fired, little one."

"I know." I noticed he was smoking a cigar. "Isn't it a bit early for that?" I said as I put the check in my purse. That's when I heard someone moving around in the bedroom and it became clear to me.

"I am on to other things," Peter crowed. "Now get the hell out of here!" He practically shoved me into the hall.

I DIDN'T TELL Mel any of this. Luckily not long after Peter fired me, Roger Stevens asked me to go into one of his biggest hits on Broadway, the comedy *Mary, Mary* by Jean Kerr. My job: double understudy to the star of the show, Barbara Bel Geddes, as well as to the ingenue Betsy von Furstenberg, who played Tiffany.

The pay was good, $200 a week. I said yes. I expected *Mary, Mary* would be temporary. I had no idea I'd remain a double understudy for close to four years.

My routine was simple. I had to be in my dressing room from 7:30 to 11:00 p.m. Monday through Saturday and matinees. I'd rehearse twice a week, two complete run-throughs. In the first months I'd stand at the back of the house listening to the dialogue until the lines were part of my bloodstream. Laughs came from the audience with the speed of machine-gun bullets. Jean Kerr had a gift for writing crisp, witty speeches that were both funny and shrewdly observant. The character of Mary was hilarious, and as Barbara Bel Geddes played her, she was also very touching. The plot revolves around Mary's coming to see her ex-husband supposedly to clarify certain tax returns. In reality she hopes for a reconciliation, but then she finds he's engaged to party girl Tiffany.

As Mary, Barbara never missed a trick. I loved watching her. She was a beguiling actress with a husky voice and mischievous eyes. She must have been close to forty, but there was still something very girlish about her. She once told me bitterly that she couldn't seem to outgrow ingenue parts, even though she'd created the fiery role of Maggie in *Cat on a Hot Tin Roof*. She longed to be given another chance to explore the angry sexual side of herself. I too had been imprisoned by my angelic blondness. When I told Barbara that, she nodded. "Your looks can really fuck you up."

OFFSTAGE BARBARA LOVED her liquor, which is why I went on for her one night. She called in with the worst hangover of her life. It happened on my twenty-eighth birthday. I'd been with the show six months. Jack Devereaux, the stage manager, had agreed to let me go out to dinner with Mel at Dinty Moore's next door to the theatre. I'd just downed an entire goblet of red wine when the maître d' hustled me over to a phone.

"Patti," I heard Jack's crisp voice say, "get over here fast. Barbara can't make it. You are going on as Mary."

Oh my God, I thought. Yes, I'd been rehearsed well, and yes, I was in the habit of mumbling my lines like prayers, but I'd no time to psych myself up or rehearse with lights and cues, let alone with the rest of the actual cast. I dashed to the Helen Hayes past crowds moving into the theatre proper. Barbara's maid rushed me to the star dressing room, which was right onstage, since Barbara had so many changes. I was helped off with my clothes and started trying on Barbara's costumes. They hadn't gotten around to making understudy costumes yet. Barbara was heavier than I was, so I was pinned into the first outfit, a trim snappy suit. I was able to get my makeup on and then Barbara's hairdresser popped in to give me a comb-out.

Well-wishers kept knocking on the door. Ward Costello, another understudy who had the dressing room next to mine, called out, "Break a leg!" and Jack Devereaux rushed in to ask if there was anything I wanted to go over.

"I'd like to go over any number of things," I answered, "but there is no time."

Then Barry Nelson, the wonderful actor who played Mary's husband, poked his head in and said reassuringly, "You'll be okay, kid." And just then I heard, "For this performance the part of Mary will be played by Patricia Bosworth," followed by groans from the audience, since Barbara Bel Geddes was the star draw. I found myself quaking in the wings, waving my hands up and down, up and down, as I'd seen Barbara do, and then I marched across the stage and made my entrance to deathly silence.

I seemed to slip into a zone of semi-reality. The lights were blinding hot. I saw a blur of faces out front and then I said my first line and got a laugh. I continued to get laughs where I was supposed to. The role of Mary is a smart, wacky one; she has hilarious comebacks for every occasion. As time went by, I loosened up and even started to enjoy myself a bit.

The theatre turned dead quiet during Mary's poignant monologues. I did make mistakes, a lot of wrong moves onstage, and Barry had to say a couple of lines for me when I went up in my cues, but overall, when the curtain came down, the applause seemed enthusiastic.

Afterward I sat in Barbara's big dressing room drained and exhausted, sweat streaming down my face. I felt like a real professional. I'd been tested on everything I'd ever learned.

Mel ran in with a bunch of flowers and we hugged. "You were wonderful, sweetheart, just wonderful!" And then the playwright Jean Kerr appeared. I recognized her; a big Valkyrie of a woman, she'd just been on the cover of *Time*. She was currently one of the most famous humorists in America and the author of *Please Don't Eat the Daisies*. She said she'd decided to catch the show because she'd never seen anyone but Barbara play Mary.

I knew she was Catholic, so I joked, "I hope you prayed for me."

"Pray for you?" She laughed. "I went to St. Malachy's and lit a dozen candles." Then she patted my shoulder. "You were fine, Patti, just fine." And she was gone.

I had lived through the understudy's nightmare and survived. But the earth didn't shake and nobody knew or cared that I'd gone on. Of course I'd momentarily fantasized that some important person would see me and star me in another show. But my life didn't change (unlike Shirley MacLaine, who subbed for Carol Haney in *The Pajama Game* the night Alfred Hitchcock was in the audience). I went back to reality and continued to be the double understudy, and in time I'd go on as the ingenue Tiffany and then for other Marys in the star role.

*   *   *

MONTHS WENT BY. I was securely stuck as a double understudy and I felt more and more like a ghost. I didn't exist in the production unless I went on in a role. I was paid for doing nothing, essentially, and when I did go on, I basically just did the show. Part of me lived in a kind of limbo of expectation and dread. My agent would send me on auditions, but with Daddy gone, I found I'd lost my ambition to act.

Eventually I brought my typewriter and some favorite books to my dressing room on the fourth floor of the theatre. It was a good-sized space with a cot, a washbasin, and one barred window that looked out on a fire escape.

"Reminds me of a prison cell," Mel joked.

To liven it up a bit, I began papering the walls with photographs of Jackie Kennedy in all her youth and sphinx-like glory. Like millions of Americans I was a Jackie watcher, a Jackie junkie. I loved contemplating the images of Jackie in all her configurations: Jackie in riding togs, Jackie in her satin Givenchy greeting General Charles de Gaulle in Paris, Jackie in that brilliant orange dress she wore in India, where she rode on an elephant with her sister Lee Radziwill. Jackie in dark glasses, Jackie in her pillbox hat, Jackie in turtlenecks.

For the next four years I hid from the world in my dressing room, surrounded by Jackies, writing and grieving for Daddy, although I didn't realize that's what I was doing at the time. While I was there I finished my novel, although it went unpublished, and then I began making notes on what I remembered about the city of my childhood, San Francisco.

"The smell of eucalyptus leaves ... The predawn hush of Golden Gate Park as my friend Terry Ashe and I exercised the polo ponies, their hooves clop-clopping across the soft, dark earth of the bridle paths. Once we saw a squirrel sitting unafraid in the middle of the silent road."

Then I slowly, laboriously began a roman à clef about growing up in California with my brother, and I began retracing Mama's dreams and watching my father's rise in politics. I titled it *Anything Your Little Heart Desires.*

Chapter Twenty-Four

MEL AND I had been together for three years; we were both poor, but we managed. He kept asking me to marry him. Our relationship was the most sustaining one I'd ever had, but I kept putting him off. Even though I loved him, I was worried about money. Then I got the *Mary, Mary* gig and Mel began writing for the CBS-TV soap opera *Search for Tomorrow*.

It was grueling work; the pressure was intense and Mel complained as he batted out three scripts a week, attended story meetings, wrote up outlines for future plots. His ability to write good characters with big problems and fast-paced dialogue to match soon brought him the offer to be head writer. This meant he'd be earning over $100,000 a year and then some. I thought this would be the answer to our financial problems, and maybe then I would marry him. Yes, I loved Mel, but I had to be practical; I was supporting my mother and worried about money, as always. It *did* make a difference to me if he was financially stable.

After the offer came, we were invited to dinner with the head writers he was being groomed to replace, a middle-aged husband-and-wife team who'd been grinding away on this TV soap for over twenty years. They were millionaires, with a condo in Florida along with their big Park Avenue duplex. They assumed Mel would jump at the chance of taking over the show, and they praised him for his writing, saying he was "perfect for the job."

Mel listened, tight-lipped. Writing soaps was like writing pulp fiction, he'd told me. "It's nothing to be proud of." He wanted to be compared to Hemingway and F. Scott Fitzgerald.

So, in spite of my pleadings and the pleadings of the head writers, Mel quit the job after four months. "It's killing me," he said, and besides, he had to go back to his mystery novel. His agent, Annie Laurie Williams, hadn't sold it yet, but he knew she would if he had the time to finish it. So if I would lend him the money to help support him . . . just for a couple of months. I did so immediately.

I TRIED TO justify loaning him the money, first in my journal: "Now I'm paying Mel's (admittedly small) rent and his phone bill . . . and I am doing it because I love him and he has to finish that novel," and then more heatedly during one of my extended conversations with my brother. I maintained I'd never have worked so hard if I hadn't had to be responsible for so many people—before it had been Jason; now it was Mel and Mama. "But I am naturally lazy," I concluded.

With that, Bart broke in with a curt, *You are a compulsive giver. Mel could drive a cab and Mama could wash her own hair. You've been a fool about money and maybe you'll always be a fool about money, all in the name of love.*

In the end, although I did resent loaning the money to Mel, I didn't tell him. Dr. Rado said, "You're afraid of being abandoned again; you have already been abandoned by your brother and your father." At that time I wasn't sure he was right, but now I think maybe he was.

MEL WAS GROWING more reclusive. In the evenings I would get back from the show and beg to go frugging at some disco; he would want me to stay with him while he read his latest draft. I got frustrated. Once I went off defiantly to have drinks with a nightclub comic because he made me laugh, and then I wrote about him in my journal and left it open on my desk for Mel to read. (Now what was that about?) Mel went ballistic; we fought about what he called my "roving eye," my furtive need to have other men in my life. Mel's beef was that I couldn't be up-front about it.

"At least be honest with me!" he'd shout. "I'm faithful to you."

I was faithful too, I'd scream. Until once I wasn't, and then I told Mel, so he went off with someone else. Then we made up in bed and vowed we'd always be faithful—always, always, always.

Fidelity. How did I really feel about it? Extremely ambivalent. I had the example of my mother in front of me; she was a rebel and I disapproved of her behavior when I was a kid. But now I was beginning to understand how enticing it was to succumb to someone new. I got such an actual *rush*—it made me feel so alive—and then if I did allow myself to be seduced, the sex could be so passionate and fresh. I never told Mel any of this. I was terrified I'd lose his love, so I controlled myself—most of the time.

As the years passed, I began to realize that long-term passion was very rare, and that passionate sex was not necessarily about intimacy, but about something more immediate and raw and mysterious. That said, women have never been able to express their true sexual natures without being scared shitless. We're afraid that we'll lose our lovers or husbands, as well as our reputations, and we might even suffer physical abuse. Even today, most women don't talk openly about what they like to do in bed. The deepest truth about female sexuality is that we have never had the freedom to shape it.

SO I KNEW I was in love with Mel, but I also knew that things were starting to fall apart. We both knew it and we worked like hell at staying together, but the efforts left us stressed and skittish. In the meantime, after all this Sturm und Drang about money and staying faithful and God knows what else, Mel's relentlessly hard work paid off. G. P. Putnam's Sons bought his mystery novel *Freak Out,* and they optioned a sequel called *The Death Collection.* Otto Preminger expressed interest in a rough draft of a play called *The Castro Complex*, about a girl who gets turned on only when her lover dresses up as Fidel Castro.

To celebrate his good fortune, Mel surprised me with a weekend in Montauk. He rented a car, reserved a big room at Gurney's Inn. We started off late at night. When we stopped for gas, the attendant gave us the wrong directions. We lost our way and didn't get to the beach until dawn. I was sick with fatigue.

I remember flopping down on the bed and hugging a pillow.

Mel nuzzled me. "Sweetheart, don't go to sleep yet." He sounded wide-awake; his voice was urgent.

"Let me sleep just a little," I murmured.

"Not until you say you'll marry me."

"Oh, Mel—not now."

He pulled me into a sitting position. "Marry me, sweetheart! Make an honest man out of me."

I didn't say anything. I felt groggy.

He waited and then he asked me again. This time his voice was irritated. "Will you or won't you?"

I rolled over and put the pillow over my head. "I'm tired, so tired. Please don't make me answer you now."

With that he grabbed my arm so hard I cried out, "You're hurting me! I just have to sleep."

Mel stared as if I'd hit him. Then he retreated back into himself. "I'll get some breakfast downstairs," he said as he started out the door.

As he left the room, I called out, "I love you!" Of course he didn't reply.

*　　*　　*

MEL KEPT TO himself for the rest of the day; he walked along the beach for hours. I slept most of the time. We didn't see each other again until we were ready to return to New York. As we drove back in the pouring rain, we were both in a terrible mood.

Approaching the Midtown Tunnel, our car skidded. Mel managed to steer us to safety between two other cars. (Some mysterious force saved us from crashing through the windshield; cars didn't have seat belts then). After we left the tunnel, we drove in silence to the Helen Hayes, shaken by our near accident and the botched-up weekend.

That same night Mel dropped by my dressing room after the curtain came down. He then announced that he was leaving for the West Coast. "More TV prospects—got to follow them up." He said he might be gone for quite a while.

"How long?"

He shrugged; he didn't know.

I was the one who challenged him with "Is this the end for us?" and he answered that he wasn't sure. Then he added, "Look, we both know it's not working anymore, because I love you more than you love me." He went on to say quietly, "I'm not blaming you or me. I'm not whining. I'm just telling you how I feel." Before I could interrupt, he went on, speaking very slowly so he wouldn't stutter. "There . . . is . . . always one person . . . in a relationship who loves more. I've always known I loved you more than you love me."

"That's not true. I love you very much," I exclaimed. "Is this because I won't marry you now? That I want to wait? My God, Mel, I love you with all my heart and soul."

"You love the way I look. You keep telling me I'm so beautiful." His tone was contemptuous. "You know something? Inside I'm a fat, insecure little boy. I was a very fat kid when I was growing up."

"I didn't know that."

"I never told you," he retorted angrily. And he left, calling out "Bye-bye"—something he always said and that didn't fit with his tall gangly frame.

I WENT HOME and fell into bed, but I tossed and turned. I missed Mel's body next to mine, so big but strangely soft and warm against my skin. I'd always slept like a baby in his arms. Now that he was gone, I was wide-awake and anxious, my heart beating rapidly.

Around four a.m. I rose and drank some brandy and then returned to reading Doris Lessing's *The Golden Notebook*, the novel that was becoming the Bible for many of my female friends. I'd been reading it for weeks. In it, Lessing writes profoundly about the split between women's sexual and emotional identities. She seemed to understand the anguish of women who hide out in bad relationships because they don't want to be alone.

By dawn I was telling myself that I'd made the right move to say no to Mel. I wasn't ready to settle down and get married yet. I didn't know what I was going to do next, but I knew I had to do whatever it was by myself.

In the next weeks I held to my routine and that saved my sanity. I attended sessions at the Studio, and then I had understudy rehearsals, and had to be at the theatre promptly every night. I felt edgy and overprepared in the event that I had to go on, but I rarely did, so I'd hole up in my dressing room, tacking up new Jackie pictures and trying to write.

I hadn't expected Mel to walk out. The breakup had taken me by surprise, so I did what I always did when surprise turned to upset. After the curtain came down, I'd wander over to Downey's, sit at the bar, and have a whiskey sour, or I'd move in and out of various parties. But I couldn't avoid the loneliness, and I didn't, nor the frightening silence of my apartment when I entered it. I felt as if I was winding down and moving onto a different track. The intensity of my feelings for Mel hadn't lessened. I loved him as much as ever and I missed him terribly.

There was something else that was making me slow down. I'd been having persistent gynecological aches and pains; sex with Mel hadn't always been that enjoyable of late. I blamed it on the abortion. In the past I'd relied on Marcia and Lils for doctor recommendations and medical advice, but they weren't much help. We all had a historical lack of self-knowledge about our bodies.

Lils did give me the name of one male gynecologist; when I went to see him, he discovered that I had a vaginal cyst that had developed into an infection. He started me on expensive heat treatments designed to "burn the infection out." He knew I was an actress and that I didn't have much money. I can still see myself wrapped in a sheet on his examining table while he stroked my arm and murmured that I could come to the office for free heat treatments if I gave him a kiss and maybe more.

He was a middle-aged man with a pencil-thin mustache and very chilly moist hands. I slid off the table and told him, "No, thank you. Thank you, no." I dressed and was out of there in record time (as an actress I was master of the quick change).

I never saw that doctor again, but luckily I eventually found a wonderful doctor, Norman Pleshette, who answered my questions and helped heal my body. I was his patient until he died.

IN *The Golden Notebook*, Lessing's heroine Anna Wulf keeps several notebooks of different colors—black, yellow, and blue—which deal with different aspects of her life. I too had notebooks dated by the year and labeled "Quotes" and "People I Love," and then there was one marked "Fate." I'd scribbled only a couple of sentences in it about predetermination.

I decided I should take a writing course. Maybe that would help me focus. All the while I tried not to think about Mel. I did love him so and would probably never love like this again.

I enrolled in a memoir workshop at Columbia that was taught by the soft-spoken, white-haired cultural critic Gerald Sykes. At the first class, Gerald defined memoir for us as "a corner of your life that is especially vivid and intense and framed by unique events."

Other members of the class included a retired policeman, a former ad executive, and a divorcée who had a bright pink rash on her cheeks. One by one they read their little pieces. And then I read mine.

It was the rough draft of a story I'd set in San Francisco, when we were living in an apartment overlooking the marina. My father and Bart were playing chess together there on a gray, rainy afternoon. They played together only once, so I cherished the memory.

I can still hear the foghorns as they hooted from the bay, can still hear the sea gulls. Our windows faced the Golden Gate Bridge and, directly below us, Fisherman's Wharf. Bart and Daddy were by those windows, hunched over the antique chess table, totally engrossed in the game.

The table itself was a thing of beauty (Mama's words). It was small and dainty, with a chessboard grid of sixty-four squares; each square appeared to be a different shade of wood—blond, mahogany, tan, taupe. Bart loved polishing the board to a fine sheen before he played on it.

Father and son began cautiously. Bart would later say to me excitedly, "I couldn't believe I was playing chess with Daddy!" It was one of the few times they were connected and working in harmony. Such concentration—they seemed to know the game was all about control and vulnerability; wasn't that part of their complicated relationship?

The game had gone on for hours. It was tedious (Bart told me later he was sure that "Daddy was assessing me, his opponent—

trying to figure out if I prefer knights to bishops. That was my bluff . . ."). I tried to write about the intricacies of their game—bishops, kings, rooks, with a key breakthrough for Bart when his three rooks seemed unstoppable; all the while Daddy was chain-smoking and sipping his bourbon on ice.

My story ended with Bart winning the game and Daddy congratulating him. He put his arm around his son's skinny shoulders, and Bart was beaming.

Ken McCormick, a senior editor from Doubleday, sat in on Gerald's class the afternoon I read that story, and afterward he came over to me and said he was going to arrange for me to receive a Columbia Doubleday fellowship. This meant my writing course would be paid for, and he added that he'd like to see my book when I finished it. He gave me his card.

Gerald explained that this was great encouragement. I returned to the theatre feeling hopeful about myself for the first time in a long time.

Chapter Twenty-Five

ALTHOUGH I TRIED to ignore her, Mama was still on my case phoning me, writing me, bemoaning the way I lived and loved, wondering why when I'd "started off like a bright comet in the theatre" I'd "fizzled and died." Oh, Mama could be tough and Mama could be cruel, but her remarks no longer hurt. I was so used to them that they barely registered, and what's more, ever since I'd become responsible for her financial survival, our positions had reversed. I was more the parent than the child.

The one subject that we could always return to without friction was Bart. We met on his birthday and on the anniversary of his death. Mama would recall where she'd heard about Bart's suicide. She'd been at Bloomingdale's Gourmet Shop lecturing to customers on how her celebrity chef, Rudy Stanish, prepared his omelets. Neither one of us could ever eat an omelet again.

We were both consumed with keeping Bart alive in photographs. Between us we'd been adding to various scrapbooks for years. One afternoon Mama came over to my apartment with an envelope of rediscovered snapshots of us as children. She threw them down on my coffee table.

There was four-year-old Bart, solemn and pudgy, standing in

shadow next to me in the garden at Berkeley. I seemed to be lording over him in the sunlight. There was Bart cuddling our cocker puppies, grinning from ear to ear. In some images my brother seemed wistful, timid; in others he seemed exultant, as when he caught his first fish at Tahoe. His expression changed as he grew older; he was no longer smiling and appeared wary and watchful by the time he turned eleven or twelve. And then there were the final pictures with me the summer after the tragedy at Deerfield. He seemed both despairing and angry, gazing balefully into the camera. Then there was his passport photo, so incredibly bleak. After that summer he'd refused to pose at all.

"Where are the pictures with Arthur Mehija?" I asked. I remembered taking them with my Brownie camera. The boys had posed side by side with their tennis rackets, Arthur gazing longingly at Bart. They were both about thirteen, both about to go off to Deerfield. I remembered Bart's expression. He seemed aloof, as if he didn't notice Arthur's show of affection.

I thought of a conversation I'd had with Arthur long after the tragedy at Deerfield, and I tried to reconstruct it for Mama. Arthur admitted he was gay and that he had been in love with Bart. But he hadn't told him; he was too uptight. So it had been love from afar. They were both so naive and innocent; sex was a mystery, and of course sex was taboo. At that time sex with another boy was criminal, but yes, they'd fooled around a couple of times in the privacy of their rooms because it was a natural impulse. They just couldn't help themselves.

Arthur didn't know when Bart and Clark found each other. It was a meeting of the minds; they both were exceptionally bright, and Clark had a wonderful sense of humor. Clark was Bart's first and only love, Arthur concluded. Their feelings for each other were so intense you couldn't intrude. It all happened so fast, and then they were discovered in the gym.

Mama looked very sad. "Do you think he was a homosexual?" she asked. She'd never asked that question before.

I told her I wasn't sure, that Bart might not have known yet.

Mama began pacing. She admitted trying time and time again to bring up the subject with Daddy, but he would not deal with it. He was a homophobe, she told me. He was a homophobe because he was afraid he might be gay himself.

"Oh, Mama!"

"Don't 'oh, Mama' me. There were too many instances. He'd had a crush on his boss, John Neylan, when he worked for Hearst. Then there was Willkie . . . Of course that was unrequited . . . but so many men had a thing for your father," she went on. "The terrible part is, if he hadn't been so confused about his own sexuality, he might have been able to help. Maybe then your brother wouldn't have killed himself."

"Have you finally come around to accepting the fact that Bart committed suicide?"

Mama bowed her head. "It's difficult for me, but now I accept his suicide as a fact, yes." She turned back to the pictures and briskly changed the subject. "It's been a good idea to organize the snapshots. Makes me feel better somehow when I study the images of you when you were young, when we were all young . . . You were such beautiful, gentle creatures."

Mama left me alone with the pile of photographs; I would soon paste them into yet another album.

Afterward I thought about what she'd said about my father and his sexuality. I thought of Kal Nulman, a lawyer now long dead. I saw him a lot right after my father died. Kal was a balding, kindly man who was Daddy's drinking buddy. They drank almost every afternoon at the St. Regis bar. Kal lived by himself on Park Avenue and practiced law in New York City and on Long Island. He called himself my father's best friend. He kept a picture of himself and

Daddy in his office, taken at a party; they are both wearing funny hats and laughing uproariously. They had met in Washington during World War II and were in constant touch. Kal was devoted to him. Daddy had phoned Kal the day my brother shot himself.

"I said, 'What do you want me to do, Bart? I'll come out to be with you right away.' And he said, 'No, Kal—just talk to me.' He was very broken up and there was nothing I could say—could ever say."

Kal maintained my father's reach exceeded his grasp of things. "He wanted to do so many things he wasn't able to. He was a decent, good man. Terrible things happened to him and they shouldn't have. He was an innocent."

Kal maintained he knew nothing about my father's addiction to liquor or pills. He even brought him a bottle of bourbon when he visited Silver Hill, "because he asked me to."

Once when we were having lunch, Kal confided, "Your mother thought your father and I were lovers. But we weren't." And then he added, "But I loved your father more than I ever loved anyone in my entire life."

Chapter Twenty-Six

Mid-november 1963 and I was still in *Mary, Mary*. By now the original cast had left the show. Barbara had been replaced by Diana Lynn, who'd been replaced by Nancy Olson, and there were numerous Tiffanys after Betsy von Furstenberg, including the ubiquitous Carrie Nye, who kept an iguana in her dressing room and ultimately married Dick Cavett.

But the understudy job wasn't leading anywhere and I knew it. I went on in both roles at one time or another, and every so often as I was being rushed into the star dressing room it reminded me that I'd grown up in a climate of expectation and dread my entire life. It was Daddy's fault. Oh, I didn't blame him—I loved him too much to ever blame him for the atmosphere he created around us—but things had never been calm at home. We'd lived in a heightened kind of reality. I'd grown used to it; it was a habit, a need almost. Maybe that was why I'd resisted Mel's slower, contemplative, quiet way of existence at first. But as I spent long hours alone in my dressing room, I realized that I enjoyed being by myself more and more.

Between the matinee and evening shows I would wander around Times Square, ending up at the familiar "bow tie," the area between Forty-Second Street and Forty-Seventh where Broadway and Seventh Avenue intersect. Crowds of tourists moved along with me; we were flanked by cheap hotels and garish movie palaces. I would always meet somebody I knew—Liz Ashley on her way to go on in *Barefoot in the Park* or Bobby Morse, the gap-toothed star of *How to Succeed in Business Without Really Trying*.

This particular night it was Bobby; he was practically jumping up and down with excitement. "Jackie and the president are coming to see the show tonight," he exclaimed. "At the curtain call I'm gonna sing to them directly." He stopped. "Your show ends before mine. Come backstage and you can see me perform for the Kennedys." He darted off.

I could hardly wait. As soon as the curtain came down, I dashed from the Helen Hayes to the Forty-Sixth Street Theatre, just beyond Dinty Moore's. I was able to slip into the wings just as Bobby begain belting out "I Believe in You," the signature number. I peeked through the curtains; the houselights were up and everyone in the audience was gazing at Jack and Jackie. They positively glowed. The president had a tan; his white teeth flashed. Jackie was in pastels, her handsome face surrounded by dark upswept hair.

When Bobby finished singing, the president and First Lady stood up and basked in the cheers and huzzahs that shook the very foundations of the theatre.

THREE DAYS LATER Kennedy was assassinated in Dallas. I heard the news on a radio that was playing in a Greek restaurant on Eighth Avenue and Forty-Fourth Street. I'd been having lunch with Brenda Vaccaro and Marty Fried after a session at the Actors Studio. We stared at each other in disbelief.

We paid the bill and wandered off on our separate ways. All I could think of was Jackie. I passed the Martin Beck Theatre, where *Ballad of a Sad Café* was playing, and the actor Lou Antonio, who was in the play, burst out from a dressing room; he had the dwarf Michael Dunn on his back, and the two went galloping down the street with Michael raging and shaking his tiny fist. I assumed they had heard the terrible news.

Then I walked over to Times Square. It was eerily quiet even though cars, buses, and taxis were progressing down Broadway and Seventh, but at a snail's pace. Crowds milled on the sidewalk; many had gathered underneath the gigantic Bond Clothes billboard. Everybody seemed to be looking up at the Times Tower, where the revolving electric news bulletin sign kept moving around and around, repeating the same horrific bulletin: PRESIDENT JOHN FITZGERALD KENNEDY DIED AT PARKLAND MEMORIAL HOSPITAL IN DALLAS, TEXAS, AT 12:30 PM EASTERN TIME.

On an impulse I phoned Danny Massey, who was in the musical *She Loves Me.* His wife, Adrienne Corri, was in *The Rehearsal.* Danny told me, "The producers want us to play tonight. We don't want to."

Late that afternoon there was a meeting between Actors Equity and the Broadway League. It was decided that the theatres would stay open, although every cast in every show on Broadway wanted to mourn. But we all went on that night. (I was subbing in as Tiffany.) Every performer, whether in a musical or a straight play, wore a black armband.

After my show I ran over to see Bobby in *How to Succeed.* I caught him just in time to see him singing "I Believe in You," but this time he had tears streaming down his face.

WHEN I GOT home, the first thing I did was turn on the TV. Bobby Kennedy was meeting Jackie at Andrews Air Force Base; together they watched JFK's coffin pushed off of Air Force One.

Just then the phone rang. It was Mel.

"Are you okay, sweetheart?" he was asking, trying not to stutter. "I know how you feel about the Kennedys."

I heard his familiar voice, but my concentration was focused on Bobby and Jackie walking hand in hand behind the coffin.

"It's terrible—I can't stop watching TV." I began to sob. "I'm so glad you called."

"You sound the same. Are you the same?"

"Not the same without you."

There was a pause and then Mel told me he was calling me from a pay phone at the airport and he was about to take the red-eye back to New York. "I'll see you soon."

I sank down on the couch. *He's coming back*, I told myself. *I can't believe it. He's coming back to me.*

TEN HOURS LATER Mel was standing in my apartment, out of breath and unshaven. He had his Olivetti in one hand, his battered suitcase in the other. We didn't embrace. He joined me on the couch and we watched TV like zombies. We didn't speak until after Oswald was shot by Jack Ruby.

Then Mel turned off the TV set. "Jesus," he said.

We began to discuss the assassination. Mel guessed it would probably be the most traumatic event in our lifetime. It was difficult to bring the subject back to ourselves.

We sat quietly for a while and then Mel said, "We could have a future together if we'd stop screwing around." He went on to say, "I know what I want and I want you and need you. But if we get married we have to strike a balance of power between us, and the balance should be based on an understanding about what's most important to each of us. For me it's work—even second to creating a family." He looked very serious when he said that.

There was a long pause and then he added, "I know you hated loaning me that money."

I stared at him.

"I'm not stupid." His tone was impatient now. "The bottom line is that all artists have money problems. Sometimes the wife does make more money than the husband, and then the situation reverses and the husband brings in the dough. But financial insecurity is something we have to face and accept. It's always going to be part of our life."

When I didn't answer, he prodded me, "Aw, c'mon! Now what?"

I told him that I hadn't been ready to commit myself to one man for the rest of my life.

"It sounds like a prison sentence. You're a free woman, free to do as you please—within reason."

"What would you do if I slept with another man?"

"I'd kill him."

"Would you leave me?"

"Depends on the circumstances. But no, I don't think so. But I'd be very disappointed."

AFTER MEL LEFT to go back to his apartment, I fell back on my bed and rolled over to study my favorite photograph of Bart. It was a close-up taken of him when he was around eight or nine—he's drinking a glass of Coca-Cola and is looking over the rim of the glass. He has just come from swimming, so his hair is wet and close to his beautifully shaped head. His eyes are enormous, as if he can see the entire world ahead of him.

"So," I murmured in our private language.

So, he answered.

"I'm back with Mel. He loves me and I love him, and I feel committed; I don't feel ambivalent. For the first time in my life, I don't feel ambivalent."

Because you know you are making a rational decision. You know you love him. You know you will be spending your life with an honorable man.

"Will I be happy?"

Is the Pope happy?

"Okay, stupid question. But will it work?"

Again, stupid question.

"Let's change the subject."

Good idea.

MEL AND I started planning. We decided we'd get married the following spring. Howard and Elena offered to give us a reception in their apartment in the Dakota. When I spoke to my brother, I asked if I should tell our mother.

Not yet, he cautioned. *Wait till the last minute. Otherwise she'll bug the bejesus out of you.*

I took his advice.

Chapter Twenty-Seven

I HAD ONE LAST big audition as an actress, reading for Ophelia in Richard Burton's *Hamlet*. It was the most anticipated show of the 1963–64 season, so I prepared assiduously, working long hours, even hiring Peggy Feury to coach me. The result: I created a truly frazzled Ophelia, crazy about Hamlet even though she knows he doesn't love her, guilty that she's let him take her virginity.

I started getting excited all over again about being in theatre because I realized this could be a career-changing role, and part of me wanted it desperately. After almost ten years in the business, hadn't I paid my dues? I'd always dreamed of appearing in a distinguished production. Then I could leave the business, having made my mark, and devote myself to writing.

I read four times over many weeks for the director, Sir John Gielgud, and for Burton as well. It came down to me and another actress. I was sure I would get the part. But I was rejected and it devastated me. I could not understand why I'd failed.

(Decades later I was interviewing Richard Burton for the *Times* just before he returned to Broadway in *Equus*. I couldn't resist. I had to ask him why I hadn't been cast as Ophelia.

Burton maintained he'd wanted me. I wanted to believe he meant it. "You were wonderful in those readings, luv," he insisted in his Welsh-accented voice. "But Sir John wanted to go with a brunette."

A brunette? Was that enough of a reason? I could have dyed my hair.)

I'd had enough of auditions, of the frustrations, the craziness, the feeling that no matter how good I believed I'd been, I'd somehow failed. I hated the lack of control. I didn't want to go through it anymore. That's when I made up my mind: I would leave acting.

I'd also taken my first baby steps into journalism. I'd been interviewing theatre friends for a collage of Broadway circa 1964. I spoke to legendary press agent Sam Friedman and the angular dark-haired Marian Seldes, who was appearing nearby in *Death Trap* ("What was it like to remain in a show over a thousand performances?"). I even managed to spend an afternoon with Gore Vidal, whose most recent play, *The Best Man,* had capitalized on the drama of an old-fashioned presidential election. I ultimately showed my attempts to Clay Felker, who was beginning to reshape journalism in *New York*, his lively Sunday magazine for the *Herald Tribune*. It was a virtual showcase for young, ambitious writers. Clay took a couple of my jumbled, disorganized pieces and said he would try to pull them together.

MARY, MARY was winding down. I'd been with the production four years. Roger Stevens came to me and said everybody—and that included Jean Kerr—had decided I should play Mary for the last months of the run. It would close in July.

I thought that by now playing a starring role on Broadway on a regular basis would be anticlimactic, but it wasn't. It was thrilling. I was achieving a dream I'd had ever since I was a kid. I loved walking into my big dressing room backstage, being fussed over immediately by a maid, getting my hair done, and being served a light supper on a tray from Sardi's after every matinee.

I'd grown into the part. I was thirty; I had more confidence in myself as a performer—actually I had more confidence in myself, *period*. I was more relaxed (Lee had taught me that); I didn't suffer from such crippling stage fright, so I could focus on the role. It felt good to belt out the laugh lines and hear the audience roar as I bantered back and forth with the current "Bob" (Murray Hamilton). I liked having the power to make the house go totally silent when I recited Mary's poignant monologue in the second act. As a character she has always hidden behind wisecracks; now she gets serious, almost emotional, when a stranger gives her a sudden kiss.

The curtain would go down and I'd take my solo bow, my heart pumping from exertion. The applause was enthusiastic; lots of my friends from the Studio came to cheer me on, like Marty and Susie and Lils. So did many of my former Sarah Lawrence classmates. Garson Kanin came with Ruth Gordon, and afterward they took me out to the Russian Tea Room to celebrate.

Across the street at the Lunt-Fontanne, Richard Burton was starring as Hamlet. Every night I'd leave my show and immediately be engulfed by hundreds of fans waiting to catch a glimpse of Burton with his new bride Elizabeth Taylor on his arm.

As I pushed my way through the crowds to the subway I thought, *How ironic*. I'd just played a starring role on Broadway and nobody cared. That's when I knew I'd made the right decision to leave acting.

NOT LONG AFTER that, Clay phoned to tell me that he'd taken the rambling, unfocused character sketches I'd written about egomaniacal Broadway stars and edited their stream-of-consciousness dialogues into two snappy features. He then published them in *New York* and they attracted some attention.

The day the magazine came out on the stand, I was in

Bloomingdale's going up on the escalator when I ran into Diane Arbus. I hadn't seen her for a number of years. She immediately congratulated me on the pieces and said she liked my writing.

"It's so alive," she said.

OF COURSE, I wasn't an overnight success as a writer. It took me fifteen years to get my first book published. I fell into jobs: one at *Holiday* (a travel magazine), where I learned to compose elegant captions and short takes; then I graduated to movie-star profiles and editing astrology columns when I moved to *McCall's*.

But I never left the theatre world. I became part of it in a different way while I freelanced for the *New York Times* under the guidance of arts editor Seymour Peck, who became my mentor and taught me how to research and shape a piece. Sy gave me dozens of assignments—about Harold Pinter, Kurt Vonnegut, the rise of black theatre, and Joe Papp taking over Lincoln Center. I found myself reporting smack-dab in the middle of a huge cultural shift. I had tea with the Beatles in London at the height of Beatlemania; their earlier triumph in America had made them a worldwide phenomenon.

And I got married to Mel on February 15, 1966. Howard and Elena gave us a reception at their apartment in the Dakota and, although Mama disapproved, she behaved herself and concocted some delicious hors d'oeuvres.

I was in a momentary state of bliss. I'd had my hair done à la Jackie Kennedy and I wore a violet silk shift. As we were having our pictures taken, I looked at my new husband and thought, *You are so beautiful and we love each other. You understand me. Isn't that the important thing?* Then I thought some more as he hugged me tight and I said to myself, *And he's a writer! How could I not be married to a writer? Who else is going to put up with my self-absorption?*

* * *

WE MOVED INTO a floor-through on West Thirteenth Street and went on with our lives. By now, the war in Vietnam was escalating; Mel and I joined demonstrations and once even traveled to Washington, DC, to hear veterans speak against the violence.

In the midst of this we were trying to have a baby. I had a hard time conceiving. We went to fertility doctors. Mel's sperm count was low because he smoked so much; I had miscarriages. Specialists said my uterus was too delicate; something might be the matter with my cervix. We talked about adoption but ended up agreeing that we didn't want to go that route. By this point I'd told Mel I'd had an abortion and Mel had admitted he'd found his schoolteacher ex-girlfriend in L.A. and she'd had his child, a son.

"He looks like me except he's black as the ace of spades," Mel told me somberly.

He would send them money every month, and I assumed he saw his son whenever he went to California to write a TV show, but he never mentioned it. I felt very, very sad. I once asked, "Why can't I meet your little boy? Could you ever bring him to New York? Maybe we can take care of him for a while." Mel shook his head.

It was a strange melancholy situation, one we never shared with anyone. I felt guilty about not being a mother, especially when one friend who had six kids clucked, "I feel so sorry for you. You have missed something very important in a woman's life." I thought I probably had.

As I grew older, when I taught creative nonfiction at Columbia University's School of Journalism, I started mentoring various students, both male and female. I became close to some of them; I'd bring them home and feed them, listen to their problems, try to give them advice, and I'd feel maternal and loved. I still keep tabs on some of these students. I've watched them grow up—marry, raise families, finally succeed in what they want to do. Some of them have published books. They give me great joy.

*   *   *

IN 1974, I signed a contract to write a biography of Montgomery Clift. In retrospect I'd been preparing to do this for two decades. I'd performed in umpteen shows; I'd hung around the Actors Studio taking notes, experimenting with craft, learning from Lee; I'd written a ton of journalism. When I sat down with Brooks Clift (Monty's older brother), taping the myriad anecdotes he had about their childhood, I realized that I was approaching writing as I had approached acting. I used the same tools—observing, listening, asking questions, discovering the subtext in a given situation. I'd always been insatiably curious (Mel called me "nosy"). I collected gossip and secrets; I was patient, tenacious, willful. But it took a long time piecing together the puzzle of Monty's life.

"Writing is another kind of performance," John Guare told me. "When you're a writer, you get to play all the parts."

When finally my writings about Montgomery Clift flowed onto the page, what I was trying to express blossomed in print from both an inner need and a conviction that I had been able to tell the story and solve part of the mystery of someone else's life. But not yet mine. That would come later.

Afterword

IN 1984 I flew out to Sacramento to visit my brother's grave. It had taken me many years to do this. Mel had wanted to come with me, but I decided I had to be alone and he understood.

My cousin Jim Wiard drove me to the cemetery, a beautiful, tranquil place high on a hill surrounded by gnarled old trees. I'd brought some flowers—red roses, because we used to pick fragrant baskets of them for Mama in Aptos.

So there I was, after so many years. I knelt down and put the flowers next to Bart's gravestone. The two Barts—father and son, buried side by side. It seemed ironic. In life they had never been close, never spent much time together, and now they were deep in the earth together for all eternity.

"I'm sorry it's taken so long," I whispered.

Don't apologize. You're here now. That's all that matters.

The wind rustled the leaves. Sun glanced off my arm.

"I have to ask: Were you ever happy?"

You mean when I was alive?

I nodded.

Once. When I was making those wings.

"Oh, God. I remember how you said you wanted to fly like Icarus."

He didn't know his own limits. He flew too close to the sun.

"You were determined to build those wings . . . You constructed them on the nursery floor."

Took me five goddamn months, and then they were too big. You tried to help me put them on.

"We both fell on the floor."

But I wouldn't give up.

"You tore them up and then started all over again."

Mama and Daddy used to come up to the nursery to see what was going on.

"They'd stay a short time—they were usually late for a party."

They pretended to be interested, but they really weren't.

"But they'd hug and kiss us, remember? And later we'd have our supper served to us on trays by our nanny . . . It was quite beautiful, wasn't it?" I heard my voice quavering.

Don't get so choked up. The beauty didn't last.

"But why were you so happy when you were building those wings?"

Because you helped me, stupido. I couldn't have done them without you.

I'd forgotten I'd helped. "All I did was bring you the paste and the string."

But you were the only one who believed I could do it. You were there for me. Everybody else thought I was nuts.

"I don't remember being so helpful."

Believe it. You were.

"I'm glad."

Silence.

"And now you can fly. You're an angel—you have wings."

I never said I was an angel and I never said I had wings. Don't be so sentimental, Attepe.

We both laughed. Suddenly I wondered, "Do you and Daddy talk more now?"

Long silence.

"Hey! Are you going to tell me you and he still don't communicate?"

He tries. I try. But some things never change.

"Even in heaven?"

Even in heaven.

Acknowledgments

I HAVE BEEN WRITING this memoir off and on throughout my entire life, so I have a debt to many people who helped and inspired me.

To my beloved parents, Daddy and Mama, who always believed in me. To my brother—his story inspired this book.

To friends and colleagues no longer with us, who accompanied me on my journey: Robert Anderson, Anne Bancroft, Patricia Collinge, Jane Cooper, Mildred Dunnock, Nora Ephron, Clay Felker, Marty Fried, Betsy von Furstenberg, Arthur Gelb, Barbara Goldsmith, Philip Goodman, Ruth Gordon, Marcia Haynes, Audrey Hepburn, Gene Hill, Anne Jackson, Garson Kanin, Elia Kazan, Bela Kornitzer, Warner LeRoy, Daniel Massey, Sandy Meisner, Mike Nichols, Geraldine Page, Seymour Peck, Arthur Penn, George Plimpton, Alastair Reid, Mary Rodgers, Gene Saks, Gerry Sarracini, Bessie Schönberg, Marian Seldes, Susan Stein, John Stix, Lee Strasberg, Susan Strasberg, Elaine Stritch, Gore Vidal, Eli Wallach, Tennessee Williams, Shelley Winters, and Fred Zinnemann.

I'm especially grateful to: Jenny Allen, Hilton Als, Terry Ashe-Croft, James Atlas, Thomas Beller, Susan Brownmiller,

Ellen Burstyn, Ina Caro, Robert Caro, Janet Coleman, Judy Collins, Andrew Coppa, Susan Dryfoos, Martha Fay, Emily Feyder, Jack Garfein, Leslie Garis, Gary Giddins, Lee Grant, Tammy Grimes, Molly Haskell, Linda Healey, Robert Heller, Maria Cooper Janis, Joyce Johnson, Charles Kaiser, Frances Kazan, Arthur Kopit, Wayne Lawson, Susan Lehman, Aaron Lehmann, Lily Lodge, Philip Lopate, Jane Maas, Daphne Merkin, Edmund Morris, Richard Morse, David Nasaw, Victor Navasky, Estelle Parsons, Austin Pendleton, Barbara Quinn, Anne Roiphe, Lucy Rosenthal, Mark Rydell, Joan Schenkar, Gail Sheehy, Dinitia Smith, Gloria Steinem, Gay Talese, Nan Talese, and Robert Weil.

During the years that form the setting of this memoir, I was fortunate enough to meet the fascinating individuals who would become the subjects of my biographies: Montgomery Clift, Diane Arbus, Marlon Brando, and Jane Fonda. I owe them enormous thanks; writing about their amazing lives helped me to inform and shape my own.

I owe a special debt to my assistant, Jaime Lubin, tireless, steadfast, and true. Dedicated to accuracy, she worked with me on every draft of this memoir and helped me discover essential truths.

Special thanks to Till Osterland, who keeps my office running. He is my go-to expert on technology and the calm in the eye of the storm.

I am forever indebted to my agent, Betsy Lerner. She believed in this book since its inception.

Heartfelt thanks to Douglas Schwalbe.

Last but not least, to my wonderful editor, Gail Winston, whose enthusiasm for this project never waned. Patient and gentle, she has guided me through every level of this memoir, helping me be specific and giving me valued perspective on the huge amount of material that I had to draw from. Thank you for always being there for me.

Index

Note: Fictional characters and people with unknown surnames are listed under first names.

About the Author

PATRICIA BOSWORTH was born in San Francisco and is a graduate of Sarah Lawrence. She is a contributing editor at *Vanity Fair* and lives in New York City. Patricia has taught literary nonfiction at Columbia University and Barnard College and is a winner of the Front Page Award. A longtime board member of the Actors Studio, she ran the Playwrights-Directors Unit there. Her first memoir, *Anything Your Little Heart Desires: An American Family Story*, was about her family and the Hollywood Blacklist. She is also the author of bestselling biographies of Montgomery Clift, Marlon Brando, Jane Fonda, and the photographer Diane Arbus. Her Arbus biography inspired the 2006 film *Fur*, starring Nicole Kidman and Robert Downey Jr.